GENIUS OF GUINNESS

THE ENDURING LEGACY OF AN IRISH DYNASTY

Enjoy!
Michele Guinness

MICHELE GUINNESS

AMBASSADOR INTERNATIONAL
GREENVILLE, SOUTH CAROLINA & BELFAST, NORTHERN IRELAND

Blessed is the man that walketh not in the counsel of the ungodly, nor standeth in the way of sinners, nor sitteth in the seat of the scornful. But his delight is in the law of the LORD; and in his law doth he meditate day and night. And he shall be like a tree planted by the rivers of water, that bringeth forth his fruit in his season; his leaf also shall not wither; and whatsoever he doeth shall prosper.

PSALMS 1: 1-3

GENIUS OF GUINNESS

The publisher has acknowledged copyright holders for various quotations within this book. These quotations comply with the copyright principle of fair comment or fair usage.

ISBN 1 932307 39 7

Cover design & Page Layout by
Andrew Ramos of A&E Media

Ambassador International
427 Wade Hampton Blvd.
Greenville, SC 29609, USA
www.emeraldhouse.com

Ambassador Publications
a division of
Ambassador Productions Ltd.
Providence House
Ardenlee Street
Belfast
BT6 8QJ
Northern Ireland
www.ambassador-productions.com

The colophon is a trademark of Ambassador

TABLE OF CONTENTS

INTRODUCTION
AN INTRODUCTION TO THE FAMILY

I was walking down O'Connell Street in Dublin, enjoying an hour's retail therapy before speaking at a Women's Luncheon Club, when the strap on my sandal snapped. They were the only shoes I had with me, and my meagre resources in those early-married days couldn't possibly rise to a new pair. My hostess, an American missionary, shared my pennilessness, and we rushed into the first shoe repair shop we could find.

"Could you do something with it now?" I asked urgently. "I've no other shoes with me."

The assistant shook her head slowly, unmoved by my predicament, or (so it seemed) by any other emergency that might cross her path that day. Time has no meaning in Ireland.

"There's a long waiting list. Sure, it'll take two days."

"Two days!" I groaned. "It only needs a stitch."

There was still no response, and I would have marched out of the shop with my head in the air, were it not for the fact that you can't go far—let alone with dignity—wearing only one shoe. That fact appeared to dawn upon the young woman, as she observed with some surprise that I was still standing, or rather perching like a pelican, on the other side of the counter.

"Name?" she asked suddenly.

"Guinness," I said.

There was a moment's silence, and, when she lifted her head, a perceptible change of expression appeared on her face.

"Your shoe will be ready in five minutes, Mrs. Guinness," she whispered deferentially.

And sure it was.

My companion was awe-struck. "Oh gee," she gasped, as we walked back out into the street, "it's just like being with one of the Kennedys in New York."

I felt slightly punch-drunk, too. My name had never had that effect before. Admittedly, when my husband, Peter, and I got engaged and he handed me a copy of his pedigree, I was impressed. Not many girls are given an official, published family tree, containing three peerages, two baronetcies, and a heavy smattering of royalty—foreign, admittedly. It was heady stuff for the granddaughter of working-class Jewish immigrants. But though the *Daily Express* claimed in 1969 that "all the members of the world-famous Guinness family are reputed to be worth a fortune in the region of £200 million," I had never seen any of it. Great-great-grandson of Arthur Guinness, founder of the brewery, my Peter may well have been, but he was a comprehensive schoolteacher in Stockport when I married him, a fact not lost on my father. When I tried to soften the blow of "marrying out" by telling him he would have his place in the Guinness family tree where I would be described as "daughter of," he replied wryly, "And did you have to pick one of the poor members of the family?"

During the early years of our marriage, in the evangelical church circles in which we moved, I discovered, to my surprise, a certain prestige attached to the name of those "poor relatives"—pronounced Guinness, with the emphasis on the "ness," to dissociate it from its other, less acceptable spiritual connections. The kudos stemmed from the long involvement of the Grattan line of the family in church and missionary enterprise. At conferences I was forever being asked how my husband was related to Canon Gordon Guinness, Howard Guinness of the Inter Varsity Fellowship; or Desmond, ex-Vicar of Staines; or other clergy like

Robin, Garry, and Chris; or Os Guinness, the theological writer—so much so that I used to threaten to pin a copy of the family tree to my back.

But a sense of belonging to the wider clan was reserved for that moment in the Dublin shoe repair shop. In Dublin the name is inescapable, emblazoned on illuminated clocks and signs. Statues of Guinness benefactors look smugly down on the buildings, parks, and cathedral bounteously bestowed upon the people. Pilgrims from far and wide travel to St. James' Gate for the mystical "Guinness Experience"— a brewery tour and a pint. The name, the firm, the family are deeply embedded in the history of the city. In Dublin, for the first time I understood something of my husband's pride in his heritage.

In time-honoured tradition, and not just in the Grattan line of the family, Peter became a church minister, one of more than twenty in the family, not including the other twenty or so acquired by marriage. Over the years, his family pride, resting on its reputation for uprightness and honesty, generosity and philanthropy, has been severely tested by an apparently endless stream of scandals and tragedy. There were so many bizarre Guinness deaths in the 1970s and 80s that my parents began to wonder if their son-in-law had been watching the film *Kind Hearts and Coronets* on the television, and was making a bid for a peerage by removing the obstacles one by one. (The great British actor, Sir Alec Guinness, whose relationship to the family remains a best kept secret, played each of the victims.)

From the moment the first Arthur went forth into Dublin and multiplied, procreating was a more hazardous business than brewing. Three of Arthur's grandchildren become alcoholics. Two more ended up in mental institutions. Some were reduced to insolvency and begging. But one had a profound impact on the birth of the world church. In 1880 few ordinary people would have heard of Lord Iveagh, owner of the Guinness brewery. But everyone throughout the United Kingdom, Ireland, and the USA would have heard of Henry Grattan Guinness, the legendary preacher whose influence was more extensive than Guinness beer imports, and the catalyst for most major faith missionary societies including Barnado's Homes, AB Simpson and New York Bible College, and the Moody Bible College, to name but a few. The entrepreneurial skills and determination which earned the brewing Guinnesses their millions were alive and well in the Henry Grattan Guinness line—though serving another kind of spirit. Yet few today know the story of his family, or what it cost them to achieve what they did. I have therefore chosen to focus on this line of the family, comparing their extraordinary hair-raising missionary adventures with the enterprise of their brewing cousins.

The discovery of the raw material for this book was in itself the stuff of storybooks. On honeymoon in Ibiza in my parents-in-law's retirement home, I wandered up to my father-in-law's rooftop study during siesta hour, when all the house was quiet, and idly began to explore his bookshelves, looking for something to read. An old, musty-scented biography caught my attention. I took it down and began to read—and was still sitting on the floor several hours later when Peter came to find out where I was. "I had no idea of the risks your relatives took," I said to him. "Why does no one read these books today?"

At dinner, my father-in-law mentioned in passing a trunk in his study cupboard, "full of bits and pieces," he said with a dismissive wave of the hand—poems, letters, the memorabilia his mother had collected over the years. He wasn't sure what was in it. He had never been terribly interested. She was a great hoarder.

I rushed to the top of the house as soon as the meal was over, heaved a large, antique trunk out of the study cupboard, pried it open and could hardly believe what I saw. The trunk was stuffed to the brim with papers, withered with age and the drying effects of the heat. There were letters dating back to the eighteenth century, some in packs tied up with ribbons; newspaper cuttings from as early as 1815; volumes of poetry, postcards, diaries, and notebooks. Grandmother Gracie had married the legendary Henry Grattan Guinness, Peter's grandfather, in 1903, when she was 26 and he was 67. They had two sons and a mere seven years together before his death. Everything in her possession relating to her marriage and her husband's family history had been carefully preserved—as if she knew that one day someone would recognise its importance.

I knew then, in 1975, that I would write their story. It was a long time in the making. During that time the family name lost its lustre in the aftermath of events surrounding the Distillers' takeover, and the arrest in 1986 for the unfair share dealing of its then Chief Executive, Ernest Saunders. But though 7.5 million pint glasses of the beer are consumed every 24 hours, the Guinness story consists of so much more than brewing.

One of my favourite family characters has always been Jane Lucretia Guinness, Henry Grattan's mother and my husband's great-grandmother. Os Guinness, another of Jane's descendants, maintains that she prayed that at least a further seven generations of Guinnesses would be totally committed to Jesus Christ. That prayer left a profound impression upon all the family—as did a large oil painting of Jane Lucretia which Peter remembered seeing as a boy in his uncle's home in the south of England. The artist had captured a radiance in her face that, once seen, could never be forgotten. But while the twin portrait of Captain John Guinness, her husband, was left with cousins in England, hers went to the USA with a part of the family which wasn't particularly sympathetic to her uniquely Christian outlook. There was also a strong possibility that she had been born into a Jewish family. We very much felt she belonged with us, but never imagined it possible.

One day we arrived home from work—and there she was, on the doorstep, lovingly sent thousands of miles back across the Atlantic. And now she smiles down on us—a beautiful presence in our home, and a reminder of the impact of one woman's prayers.

One of the major strengths of the Guinness men was the exceptional spouses they picked—women whose vision and courage, expressed in diaries and letters, weave coloured threads through the story. But then, being a Guinness wife myself, I would say that.

CHAPTER ONE
1815

1.

When her first husband was killed by the famous Irish politician and radical Daniel O'Connell, Jane Lucretia D'Esterre Guinness was subjected to the nineteenth-century equivalent of "fame for fifteen minutes." The media hounded the eighteen-year-old, already the mother of one child, pregnant again, and destitute.

At the age of fourteen, Jane married a minor merchant, John Norcott D'Esterre, who was more blessed in his looks than with common sense. Like many handsome young men, he succumbed to vanity and the temptation to swagger, temptation compounded by the fact that he was also a crack shot with a pistol. When he challenged O'Connell to a duel, it was a foregone conclusion in Dublin that the Catholic leader, who had never wielded a gun in his life, was a dead man. But D'Esterre managed to miss his target, and O'Connell, who planned to miss it by aiming elsewhere, inadvertently hit a bull's eye.

The first Jane Lucretia D'Esterre knew of the duel was the moment she opened the door to allow her dying husband to be carried into their home. The scene was hardly the glittering future the society beauty and budding actress had been led to expect.

Described in an early biography of O'Connell as "the beautiful Miss Cramer of Dublin," she looked, according to one of her sons,[1] as if she had been "formed to win admiration and affection...waving locks of dark hair falling over a high, fair forehead; the eyes dark brown and bright with intelligence; the eyebrows arched; the nose slightly aquiline; the mouth fairly large with mobile lips full of expression." She was indeed a beauty, and when she first appeared on the stage of the Theatre Royal, she took Dublin by storm, even catching the attention of the wild poet, Lord Byron.

She was also an exceptional pianist. The Cramers had been musicians for generations. They hailed from Sachau, Silesia, in the south of Germany, where Jane's father, Wilhelm Cramer, had shown unusual brilliance on the violin as a child, and was accepted as a pupil by the foremost violin teachers of the day. When his son, Johann Baptist, was still a baby, the family sailed for England. King George III quickly recognised Wilhelm's musical ability and made him leader of the Court Band, the Opera, and the Pantheon. But it was his role as lead player in the Handel festivals at Westminster Abbey which brought him real recognition as a virtuoso performer. He was without rival—until his son proved himself an even more able musician. Johann Baptist Cramer was the only pianist Beethoven claimed he truly rated. Johann later founded the successful music publishing company, Cramer and Addison.

It was rumoured the Cramers were Jews. If this rumour be true, they never made it public. It probably accounted for Wilhelm's lack of good fortune in Germany, and he had no desire to suffer the same disadvantage in England. When his first wife died, he married Maria Madden, daughter of a well established Dublin Protestant family, and many years his junior. Jane Lucretia was born in 1797, two years before her father's death. Her widowed mother took the little girl home to Dublin and raised her as a member of the comfortable, but solid, Protestant bourgeoisie.

The genetic mix of Irish willfulness and Teutonic artistic flair would never allow Jane Lucretia to settle for respectable mediocrity. At fourteen, she managed to persuade her family to let her act—presumably because acting opened doors into Dublin's anglo-aristocracy, and the promise of a wealthy match. Her stunning looks and brilliant musical gifts, on the harp as well as the piano, made her a prize at many a soiree. Warm and vivacious, clever and cultured, she had just enough of an Irish pedigree to be accepted in society, and just enough of a foreign history to exert a certain fascination.

Within six months, a dashing, worldly ex-naval officer, John Norcott D'Esterre, had swept her off her feet. Though Jane was still little more than a child, she and her mother seem to have thought it an entirely desirable match. The young merchant came from a well established Limerick family, mainly composed of lawyers. His brother was a judge. In 1811 his ships' chandlery business was thriving, and his home in Bachelor's Walk would have appeared the epitome of affluence and success.

The truth was that port trade was being undermined by a deep economic depression, and there were money problems from the start of their short marriage. D'Esterre moved from one trade to another, begged and borrowed from all his friends to enable him to live up to his expectations, and finally, when he died in 1815, left nothing but debts behind.

2

In the icy winter of 1814-15 frustration was running high amongst the Catholic population. The Protestant-controlled Dublin Corporation was opposed to any concessions, and political equality seemed an impossible dream. But the Catholic majority had found a leader and a voice in lawyer Daniel O'Connell, a large, genial Irishman whose gift for the blarney was combined with a brilliant legal mind.

On January 22nd, at a meeting of the Catholic Board, he referred to the Corporation as "beggarly"—hardly the worst term of abuse he could have employed, given the man's reputation for deadly invective.

But this was a time of severe economic depression and hardship. Lord Mayor Frederick Darley, brother-in-law to Arthur Guinness, the successful brewer, was bankrupt, and utterly dependent on his wife's family to support him. Eight of the aldermen were also bankrupt; the city treasurer's accounts were under investigation; and the Corporation was in debt and couldn't pay its bills. O'Connell had touched a raw nerve.

One of the Corporation's most recent, and most hot-headed-younger members, John Norcott D'Esterre, appeared to take exception to O'Connell's remark, reported in the *Carrick's Morning Post*. The irony is that D'Esterre was one of the few members of the Corporation who had spoken up for Catholic emancipation in the past. At heart D'Esterre was not a bigot. Nor was he "gallant, but unfortunate,"[2] as his wife's family would describe him by way of apology in future years. He was a political nonentity standing for City Sheriff, a post which would confer almost instant relief from his financial worries. A show of anti-Catholic muscle—particularly after he had appeared so accommodating in the past—wouldn't do his cause any harm.

It took D'Esterre three days to demand an apology. O'Connell replied that although he agreed there were no doubt one or two invaluable persons on the Corporation, in view of its treatment of the Catholic community, "no terms attributed to me, however reproachful, can exceed the contemptuous feeling I entertain for that body in its corporate capacity."[3] All future communication was returned to D'Esterre unopened.

Word of the dispute spread quickly and fed the tension in the deeply divided city.

On January 31ˢᵗ D'Esterre swaggered down the centre of Dublin towards O'Connell's chambers at the Four Courts with a whip and pistol in his hand, threatening to shut the loud-mouthed O'Connell forever. The lawyer was twice the size of the wiry little merchant, and Dublin Catholics might have been amused, were it not for D'Esterre's reputation with a gun. In 1797, as First Lieutenant of the Marines, he had played a heroic part in suppressing the mutiny of the Nore. Legend had it that the mutineers had put a rope around his neck and threatened to hang him if he didn't join their side. "Hang away and be damned," he had cried, and they had been so impressed that they had changed their minds.

Crowds turned out to witness the confrontation. D'Esterre lured O'Connell into Grafton Street, where Unionists were ensconced in shop windows ready to watch the fun. As O'Connell and his followers chased after him, D'Esterre dodged into a house and gave him the slip, narrowly averting a riot. O'Connell took refuge from the Unionists in a shop, and was bound over by a judge and ordered to keep the peace.

The following day at Morrison's Hotel in Nassau Street, Sir Edward Stanley, a colleague of D'Esterre's on the Corporation, called on O'Connell's friend, Major MacNamara, a wealthy Protestant from Clare with Catholic sympathies, and once again demanded an apology for the offensive remark. MacNamara, a practised duellist, refused, and with a speed which left Stanley breathless, accepted the challenge and insisted a duel be fought that day at 3 o'clock. Stanley tried to negotiate a postponement, but the only concession he was given was that since this was not a private quarrel, a single shot would suffice.

"No, Sir," he cried, "if they fire twenty shots each, Mr. D'Esterre will never leave the ground until Mr. O'Connell makes an apology."

MacNamara replied, "Well then, if blood be your object, blood you shall have!" and stormed out of the room.

It appears that D'Esterre never really intended a duel at all, but having dug a hole so deep, he couldn't climb out. After all, it had taken him three days to demand an apology, and a further six to confront O'Connell. But his colleagues reassured him that a man who had challenged O'Connell two years earlier had got away without firing a shot, and had been made a judge for his pains.

This was exactly what the ambitious young fool needed to hear. The Unionists were determined to destroy O'Connell, and junior Corporation member D'Esterre, with lofty aspirations and a large ego, was putty in their hands.

It was a bitterly cold February day and snow lay thickly on the ground as O'Connell's carriage rolled into the field in Bishop's Court, County Kildare, the spot some twelve miles west of Dublin chosen for the fight. D'Esterre arrived almost an hour late, at four o'clock, accompanied by Sir Edward Stanley, Mr. Peile, the Surgeon-General of the Dublin Garrison, and his brother, Henry D'Esterre, the recorder of Limerick. As the seconds wrangled over details, carriages and gigs poured into the field. Virtually the entire Dublin Corporation had turned out for the sport.

The two men appeared to be in high spirits. D'Esterre walked around nonchalantly twirling his cane, and O'Connell, seeing his tailor in the crowd, shouted, "Ah, Jerry, I never missed you from an aggregate meeting." MacNamara instructed the inexperienced O'Connell to remove his white neckerchief, since it made him an easy target, and to take off his fob, since it could inflict a worse wound than the bullet.

D'Esterre won the toss and the two men moved into place ten paces, approximately fifty feet, from each other. As the handkerchief fell, D'Esterre stepped to one side and fired. His shot fell short and ricocheted off the ground at O'Connell's feet. O'Connell lifted his pistol. He pressed the trigger, and D'Esterre fell writhing to the ground, an ever-increasing pool of red appearing on the snow. Surgeon Peile and O'Connell's doctor, Surgeon Macklin, who had been asked by O'Connell to help D'Esterre, rushed to his side, but didn't think the wound to his hip mortal.

In shock, O'Connell muttered over and over, "I aimed low, I aimed low." He wanted to see that D'Esterre was all right, but MacNamara led him quickly away.

The city erupted into a frenzy of joy and relief. The Archbishop proclaimed, "Heaven be praised. Ireland is safe," and bonfires burned in the streets, but O'Connell refused to join the celebration. He kept demanding to know whether his friends thought he might have killed a man.

D'Esterre died two days later. A press release issued by the Corporation maintained that D'Esterre was responsible for his own tragedy, and that it had nothing whatsoever to do with them. They quoted him as saying, "I was egged on by no one," and claimed his dying words were of forgiveness—like those of a true Christian gentleman.

But O'Connell never forgave himself. Consumed with a guilt which haunted him for the rest of his life, he never took the sacrament again without wearing a black glove on the hand that had killed D'Esterre. He would not bare it in the Saviour's presence. He went to see D'Esterre's widow and offered her half his income, but she refused his help. Her dignity impressed him greatly, but it didn't assuage his conscience. Eventually he persuaded her to accept a small annuity for her daughter, Amelia, which he paid until his death thirty years later.

3.

D'Esterre's reputation was ruined. The Protestant newspapers called him egotistical and foolish; the Catholic press referred to him disdainfully as a "pork butcher." The papers claimed that the bailiffs moved in before D'Esterre's body was cold, impounded his goods, and would have taken his body for medical science had not Jane Lucretia stolen it away and buried it by candlelight, in the dead of night, somewhere outside the town.[4]

According to the register, he was in fact buried in the parish church of St. Mary's two days after his death. His child, stillborn six months later, was buried close by. Some years after D'Esterre's death, a preacher denouncing the perniciousness of duelling reminded the congregation that one of the most famous victims of a duel lay within the sound of his voice.

Jane Lucretia endeavoured to cope on her own. The poet Byron asked a Dublin friend to see if he could tempt her back onto the stage at Drury Lane, but his offer was no more successful than Daniel O'Connell's. The strain of her situation, the gossip that followed her wherever she went, and the financial and legal wrangling with her late husband's debtors eventually wore her down and drove her close to despair. She began to feel as if events for which she had no responsibility might blight her life forever.

Desperate to escape for a while, she took a house in Ecclefechan in the lowlands of Scotland. One day, sitting by the river, too listless to concentrate on the novel she had taken with her, she was overcome by an almost overwhelming temptation to plunge herself into the waters and find peace at last. The idea of instant release was exerting an increasing attraction, when she was jolted suddenly back into reality by the sound of merry whistling from a field on the other side of the river. Totally unaware of her presence and absorbed in his task, a jaunty young farmer's lad had begun to plough up the soil, whistling hymns as he went about his business. She watched him for some time, marvelling at his concentration as he turned over the furrows, and at the evident satisfaction he gained from doing a simple, very mundane job.

She felt utterly rebuked for her self-pity. The young lad was probably about her age, with none of her responsibilities as a mother. If he could perform a dull but necessary chore with dedication and cheerfulness, the very least she could do was "plough the land she had been given to furrow" with courage and grace. Perhaps, one day the "blessedness of work" would be a reality for her as well.

She returned to Dublin with a new determination to earn her living as a music teacher, to support her child and pay off her debts. The farmer's boy would never know that he had given one young woman the will to live.

Only weeks later, sitting in the gallery of St. George's Church as she did every Sunday, Jane Lucretia heard words that brought joy and meaning into her life far sooner than she ever expected. Listening half-heartedly to the preacher, she was suddenly struck by his famous text as if she were hearing it for the first time. "God so loved the world that he gave his only begotten son." In that moment she understood that God loved not "the world" in general, but her in particular; that this was a love that would not let her down, as John D'Esterre's had done. This was a love that would enable her to hold her head up high, whatever the gossip and the whisperings, no matter how many doors were closed in her face.

Alluring in her severe widow's weeds and flowing black veils, she nonetheless managed to ward off a succession of suitors for fourteen years. When, finally, she did succumb, it was again to the attractions of a military man. And once again she followed her heart, rather than the dictates of financial good sense.

CHAPTER TWO
1815-1829

1.

Jane Lucretia D'Esterre married the dashing ex-army officer Captain John Grattan Guinness in 1829 at the York Street Chapel in Dublin. In many ways the match was a romantic happy ending, for life had not been any kinder to Captain John than it had been to his new bride.

John was the youngest child of Arthur Guinness, brewer of distinction, a servant and nonentity who rose to become one of Dublin's foremost merchants and city leaders. The story of Arthur Guinness, creator of Ireland's most famous stout, is the stuff of legends. No one ever really knew who he was or where he came from, and he was not of a mind to enlighten them. But when he quietly adopted the coat of arms of the Magennises of County Down—one of Ireland's oldest and most powerful Catholic clans, the hereditary earls of Iveagh—no one questioned his right to do so. How and when the family became Protestant and took the name Guinness, no one knew for sure.

Gossip suggested that a well-to-do young woman by the name of Elizabeth Read had broken her parents' hearts by eloping with the family groom, a Richard Guinness of Celbridge. After their marriage he became an agent for the Reverend Dr. Price, Vicar of Celbridge, who later became Archbishop of Cashel. It is possible that Richard Guinness, Arthur's father, may have been descended from the Catholic Magennis tribe, but he was a Protestant, and locals in Celbridge (where the vicar built his residence, Oakley Park) preferred their own story, that he was the illegitimate son of a country girl and a Cornish soldier called Gennys, left behind in 1690 after the Battle of the Boyne. The girl, they said, left her illegitimate son to be raised at the foundling hospital in Leixlip. The rumours were never substantiated, and rent collectors are notoriously unpopular. Regardless of the circumstances, however, Richard Guinness was born sometime around 1690.[5]

What is known is that when the old Archbishop of Cashel died in 1752 he left one hundred pounds to his faithful retainer, Richard Guinness, whose delicious homemade black brew had made the old ecclesiastic a favourite host with the local gentry. Richard became proprietor of the Bear and Ragged Staff in Celbridge and established its reputation as a popular coaching stop.

As for seventeen-year-old Arthur, the Archbishop left him, too, a hundred pounds, little guessing what would sprout from such a small bequest. Richard Guinness's son opened a small brewery in Leixlip and began to concoct a beer unlike any tasted before. Although these were times of great experimentation in brewing, according to public consensus Arthur's brew was by far the best. Some said it started as a mistake, that Arthur had been following his father's recipe, had burned the malting barley, and that the caramelised result had turned out richer and better than the brew he intended. Others said Arthur had stolen the recipe from monks. But no one knew for sure.

Six years later, when Arthur left the small Leixlip operation in the hands of his younger brother, Richard, and set off to make his fortune in Dublin, locals said there was magic in the holy water of St. James's well, and that it was the River Liffey which gave the beer at the new Guinness brewery its distinctive flavour. They may well have been right. The new extra-strong beer known as porter, or stout, required soft water.

The pokey little brewery he acquired for 9,000 years, at an annual rent of £45, had been shut for nine years. It may not have been the most imposing in St. James's Gate, but it was larger than many of its rivals and by Dublin standards, fairly substantial. From the moment he saw it,

Arthur Guinness recognised the unmistakable advantage of the site. From the Dublin mountains, ten miles out of the city, water flowed in plentiful supply into the River Liffey and was carried by a system of pipes right up to the western side of the property, into the city watercourse. Attached was a dwelling place with spacious gardens, a summer house, and a fishpond. Arthur Guinness was well on the way to becoming a gentleman. All he needed now was a wife, preferably one with enough income to keep him in the way to which he intended to become accustomed. This accomplishment he managed within a mere two years.

2.

Olivia Whitmore not only had a mouth-watering inheritance of £1,000; she was also related to some of Dublin's most prestigious families, including that of Henry Grattan, Ireland's greatest orator and foremost politician. She appears to have accepted Arthur Guinness with surprising alacrity. He was not exactly a handsome man, but he was personable, aristocratic in bearing, with a high forehead and an aquiline nose. The glint of steel in the eyes and the finely chiselled chin, passed on to select individuals in future generations, revealed the determination of a breed of men who knew their mind and stuck to it.

Arthur and Olivia married on 17th June, 1761, and Arthur began his meteoric rise. Within two years he was elected Warden of the Corporation of Brewers. The following year he moved out to the suburbs, where he bought Beaumont, his stately home, and began to fill it. Olivia provided the patriarch with twenty-one children, though only six sons—Hosea, Arthur, William Lunell, Benjamin, Edward, and John—and four daughters survived.

In 1790, when he was sixty-six, Arthur Guinness extended his brewery, built two flour mills at Kilmainham for an amount between £4,000 and £5,000, and expressed his gratitude to God, not only for material prosperity, but for his children—especially his second son, Arthur, now twenty-two. Arthur had "grown up to be able to assist me in the business," he explained, "or I would not have attempted it, though prompted by a demand of providing for ten children now living out of one and twenty born to us, and yet more to come." [6]

The brewer adopted as his motto "*Spes* Mea In Deo,"— "My Hope is in God." He must have been a very young man when, for the first time, he heard John Wesley on one of the preacher's many trips to Ireland. The experience profoundly affected Arthur's thinking. He was not offended to hear that the heart of a gentleman was as black and sinful as that of any labourer. On the contrary, the statement appealed to his innate sense of equality and fair play. Throughout his life, however, he remained part of the Church of Ireland in practice, and a non-conformist at heart. The Church satisfied his aspirations, the non-conformist, his integrity. Although Olivia's cousin Edward Smythe was minister of Bethesda Chapel, the leading non-conformist congregation in Dublin, Arthur was not a Methodist. Methodism was too new a movement, too radical for a man of conventional tastes who was mixing increasingly with the Protestant upper classes.

But Wesleyanism taught Arthur that wealth brought responsibility, moral obligation, and public duty. He was treasurer and later Governor of the Meath Charity Hospital. He began the long family association with St. Patrick's Cathedral, lending the Dean and chapter 250 guineas for repairs and alterations to the Chapel schools, refusing repayment and requesting instead that the money be distributed among the pupils. Then, in 1786, he founded Ireland's first Sunday School.

Unlike many of his Protestant peers, he was an enlightened and exemplary employer, treating his Catholic workforce with dignity and respect. More unusually, especially for a member of the Church of Ireland, he publicly supported the Roman Catholic majority in their struggle for equality with the Protestants, equality including full political emancipation, as long as they went about it the proper way: without violence.

In 1791, as Master of the Dublin Guild of the Corporation of Brewers, and official brewer to the Castle, Arthur Guinness began the four-year campaign that would turn brewing into one of Ireland's most lucrative industries. He realized that it was imperative that the government withdraw punitive excise duties and restrict cheap English imports. Parliament prevaricated, fearing that without regulation, Irish brewers would make poor beer.

But Henry Grattan taught his wife's cousin how to maximise political sympathy. Arthur Guinness claimed that alcohol-related problems were rising at an alarming rate, and that the real culprit was whisky, not the healthful, wholesome alternative he had to offer. Distilling, not brewing, should be taxed.

However profoundly Arthur Guinness's thinking was influenced by Wesleyanism, that influence never extended to teetotalism. But did Guinness really believe his campaign was doing the public a service? It never seems to have entered his head that men would drink themselves into a Guinness-induced stupor. To be fair, perhaps Guinness, a man who deplored excess of every kind and spoke out against the gross expenditure of the Council on gluttony and drunkenness, assumed that no one would be able to drink beer in enough quantity to get drunk. Perhaps the very idea was too upsetting to contemplate. After all, beer, not whisky, was the middle-class man's drink, seen at the time as a kind of fortified lemonade.

With all of Ireland's major problems—physical, moral, social, and economic—attributed to strong spirits, after four years Parliament finally yielded and in 1795 repealed all the taxes on beer. In a letter to the brewers, a letter which smacks with the irony of hindsight, Henry Grattan hailed the action as a major piece of social reform. "It is at your source the Parliament will find in its own country the means of health with all her flourishing consequences, and the cure of intoxication with all her misery."[7]

Thus another Guinness family legend was born, a legend popular especially with the descendants of the teetotaller Captain John, founder of the missionary branch of the family: Guinness beer was brewed in the spirit of true altruism, to combat the worst social excesses of whisky drinking. "Beer," said Henry Grattan, "was the natural nurse of the people," and his sentiment was echoed by many an Irishman over the years as he sat finding comfort for his sorrows in a pint, or two, or three.

If Arthur Guinness stands convicted of compromising his Wesleyan values to suit his capitalism, judgment followed. Four of his grandsons had to be dismissed from the brewery for drunkenness and related problems. The patriarch was probably turning in his grave.

When Arthur Guinness died in 1803, his estate was valued for probate at £23,000, a small fortune for the time. In forty years he had turned a white elephant into the biggest business enterprise in Ireland.

His extraordinary entrepreneurial skills had been matched by those of brother Samuel, a prosperous goldbeater. Samuel was to found a line of successful bankers known as the Rundell Guinnesses. Many years later one of Samuel's descendants, the lovely Sabrina, would date that most eligible of bachelors, Charles, the Prince of Wales.

Meanwhile, the brewery passed to Arthur's second son, Arthur. Arthur Sr. had never anticipated the church's depriving him of the natural heir to his business. In his will he bequeathed Beaumont, the family home, to his eldest son, Hosea, who, as rector of the prestigious St. Werbergh's in the city centre for thirty years, was "not...in any line of life whereby he [was] likely by Industry to enlarge his Property."[8] One clergyman in the family for form's sake might be a blessing, remarked old Arthur dryly, but one was enough.

To his relief, old Arthur's second son, Arthur, was as like his father in nature as in name and had inherited what would become the quintessential Guinness flair for business. The physical resemblance was remarkable: the same long, pale face, its length emphasised by a receding hairline and an aquiline nose. The eyes, more hooded than his father's, glinted warily beneath the heavy lids. The set of the jaw gave an impression of dignity and determination, and only a slight curve of the mouth hinted at a carefully concealed store of compassion and generosity.

To this son, Arthur bequeathed the treasured silver salver, presented to him by the Corporation of Brewers of the City of Dublin, to keep in perpetuity as a sign of particular respect, and "to go to the Eldest Male Branch of my Family...who shall be in the brewing trade." [9] Arthur the Second, wearing his father's mantle, stepped into the role which should have belonged to his elder brother, assumed the running of the brewery and with it, the headship of the family. For the first, but not the last time, God had come between a Guinness and his earthly inheritance.

3.

Like his three remaining older brothers, John received a bequest of £1,500. He had by then joined the twelfth regiment native infantry of the Madras Army, undeterred by injuries he had received in the 1798 Dublin uprising when he was only fifteen. Fired by the French revolution, Presbyterians in the north and Catholics in the south had joined forces to establish a democratic Irish republic. A yeomanry was raised to defend the city. Two of Arthur's sons, Edward and William Lunell, volunteered immediately, while Arthur and Benjamin were left behind to look after the brewery. Young John, desperate to see some action, had ignored family warnings to stay away from the defences and was severely wounded carrying dispatches. His father was furious, not only with him, but with all violence and the bloodshed it caused.

John did not share his father's distaste, and his yen for adventure took him to India, home from home for many an Irishman with military ambitions. By the turn of the century the 250-year-old Mogul Empire had collapsed, and the country was divided into a number of warring princely states. It was a prime opportunity for European imperialism.

The East India Company, which recruited the young John Guinness almost as soon as his wounds had healed, had been created as a trading company during the reign of Elizabeth the First. By 1765 it ruled the vast province of Bengal, reducing its mighty princes to mere dependents. Every rapacious director, civil servant, merchant, or army officer grasped at a piece of this exotic land. Every Muslim sultan, Hindu rajah, marauding thug and bandit was equally determined to make them release their grip.

When war broke out between England and France, Tippu Sultan, Rajah of Mysore, a clever and powerful prince, recognised a chance to manipulate the situation for his own ends and made a treaty with the French. In 1798, to bring him to heel, the English sent one of their most famous Irish soldiers: Arthur Wellesley.

Wellesley, later Duke of Wellington, had been Viceroy of Ireland and was excruciatingly bored at Dublin Castle, where, apart from the republican uprising, life consisted of little more than handing the ladies of the Anglo-Irish ascendancy in and out of their carriages. He was no doubt unaware that his brewer's youngest son, also desperate for action, had followed him out.

In India that young son—a tall, dark, rather good-looking teenager—found plenty to satisfy his appetite for excitement. Fighting methods, stretching every nerve until it was taut, were mean and underhanded by gentlemanly British standards. An unwitting soldier had a nail driven into his skull; another had his neck wrung by Hindu strongmen known as Jetties. A prisoner was subject to prolonged torture.

After a lengthy siege, Wellesley took Tippu Sultan's capital, Seringapatam, installed himself as governor, and appointed a new rajah. One of Tippu's supporters, a brigand from Mahratta with the unlikely name of Dhoondiah Waugh, managed to escape during the English assault and, gathering a band of Tippu's men around him, made a series of successful guerilla raids across the border from Mahratta into Mysore, inflicting serious losses on the English army. Wellesley was instructed to hang Dhoondiah Waugh from the highest tree.

In years to come John Grattan would regale his children with romantic tales of following the great general in the chase which would make Wellington's military reputation. The reality was far different from the romance: mile upon mile of marching in intense heat, freezing nights, and constant danger from bandits. Dhoondiah and his untrained thugs were no real contest for the English, and his mission accomplished, Wellesley led his victorious fighting force back to Seringapatam.

John Grattan's two years in the garrison there, restoring law and order to the province were among the most difficult he had ever known. The natives were easy to manage compared with the troops who bullied and threatened them, engaging in looting, drunken brawling, and debauchery as soon as Wellesley's back was turned. The youngest son of Arthur Guinness was deeply disillusioned. The Honourable East India Company was honourable in name only. This assignment was not the glorious victory he had painted in his vivid imagination. He longed for action and was relieved when, in 1803, Wellesley decided to deal with the violent princes of the Mahratta states once and for all. He assumed it would be as easy as the defeat of Dhoondiah Waugh, but he was wrong. In two years the French had transformed the marauding hordes of Mahratta into an intelligent, well-disciplined fighting force, equipped with skills in military intelligence and the latest weapons. As the English tried to navigate a treacherous system of river tributaries, the Indian troops advanced, inflicting huge casualties at Assaye. John Grattan survived the carnage, helped to subdue the enemy princes—and won his commission. His greatest disappointment was that his father had not lived to see his success.

In 1805 Wellesley was recalled. Captain John stayed on, determined to live the kind of upright life his hero commended to his officers. One day he received a letter from brother Edward, enthusiastic about the potential of two large ironworks in Palmerston and Lucan. Edward wanted to buy them but hadn't enough money. Arthur, William, and Benjamin were too strongly committed to the brewery to help, but John still had his inheritance. He didn't need it in India, but well invested, it would be worth a great deal more when he came home. Captain John, naive in all but military matters, unaware of his brothers' lack of confidence in Edward's business ability, willingly handed his legacy over. Whatever shrewd financial sense old Arthur possessed had been absorbed by the rest of the family before it reached the youngest of his sons.

When Captain John came home on leave in 1810, he met and married Susanna Hutton, daughter of a local alderman, but any thoughts of settling down to a more quiet life were shattered when the ironworks collapsed. Hounded by creditors, Edward fled with his wife, Margaret, and their five children to Dundalk, where, in terror of debtor's prison, he besieged his brewing brothers with demands for money. His letters were full of a sanctimonious self-pity and piety. "I must wait for the Lord's good time and use reasonable means to save my person,"[10] he wrote. Edward certainly wasn't bothered about his brother John's person, and in 1813, left him, Susanna, and their two baby sons in Scotland,[11] while he escaped to the Isle of Man, a safe haven from the Insolvent Act.

Worn down and more than a little irritated by the constant barrage of requests, Arthur finally paid off his brother's exorbitant debts, putting the very future of the family business in jeopardy. He found Edward a job at the brewery as a clerk, a position Edward regarded as beneath him. But the destitute Captain John—father of two small sons, John Grattan and Arthur Grattan—had no alternative but to return to India where the army would divest him of his health and another fourteen years of his life.

4.

John could no longer cope with the climate, his wrecked digestive system, or the constant massacre of human life. The conquest of northern Burma in 1824 under Lord Moira almost broke him. Fighting had lost its appeal.

Wesleyan teaching was having a having a profound impact on an ever-increasing number of officers in the mess, and Captain John was no exception. Wesley was dead, and Methodism had been outlawed in 1810. Meetings were broken up, their leaders beaten and imprisoned; but under pressure the movement spread like wildfire—all the way to India, where disillusioned, unhappy British officers provided it with a highly fertile environment.

Even if his religion had been a mere formality in recent years, the youngest son of Arthur Guinness was highly susceptible to notions of justice, morality, and decency. Like Jane Lucretia, he experienced a revelation of God's love which changed the direction and values of his life. The Bible now appeared a much more effective weapon in dealing with the ails of mankind than did the sabre or the gun.

Captain John arrived home unwell in 1825, with a wife, two sons, two daughters, and an army pension of £100 a year, very modest by the family standards of the brewing Guinnesses. Like all his brothers and sisters, he expected brother Arthur to provide, and Arthur complied. He was in the process of expanding Guinness exports to England, and there was a vacancy for an astute young businessman at their agency in Liverpool, run by his partners, Bewley and Neville, at 29 Manesty Lane.

Captain John's brief was to make the agency self-supporting as quickly as possible. The retired soldier did his best, but it soon became apparent to Bewley and Neville that their new manager wasn't made of the same stuff as his elder brother. Despite his recklessness in battle, the captain was a mild-mannered man without the tenacity needed in economic warfare. Nor had he the heart for it, for there was one other major problem. Alcohol was anathema to the non-conformist. John Grattan had become the first Wesleyan in his family, in worship as well as persuasion, and in so doing, had effectively snubbed brother Hosea and a host of clerical brothers-in-law by leaving the established church. He was also the first teetotaler Guinness.

He suggested to Bewley and Neville that they might like to replace whisky with another commodity—food perhaps? The idea was not financially viable, however, and in the end, rather than place them in an embarrassing position, Captain John withdrew from the partnership. A few months later, when Susanna died, brother Arthur agreed to take on Captain John's eldest son, John Grattan Junior, as an apprentice at the brewery. And Captain John decided he himself was suitable for very little other than to lead the life of a retired officer and Christian gentleman.

In middle age he was still the most handsome of the Guinness brothers, with an erect, military bearing and a strong, dignified face set off by the high collars and cravats he wore. There was no hint of grey in the dark hair, even in the long sideburns, and the only suggestion of the trauma of past years was the unusual pallor of his complexion. His youthful drive and bravado had long burnt out, leaving a shy man who often hid behind spectacles and preferred the simple, solitary pleasures of reading and walking to the high life of Dublin society. In this refined, gentle man, Jane Lucretia D'Esterre found the qualities she most admired. Elegant and vivacious, she bowled him over at once, but he saw beyond the mystique of her notorious past to the depths of her character, moulded by hard experience and her evangelical Christian faith. In many ways it was an ideal partnership. He needed her to stir him from his phlegmatism. She needed his quiet strength. But that was all Captain John Grattan had to offer. Jane Lucretia was destined to marry men without the capacity to earn a regular income.

CHAPTER THREE
1829-1845

1.

Captain John was not the only family member to turn for help and support to his elder brother, Arthur Guinness the Second. The new patriarch was afflicted with a host of difficult relatives. Since the bankruptcy of brother Edward, a steady stream of brothers, sisters, nieces, and nephews tugged at his heart, as well as his purse strings.

An instinctive sense of duty and decency would not allow Arthur see any of his family destitute. Besides, he loved his nine brothers and sisters, and he genuinely wanted to do his best for them and their offspring. A veritable army of nephew-apprentices was now working at the brewery with a view to developing their managerial and business potential. They were carefully supervised by John Purser Junior, a formidable Guinness partner; and woe betide them if their behaviour did not enhance the brewery's reputation and moral standing in the community. Arthur Guinness's charity would not stretch to anyone whose conduct impugned the firm's good name.

Even Hosea, Arthur's eldest brother, was not above asking for a supplement to his stipend. Times were hard for the clergy in Ireland. They were accustomed to a high standard of living, but stipends were drawn from the compulsory tithe, imposed since the Act of Union on Protestant and Catholic alike. Understandably, the Catholic community bitterly resented being forced to support a church they despised, and as relations deteriorated, the Catholics withheld the tithe as a means of protest, leaving a host of clerical Guinnesses in pecuniary distress.

In 1819 Arthur's own eldest son, William Smythe Lee Grattan, as his Uncle Hosea had done, announced his intention of foregoing his natural inheritance in the family business to enter the church. Such was Arthur's personal faith that he could hardly be surprised or disappointed. And once again, there were more sons at home to join their father at the brewery.

With his wife, Anne Lee, whom he had married in 1793, Arthur had three sons, William born in 1795, Arthur Lee in 1797, and Benjamin Lee in 1798. The couple also had six daughters between 1804 and 1814, raising them at Beaumont, which Arthur had bought from Hosea, who could not afford to run it and needed extra financial help when his daughter, Olivia, became mentally ill.

An affectionate husband and father, Arthur was devastated when his Anne died, and shortly afterwards he married her closest friend, a respectable spinster by the name of Maria Barker. Unlike her future sister-in-law, Jane Lucretia, the thirty-eight-year old Maria did not provide her husband with a second family, which was probably just as well since Arthur already had more than enough relatives with claims on his time and his bank account.

The potential he expected from his apprentice-nephews failed to materialise. Many left in disgrace because of their drunken behaviour. Small wonder that Arthur wrote to his sister-in-law Jane Lucretia, as she was starting out with a young family all over again, "Early control can alone secure, under God's blessing, obedience and steady conduct."[12]

Arthur's family seemed to be acquiring as many clergy as black sheep. His own eldest son, Hosea's eldest son, and William Lunell's only son had all chosen careers in the church. Three of his daughters married Church of Ireland clergymen. It was becoming increasingly difficult to ensure a succession of reasonable, let alone feasible managers for the brewery.

And both sorts of Guinness, clerical and lamentable, pursued Arthur as if his pockets were bottomless. Any tussle for his soul between God and mammon was doomed from the start by a clan who knew how to manipulate his Christian conscience.

2.

Like his father, the second Arthur Guinness was a man of immense integrity who did what he deemed right, whatever the cost. At one point that integrity almost cost the brewery its very existence.

The early years of the nineteenth century were boom years for the brewer. He took advantage of the war between England and France to extend imports across the Bristol Channel. What better way to put strength into the young men resisting Napoleon's steady advance across Europe?[13] The end of the war with the defeat of Napoleon in 1815, and the subsequent unemployment created a severe economic depression throughout the whole of Britain, particularly in Ireland. To make matters worse, in 1817 and 1819 the potato crop failed.

The Guinness brothers were appalled by the poverty and human misery all around them. They served on a host of charitable committees, Arthur as founding member of the Society for Improving the Conditions of Children Employed as Chimney Sweepers, and William Lunell on a committee to end begging. But committees were impotent in the face of such distress. A radical economic policy was called for.

As Governor of the Bank of Ireland, Arthur was determined to introduce whatever stringent measures that policy required—even at the cost of his own interests. Wearing his banking rather than his brewing hat, he united the Irish and English currency, causing widespread deflation and ten very lean years for the family business. Settling brother Edward's debts compounded his financial problems. Surviving against overwhelming odds was a close-run affair, but Arthur had proved that he was a man of principle, prepared to put his country and his family before his own material prosperity. Writing to his teenage son, Benjamin Lee, he noted with pleasure the improvement in young Ben's handwriting and the care he was taking with his schoolwork, but added this proviso:

"My dear Ben,...recollect that although diligence in our worldly calling is our indispensable duty as Christians, yet we have a higher than these to engage our attention, for we have a heavenly calling in Christ Jesus and to this our supreme diligence is required."[14]

Arthur's colleagues at the bank were quite well pleased with their Governor's fiscal skills at first. Their pleasure diminished rapidly when he vetoed a rise in salary—his and theirs. Heaven knew his own financial situation could have benefited from a larger salary, but he was only too well aware of how it would look. The public would presume the directors had an ulterior motive for the currency reforms he had introduced. Arthur Guinness would not be the beneficiary of a nineteenth-century "fat cat" pay-out. The man who always kept a Bible open on his desk at work and finished every transaction with a word of prayer could find no biblical justification for self-interest. Like his father before him, he was austere in his standards for men in public office.

In 1821, the state visit to Ireland of King George IV included a tour of the Bank, and it was Arthur Guinness who welcomed him and showed him round. This was the first of many crossing of the ways for the Guinness family and British royalty, and in typical fashion for a tradesman who had no time for cant or social climbing, Arthur was not greatly impressed. Years later he declined the privilege of becoming "Purveyor of Porter" to Queen Victoria, on the grounds that the position was "a useless feather, and, I think, not even a respectable feather."[15] Future generations did not share his disdain for royal patronage. They coveted a great deal more than a token feather as wealth propelled them up the social ladder.

Arthur believed implicitly in the value and rights of every human being. Unusually for a Protestant, he called himself "a sincere advocate for Catholic freedom," because he felt too much ashamed to look his Catholic neighbour in the face. "I felt I was placed in an unjust, unnatural elevation above him; and I considered how I would have felt if placed in a different position myself. Sorrow always excited my mind by such a contemplation."

But walking the political tightrope was difficult. On the one hand, the Guinness brothers had a strong sense of national pride, identifying with the Irish people rather than the English landlords. On the other, since the uprising had followed so closely behind the carnage of the French Revolution, they had been alerted to how small a spark could light a fuse. Basic human rights were one thing; an independent republic was quite another.

Arthur finally managed to win Catholics the right to admission to the Court of the Bank of Ireland, at the cost of a great deal of popularity among his Protestant colleagues. But the achievement didn't win him the warm acceptance of the Catholic community. In October 1813 the *Milesian Magazine,* a nineteenth-century Irish *Private Eye*, published this little piece of doggerel:

> *To be sure did you hear*
> *Of the heresy beer*
> *That was made for to poison the Pope?*
> *To hide the man a sin is*
> *His name is Arthur Guinness*
> *For salvation he never can hope.*

According to the writer, a certain "Dr. Brennan," Guinness beer was impregnated with heresy, since 136,000 tons of Bibles and 501,000 carloads of hymn books and Protestant catechisms were poured into the brew. Brennan's analysis of the liquid proved beyond all doubt that anti-popery porter had the power to subvert all good Catholics by inducing "a disposition to bowels particularly lax, an inclination to pravity, and to singing the Lord's praises through the nose." Dr. Brennan suggested drinking Pimm's porter instead.

The Guinnesses were not amused. Aware of an increasingly glacial feel to the wind, Hosea decided it was time to confirm the family pedigree. In 1814 he wrote to Sir William Bethan, deputy Ulster King of Arms and Herald of all Ireland, and asked for official permission for all the descendants of Richard Guinness of Celbridge to use the Magennis crest and coat of arms. Sir William replied tartly, as Hosea suspected, that there were no records to suggest he was entitled to them. But since the first Arthur had already been using them, Sir William would grant a new coat of arms. But for a minor change or two, it happened to be the Magennis crest anyway. Now the family could confidently claim Irish, not English, descent from the hereditary earls of Iveagh.

Hosea's efforts, however, couldn't spare the family further political difficulties. Over the years, Arthur Guinness's support for Daniel O'Connell, whom he helped to win a by-election, was slowly eroded by what he saw as the increasing fanaticism of O'Connell's Catholic Association. The Catholics were calling for an end to the Act of Union at any price, and Arthur Guinness saw no advantages in hot-headedness or republicanism. In the General Election of 1835, a mere five years after he had accused the government of being oppressive, Arthur not only opposed O'Connell, but seriously considered a request to stand against him. "I think," he is reported to have said, "that the time has come when it is the bounden duty of every man to speak his sentiments and to declare whether he is for the destruction or preservation of the constitution."[16]

O'Connell was devastated. His newspaper, *The Pilot*, described how for years Arthur Guinness had publicly resisted the intolerance of the Protestant Orange system. He was a man "who never committed but this one public error," and the Catholics were at a loss to know why. It could not have escaped their attention that Arthur's youngest brother had just married the widow of John D'Esterre.

O'Connell's only explanation for his one-time friend's betrayal was that his hard-done-by clergy relatives had "got about him," prejudicing him against the Catholics. It was a stab in the dark, but it may well have hit the bull's eye. In all probability Arthur Guinness was less disturbed by O'Connell's "extremism," which had barely changed over the years, than by the liberal government's plans to separate from the Church of Ireland. Eight of Arthur's relatives were clergy, dependent on tithes no longer paid by Catholics—dependent therefore on him. He could hardly have been pleased.

In the end the liberal Whig government collapsed, and a General Election brought the Tories back into power. Arthur Guinness heaved a sigh of relief while O'Connell bitterly regretted the end of their long association, referring to Guinness as "that miserable old apostate."

Small wonder that some years later, when his son Benjamin Lee was invited to stand for a Dublin seat, Arthur urged him to decline. But Benjamin Lee simply bided his time. Having witnessed his father's failure to maintain a political balancing act, he had decided on a safer option as a convinced Unionist. Never again would the Guinness family climb their way back into the Liberal fold, and one potentially moderating voice in the Catholic and independence cause was stilled forever.

3.

In 1839, financial and political crises over, Arthur was looking forward to a quiet retirement. His sons Arthur Lee and Benjamin Lee appeared to be running the brewery well. It was time to hand over the silver salver. But there was one family crisis yet to come.

One day, Arthur Lee confessed to his father that he had been leading a double life. Not only was he incompetent at managing the brewery; he couldn't manage his own affairs and was heavily in debt. Mortified by his failure, he admitted that he couldn't actually bear the trade at all. It was a daily affront to his artistic nature, and he begged not only forgiveness, but to be released from the business immediately.

Arthur was deeply shocked. It appears that he had never had the slightest inkling of Arthur Lee's emotional or economic struggles. Overspending and financial mismanagement were beyond Arthur's own powers of comprehension, yet he put aside his strict code of personal conduct, never once reproaching his son, and dealt with the situation as thoughtfully and even-handedly as he knew how.

The practicalities of enabling his son to withdraw from the brewery were complicated. If Arthur Lee took his half share he would leave Ben and the business in a perilous state. In fact there was some discussion about winding it up altogether. Arthur Lee was moved at the suggestion, but decided he would content himself with a moderate allowance rather than risk destroying the goose that laid the golden egg. In 1840 a new family agreement was drawn up, enabling Arthur Lee to take what he called "a moderate £12,000" out of the business, enough to buy Stillorgan Park on the outskirts of Dublin.

There he exchanged materialistic pursuits for aesthetic pleasures, rebuilding the house and indulging to the full a Romantic, neo-Gothic lifestyle. At last he had the proper setting for his paintings, for composing Pantheistic verses and writing letters sealed with the design of a young Greek god. Dark, slim, and good-looking, his attempts to play the part made him look more of a dandy than a classical deity or a Byron.

Arthur was mystified by his son's behaviour and wished that his veneration of the Romantic poets could be replaced by "some token of his being awakened to a sense of the value of the Gospel of our Lord Jesus Christ." He urged him to self-discipline, particularly in his passion for beautiful objects. They were all very well, but he ought to "lay something by for the evil day." But Arthur Lee had inherited his father's generosity of spirit without the prudence and discretion which made it feasible. When the "evil day" finally came in 1845 with the failure of the potato crops and widespread famine, he did everything in his power to look after his tenants. And they loved him for it, erecting a small obelisk in green Connemara marble, "to mark the veneration of his faithful labourers who in a period of dire distress were protected by his generous liberality from prevailing destitution." His memory would "ever remain green in Irish hearts"; but it was Guinness beer money which made his generosity possible.

The appalling famine did not leave old Arthur untouched. Like many of his social class living in protected seclusion in Dublin, he had no idea of the extent of the disaster until he read about it in the *London Record* while on holiday in Torquay. The English newspapers contained graphic descriptions of children lying dying on the waysides, of bodies left unburied where they had died, the stench filling the countryside, while wealthy landlords did nothing. Thousands of Irish immigrants were pouring into Britain from crowded boats, riddled with the plague and countless other diseases.

Horrified, Arthur dashed off a letter to Benjamin Lee at once. "How awful do the accounts from Ireland continue and how evident is it that the exertions of the Government need to be aided by those of private individuals." He could hardly tell a man of nearly fifty what to do with his money, even if he was his son. But Ben evidently did not take the hint, so Arthur wrote again, this time more explicitly. "May the Lord in his infinite mercy direct our Government and all individuals possessing means to do so the use of measures to relieve if possible the sufferings of our wretched poor people. I wish to know of any mode in which we might be able to aid in the work. You know my dear Ben that my purse is open to the call."[17]

Benjamin Lee now ran the brewery single-handedly, showing exceptional flair for the task. Arthur stepped back into an advisory role, watching the brewery's rapid expansion with evident satisfaction. Guinness's unique black stout was beginning to find its way all round the world. In 1837 future Prime Minister Disraeli recorded eating oysters and drinking Guinness at the Carlton Club. Michael Solomon Alexander, first Anglican Bishop of Jerusalem (whose appointment Arthur, as key member of the Hibernian branch of the Church Missionary Society, had encouraged) wrote to the old brewer, "We are daily enjoying your excellent porter, which I think has done much to keep up our strength. I regret to say we have lost some on the voyage. I have no doubt that you will be pleased that your excellent beverage has found its way to Jerusalem." It must indeed have warmed the cockles of the old man's Christian heart to know that his beer was on a vital mission to the Holy Land.[18]

"My bodily health and my mental vigour are both preserved to a degree very unusual at the age of nearly 84,"[19] he wrote, evidently with some surprise. He still served on numerous civic and charitable committees—the Farming Society of Ireland, the Dublin Ballast Board which managed the docks, an exclusive business club known as the Ouzel Galley Society, the Meath Hospital, the Dublin Society, and the Dublin Chamber of Commerce, of which he had been president for many years. "We have much cause for continued thanksgiving to our God, who giveth us all things richly to possess," he wrote in 1851 to his highly prosperous son, Benjamin Lee, Lord Mayor of Dublin. In 1855 *Freeman's Journal* described Arthur as "our most distinguished citizen."

When he died peacefully some months later, the Magennis crest was in evidence at his funeral, appropriately for one who had such a strong sense of Irish identity. Dublin mourned a man who had followed his religious principles to the best of his conscience, at great personal cost. Arthur Guinness' faith, however, did not make him a joyless, narrow-minded bigot. The evidence in his letters, often written to members of his family in their crises, reveals that "the Guinness' faith was a generous broadening one. It comforted and strengthened them." [20]

4.

While Arthur was enjoying political and financial success, Arthur's youngest brother, Captain John Grattam, and his new wife led a nomadic existence, living at first in Dublin, then Edinburgh, Cheltenham, and Clifton, constantly looking for cures for John's fragile constitution. For six years there were no children, but to the couple's delight, in 1835 (the same year that Captain John Grattan's second son, Arthur, married Jane Lucretia's daughter, Amelia), they produced a son, Henry Grattan Guinness. John was fifty-two, and Jane was thirty-eight. Their baby was born in the year of Halley's comet, a propitious omen for a child who would grow up to study astronomical charts. Their firstborn was dedicated to God at York Street Chapel, and then, while Arthur Grattan and Amelia were providing them with grandchildren, the older couple produced three more children themselves: Robert Wyndham in 1837, Frederick in 1839, and Lucy in 1841.

Captain John's favourite occupation was house-building, a vital occupation since he moved his young family so often. Cheltenham was their favourite place of residence, and they settled there for some time when the children were growing up. Its sheltered position and mild climate made it an oasis for retired officers from the East India Company. It was said that "you couldn't fire a shot-gun in any direction without hitting a colonel." [21]

It was a gracious, beautiful, old town with exclusive clubs and villas whose verandas and porches overlooked wide, tree-lined avenues, in many ways a replica of life in India. The spa waters were reputed to do wonders for a liver and stomach disordered by years of unwholesome food. If that were not enough to attract Captain John Grattan and his wife, the Madras army officers had also imported their piety, making the town the English gentleman's evangelical Mecca.

The most powerful local figure was the Rev Francis Close, Vicar of St. Mary's parish, known locally, because of his authoritarianism, as "the Pope." Though he was low church and evangelical he was too establishment for the son of Arthur Guinness, who passed him by in favour of Dr. Archibald Brown, minister of the Congregational Chapel and a liberal in politics.

The couple were very happy, he pottering, she chivvying him along, reminding him of his responsibilities to both his first and his second family, taking upon her own shoulders all the practical details of running the home.

According to his son, Henry Grattan, Captain John was a man of "decidedly religious turn." One abiding childhood memory was reading to his father in their home in Clifton, where they moved some years later, from the 21st and 22nd chapters of the book of Revelation, "the light of the street lamp shining into the quiet room where we sat together, and the solemn, beautiful imagery of the chapter relating to the New Jerusalem seeming to shed over the scene a purer and loftier light." Though he was still young, he felt as if he had entered into his father's profound admiration for the passage, and felt with him, "the vibration of a soul attuned to eternal realities." [22]

There were great similarities between father and son. Both lived half in this world, half in the next, leaving the lesser, mundane necessities of basic survival, such as food and finance, to the practical good sense of their spouses.

Jane Lucretia teased her husband for his lack of practical sense. One surviving letter between the two, written on 9th August 1842 from 5 Carlton Place in Clifton to Captain John in Ireland who was visiting the children by his first marriage and his sister Mary Anne, married to the Rev John Burke, MP for Ballydugan in Galway, reveals an affectionate couple who obviously didn't find separation easy. He had asked her to drop everything and join him. Although she misses him, she appears to find his proposition romantic, if somewhat impractical. Decent child-minding arrangements were obviously as much of a problem then as now.

> As to your affectionate invitation, would you really like to see the house, which I believe is yours, completely turned outside the windows and the children after it! "On Horror's head, horror's accumulate." I would as soon put a little lap dog over my house and family as the lady you mention..."Tell it not in Gath" that a lady of my sapient time of life should elope without ever the temptation of a lover's attendance. I have the Demon of Ruin to wave his wand over my domicile.

Jane Lucretia appears as charming and coquettish in middle age as she was when she first dazzled Irish society with her wit and vivacity. Wherever they lived, she was also well-known for performing acts of charity, visiting the sick, gathering poor children into ragged schools, reclaiming fallen women, reasoning, Bible in hand, with the Jews, and stopping to talk to people in the street about their eternal destiny. In the evening, while he read, she wrote letters and poems, painted in oils, produced an illustrated book on flora and fauna, recited poetry to her children, and sang hymns accompanying herself on the harp.

By the time of Henry's birth she had already produced a book of religious poems, dedicated to the Right Honourable the Viscountess de Vesci, "calculated to excite the best feelings of the heart," its profits "to be devoted to the aid of a respectable family in reduced circumstances."

For someone of Jane Lucretia's brilliant temperament and artistic gifts, life in Cheltenham and Clifton must have been a little dull after Dublin. She never complained of frustration, but was determined nonetheless to inspire her children with a love of the arts. Years later, Henry Grattan wrote, "Whatever love I have had for nature, for history, for literature, has been derived from her, and also whatever gift I may possess as a public speaker." [23]

The only real threat to John and Jane's serene existence was the behaviour of John Grattan junior, Captain John's eldest son by his first marriage. In 1838 he arrived on their doorstep in deep disgrace. His Uncle Arthur had dismissed him from his brewery apprenticeship for drunkenness and mixing in degraded company, insisting he leave Dublin altogether. It was the first they knew that a child of theirs was going astray and it came as a severe shock. Captain John persuaded his brother this was a temporary aberration, and begged him to give his son another chance. There were new brewing opportunities and family contacts in Bristol. Wetherman, the Bristol agent, was duly instructed to buy the young man a small brewery in the town, but there was no evidence of any reforming of John Grattan junior's character, and the brewery collapsed in 1845.

CHAPTER FOUR
1845-1860

1.

The second Arthur Guinness left £150,000. Each of his nephews and nieces received £400 in trust for their 21st birthdays. Some young men might have been impressed, but not Henry Grattan Guinness. Throughout his life money would never be more to him than a tiresome necessity.

Of all his uncles, Arthur Guinness made the deepest impression during occasional childhood visits to Dublin with his father. The old gentleman was dignified and kindly, and always commented on Henry Grattan's namesake, telling him that if he grew up with a fraction of the gift of oratory of his illustrious cousin and forebear, Ireland's greatest politician, he would go far.

Henry listened carefully to the many conversations in the family home about religion, business and politics, and especially to any mention of the notorious Daniel O'Connell, discussed in hushed voices when his parents were out of the room. History nurtured a vivid imagination, and he grew up with a deep love of the country of his roots.

After Captain John's death in 1850, contact with the Dublin Guinnesses was more sporadic. Arthur the Second rightly assessed that his youngest brother would not have left his second family well provided for, and despite his obvious failure with John's eldest son, offered 14 year old Henry an apprenticeship at the brewery. But the boy had been raised in the society of military gentlemen, who whiled away the hours recounting fantastic adventures in exotic, faraway places. Henry's dreams were made of far more exciting stuff than brewing, and he turned the offer down.

He had been a solitary child, spending hours wandering, collecting fossil ammonites and belemnites, reading or daydreaming, completely absorbed in the rays of sunshine falling on the walls of a romantic old castle. When Captain John died, it was an enormous blow. Henry, who had spent much of his childhood at school in Exeter, suddenly realised he had never really known this reserved, quiet man, and now the chance was gone forever.

The bereavement left him feeling bereft and cheated. Drowning his sorrows in some of the seedier local taverns, he fell into what he would later refer to in dramatic tones as "evil company" and "evil ways."

Jane Lucretia's anxiety about her eldest son was compounded when at 17 he decided to follow his younger brother, Robert Wyndham, to sea, sailing to Mexico and the West Indies as a midshipman, transporting thousands of pounds worth of precious cargo for owners who wouldn't dream of hazarding the dangers of the ocean themselves. He certainly found the adventure he craved. Some of the crew deserted on the way home, and it was largely thanks to his presence of mind that the ship was saved. He battled at the wheel for four hours at a stretch, fighting to keep the vessel on course in gale-force winds. Years later he claimed he could still feel, "the jerk of the wheel as the vessel bounds over the billows, leaning to leeward before a stiff breeze," and vividly recall the adrenalin rush of, "battling single-handed with the top gallant sail when sent aloft to furl it before the rising storm."[24]

After that experience, any thought of an ordinary existence was out of the question. He was no sooner back than he set off for Lough Corrib to train as a farmer with a view to emigrating to the colonies. But an unexpected event one night in 1854 changed, if not his passion for travel, than at least his course of direction.

At home in Cheltenham, at two o'clock in the morning, he and his mother were fast asleep in their beds, when they were suddenly woken by a loud banging on the front door. Wyndham was home after sixteen months at sea on the *Francis Ridley*. There were visitors in the house and the only available place to sleep was next to his elder brother. Instead of regaling Henry with tales of the countries and sights he had seen, as Henry hoped, Wyndham told him instead the story of the ship's chief mate, a man called Peek. Peek had been laughed to scorn for his outspoken Christian convictions by the foul-mouthed, abusive crew—until a storm such as Wyndham had never experienced in his life threatened to capsize the ship. While the brash and brazen crewmen clung to the masts, terrified for their lives, Peek knelt calmly on the deck and prayed for the storm to cease. When it did—almost at once—universal mockery gave way to grudging respect. Wyndham was the first convert. Which man, however hard his exterior, hadn't, in extremis, remembered his mother's prayers?

Wyndham's voiced tailed off as he fell into a deep sleep, but Henry lay awake all night, tossing and turning. He suddenly recalled having measles when he was ten, lying in a darkened room, while his half-sister, Rebecca, talked to him of the beauty of heaven. He vividly remembered the way her face became illuminated with a strange, other-worldly glow. He had wanted then that, "mental vision of moral loveliness," but it had always eluded him, leaving a deep, yawning pit at the centre of his being which none of his adventures had been able to fill.

At breakfast the next morning his younger sister, Lucy could see, despite the dark circles under his eyes, that her eldest brother was a changed man. That morning he started to read *Hawker's Morning and Evening Portion*, scribbling notes about the Bible passage of the day in pencil in the margins.

But the deep restlessness was unabated, and when news reached the two brothers that Captain Peek was looking for a crew to accompany him to the East Indies, to Jane's despair, the two brothers set off together. Henry only got as far as Hartlepool, where he was put ashore and sent home to Cheltenham, dying. But he made a speedy recovery, and in the spring of 1855, set off for Tipperary to become a farmer's assistant.

Farming was tedious. He was much happier wandering the countryside with his gun—until he fell in a ditch, sprained his ankle and found himself with time for serious reflection. What if this misadventure were not a coincidence, but divine judgement on a renegade who had frittered away twenty precious years in selfish pursuits? If that was so, what did God want of him? He spent hours alone in the woods, seeking inner peace and the way ahead.

At last, "The gates of glory and immortality opened to my mental vision and there shone before me an interminable vista of pure and perfect existence in the life to come."[25] Inspired by this new awareness of eternal salvation, he was now alerted to, "the miserable and abject slaves of Romish superstition," all around him and began to preach in the marketplace, in fields, on street corners, anywhere local people would stop and listen. And they did, in such numbers that a local priest called Father H was so annoyed, that he set off on horse-back with a whip to silence the young Protestant upstart.

When he found him, he also found most of his congregation giving the handsome preacher their rapt attention. From being a gawky boy, Henry Grattan had turned into a striking young man, tall and slim, with a mane of shoulder-length brown hair, parted in the centre, and large, dark luminous eyes.

"How dare you disturb the peace of the countryside," the priest raged at him.

Henry said he wasn't disturbing the peace, he was offering the people real peace.

"Your religion is false," the priest retorted, "a cursed lie. I challenge you to prove the truth of the Bible on which you say it is founded."

Henry was about to do so when Father H turned his horse and galloped off in fury, shouting, over his shoulder, that he would denounce the young preacher as a madman when he was next in the pulpit.

The next Sunday the priest instructed his congregation to kick Henry, to splash him with sink water or throw him into the nearest puddle if he tried to gain entry to their cottages. Henry's employer was warned that if he didn't silence his assistant, his hayricks would be burnt to the ground.

Henry enjoyed the opposition. It was confirmation that he had found his life's work, especially as many local people ignored the priest and flocked to hear him, tears pouring down their faces as he preached. He was appalled by the ignorance of rural Catholics, steeped in superstitions that held them in the vice of grinding poverty. They told him that Protestantism had been invented by Henry VIII who had imprisoned Mary Queen of Scots and married his own daughter. "These people are unconvertible," warned the Protestant governess at the farmhouse. "Thank God," Henry wrote in his diary, "she was, through my poor testimony, converted herself shortly afterwards."

Henry's employer was not pleased. His labourer now needed a bodyguard and couldn't leave the farmhouse after dark. Worse still, he was constantly borrowing money. It was time for him to go.

The story of the great Captain Gardiner who had died taking the Gospel to the Patagonians of South America had been firing Henry's imagination. Henry too could shoot, fish, ride, sail a boat on a stormy sea, and was a passable carpenter. He told his mother he was the perfect omni-competent missionary, especially now that he was taking lessons in cobbling.

South America was definitely not on Jane Lucretia's agenda for her son. She replied to his letter from Cheltenham on August 11th, 1855, his twentieth birthday, telling him his Uncle Arthur had just died, and, "it appears that you now have a prospect when of age, which is new and encouraging. The sum of money which by your late kind uncle's will is in reserve for you will enable you, if you are desirous to make a favourable commencement in a line of life for which you are now preparing."[26] Farming was a noble trade. The Patagonians were no more needy than his fellow countrymen. "In this happy and favoured land—England—the towns and villages especially are so many moral deserts. The towns corrupt, the villages in a state of brutish ignorance." Studying theology might therefore be a sensible alternative to farming, if the latter had no appeal.

She enclosed some birthday money, ordered him to pay off his debts, and told him to come home to Cheltenham, where he could be built up on a diet of "farinaceous" food—her latest nutritional fad, for Jane was in a vegetarian phase.

On his way home, he went to meet Wyndham and Peek who had just docked in London. Henry was staggered when he saw the crew again. Some of the worst blasphemers he had ever met could be heard from the quay singing hymns, "with such stentorian strength that it seemed to me they might have meant to blow the roof off the deck cabin in which they held their prayer meeting." If hardened sailors could be transformed like that, anything was possible.

2.

In January 1856, on the night before he left to take up a place at New College in St. John's Wood, Henry Grattan paced the streets of Cheltenham in a state of utter dejection, convinced he was taking a wrong turn. He was terrified that theological study would rob him of his zeal and dampen his spirit, and only made his way to bed in the small hours, when he was satisfied that nothing would stop him following in the footsteps of Wesley and Whitfield.

Prolonged bouts of academic study did not come easily to someone as active and impatient as he was. He balked at what he felt was wasted time, and at weekends and in the evenings, when fellow students were settling down to write their essays, he was out in the streets holding open air services. The dynamic young student had a magnetic appeal. Gathering a crowd was never a problem. But if the people were enthralled by his preaching, local church leaders were not. After his first official sermon at the Congregational Church in Kentish Town, they said, "his voice was too loud, and people would not be frightened into heaven."

"I am sure I should not attempt to do any such thing," Henry replied indignantly, "but if I could be enabled to point out their danger, scare them away from the pit, I should rejoice."

But no further invitations were forthcoming from the Congregational Union. Henry was disappointed, but unbeaten. No one could deny him a congregation in the open air.

To his fellow students he was a familiar sight, hobbling back late at night after tramping miles around the district, his feet crippled by blisters, especially on the Sabbath day when on principle, he refused any form of transport.

By the summer, having completed his first year and gained a second class certificate of honour, he was preaching more and more, attending classes less and less. He never finished his second year.

At home in Cheltenham he started preaching every evening on the Promenade. Thousands gathered to hear him. "He'll be a very useful man when he cools down," said his pastor, Dr. Morton Brown. "Did he really say that?" Henry asked Wyndham. As far as he was concerned, there would be no cooling down.

Every night he invited anyone who wanted a private discussion about the state of their soul to come to his house. As many as seventy "enquirers" were regularly queuing to see him. Every room was so packed with people waiting for him that Jane Lucretia couldn't move around her own home. So Henry took a room at the Town Hall, where he preached regularly, packing the place until there was standing room only.

On his twenty first birthday he noted in his diary that his only ambition was "to live preaching and to die preaching; to live and die in the pulpit; to preach to perishing sinners till I drop down dead." Uncle Arthur's bequest of £400 was now his to do with as he pleased. He gave it to his mother, and set off for Birmingham with a half a crown in his pocket.

After three weeks in Birmingham where huge crowds turned out to hear him night after night, he went to Wednesbury, descending a 600 foot shaft into a coal mine with brother Wyndham so that they could preach to "these poor, benighted men."[27]

From the Midlands he travelled to many English towns, attracting ever larger audiences as his fame grew. In Exeter hundreds had to be turned away. The more he preached the more he became aware of his growing ability to hold a congregation in the palm of his hand. But he never knew where he would eat his next meal or lay his head that night.

In April 1857 he was invited to preach at the famous Moorfields Tabernacle in London, once the base of the great Whitfield himself. Henry Grattan Guinness, denied access to so many churches and chapels, now stood in the pulpit of the most prestigious non-conformist church in the country, overawed at the thought of his illustrious predecessor whose life-sized portrait hung in the vestry, arms reaching to heaven, and whose presence still seemed to pervade the place.

Wyndham sat at the back of the gallery, waiting anxiously for the reaction to his brother's first sermon. In front of him sat two elderly ladies, one of whom turned to the other and said, "My dear, there ought to be a committee appointed to choose a suitable wife for this young preacher!"

There was no doubt that Henry Grattan now constituted a serious risk to unattached young ladies. Well-to-do women with marriageable daughters invited him to tea. According to *The Christian World*:

> The moment you observe him you cannot fail to be struck with his appearance. It is decidedly singular and rather prepossessing. In person he is tall and slender, and of an easy, graceful manner. The long, thin face, not altogether destitute of healthful hue, but sometimes tinged with a hectic flush, bears, in repose, a grave and studious aspect; and when lighted up as it frequently is, with a quiet smile of pleasure, indicates the presence of a genial spirit. The long, dark hair, parted in the centre and thrown backwards, gives to the preacher a rather womanish aspect; but his voice is by no means feminine, for it is full and loud. Indeed, we do not suppose that there is a church, chapel or hall in London, or elsewhere, in which he could not make himself heard to the remotest corner; albeit he is sometimes so rapid in his utterance, that the words unite and become indistinct...[28]

It was whispered that a Wesley and a Whitfield were about to have their parallels in a Spurgeon and a Guinness. But not everyone shared that view. Some were bitterly disappointed and thought him eccentric.

Sometimes he spoke too fast, and at other times the pauses in his address were so long that many in his audience would think he had lost his place.

The pastor of Moorfields Tabernacle, Dr. Campbell, felt that these were merely signs of immaturity and was so impressed with the young man that he invited him to stay on as a permanent minister. It was a very tempting offer, holding out security and prestige, but after a lengthy inner struggle Henry Grattan declined. He could not be tied to one church. On July 29th he was however ordained there in front of a large congregation as an itinerant, interdenominational evangelist. The following day he went to Cheltenham to say goodbye to his mother, then set off on a three-year preaching tour which would take him half way around the world.

The rumblings of the mighty religious revival of 1859 which would shake most of the USA, and large parts of the United Kingdom and Europe were just beginning. Crowds thronged to hear the young preacher, breaking down and weeping openly as he spoke. In Wales Henry preached in 80 different locations, 140 times to a total of about 100,000 people. In Aberdare, when he invited members of his audience to come forward in repentance, all 10,000 of them responded at once, mobbing the platform which promptly collapsed. He was dragged to safety, fortunate to escape with a minor leg injury.

In Scotland, he packed the churches of famous past preachers like Haldane and Murray McCheyne. Year later, he would still describe, "the rustling of the leaves of the Bible at Bannockburn on a Sunday morning as the whole congregation turned simultaneously to the chapter read." *The Glasgow Examiner* approved of his zeal and fervour, but felt, "a little modification of its tones would make a still deeper impression."

In January 1858 Henry Grattan travelled to Paris, where his most influential convert was Jane Bonnycastle, the future, doughty female evangelist to Algiers; then on to Boulogne and Geneva, up into the Alps and across frozen streams on mule-back to Chamonix. It was while he was in Switzerland that Henry received the most enticing invitation of all—to Dublin, his birthplace.

3.

Meanwhile, back at the brewery, in the Dublin of 1857, Benjamin Lee Guinness, compliant son, dutiful husband, and responsible, recognised leader of the city's merchant classes, was recreating himself after his father's death. He was 57, but until that moment, had lived a prescribed existence. At 16 he became an apprentice, at 24 a partner, and at 40, the undisputed head—but only as prince regent, deferring in all major matters to the king. Once his father died and the kingdom was truly his, a cautious policy of steady growth was suddenly upgraded into determined expansionism. Within a few years the growth of the Guinness export trade would make him the richest man in Ireland.

His private life mirrored this subtle, but definite change in style. In his father's lifetime, he lived fairly quietly with his growing family at St. Anne's, Clontarf, opulent in many ways, but a comparatively small estate for such a wealthy man, about two miles from Dublin, four from the brewery.

The year after Arthur's death he bought a property much more in keeping with his aspirations, in the most fashionable of Dublin's elegant, Georgian squares, 80 St. Stephen's Green. This imposing, three-story palladian mansion with a projecting portico, supported by four columns, the first to be built in Dublin, cost him a mere £2,500 as its previous owner was bankrupt. As soon as number 81 became available he acquired that too, dismantling the adjoining walls to make one large dwelling, later known as Iveagh House, with thirty bedrooms, accommodation for twenty servants, and its own sheltered garden, It was here he began to entertain on a lavish scale, and the legendary Guinness hospitality was born.

Family fortune was manifestly increasing at a considerable rate, as he decided to invest, "a small sum, (say £20,000 to £30,000) in the purchase of land,"[29] and bought an estate in Ashford, County Galway, on the shores of Lough Corrib, the ultimate seal of the slow metamorphosis of a family of tradespeople into the landed gentry. All Benjamin Lee needed now was a title.

He could afford to look a little pleased with himself, as his portrait suggests. He had the same determined chin, prototypic Guinness jaw and aquiline nose as his father and grandfather, the same tight-lipped smile, but his face was fuller altogether, and there was something about the way he held his head which suggested a man confident enough to look the Irish aristocracy firmly in the eye.

His wife, Bessie, struggled with her husband's apparent enjoyment of luxury and status, being a stalwart nonconformist and attender at Bethesda Chapel. The daughter of Arthur and John's bankrupt brother, Edward, raised in relative penury by parents on the run from creditors, she knew and feared the seductive, destructive power of riches, and worried continually about the effect of such a lifestyle on her children.

There were a daughter and three sons, Anne Lee in 1839, Arthur Edward in 1840, Benjamin Lee in 1842, and Edward Cecil, the future first Earl of Iveagh, in 1847. Benjamin Lee appears to have adored his wife and children, and liked nothing better than to spend time alone with his family at St. Anne's or at Ashford. He would never give himself over completely to unabated or frivolous socialising. It was not in his nature. Temperamentally, he manifested the uneasy ambivalence which haunted successive generations of heads of Guinness. Success necessitated gregariousness, but innate shyness drove them to take refuge in privacy and solitude. He seems to have convinced an uncertain Bessie that entertaining was at best his duty, at worse, a necessary evil.

She remained "frail" after the birth of their children, a common euphemism for all sorts of conditions afflicting women at the time. In 1852 Arthur turned down a request to persuade his son to stand for Parliament as a Conservative on the grounds that he was "a devoted husband of a wife suffering extreme delicacy of health." Benjamin Lee bowed as ever to his father's wishes and refused the invitation, either to give his undivided attention to his wife, or more likely, because he was far-sighted enough to see that the time for a Guinness MP had not yet come. Outspoken Conservative political allegiance could damage trade in a nationalistic Ireland.

Bessie lived in daily fear for her husband's eternal soul, painfully aware of the moral dangers waiting in snare for a man of his wealth and prestige. If she were to die, and it must have seemed imminent, where would he or her children be without her spiritual protection and guidance? To her growing son, Arthur Edward she wrote:

> Do my darling avoid bad company, I mean worldlings, for there will be plenty anxious to come here, and do guard darling papa from designing, worldly women, for he will be much set on and might easily be taken in. I do not mean that he should not marry, but that he will get one who will help him on to that future world and not lead him to think of or live for the present.[30]

Her anxiety was compounded by the fact that along with the other changes in his life, Benjamin Lee was becoming less non-conformist, increasingly conservative in religious observance. He would say to her that a Church of Ireland threatened with disestablishment needed a staunch defender. And, after all, they were surrounded with clergymen— one of his brothers, and all but one of his brothers-in-law. But she saw that evangelicalism and increased sophistication didn't mix easily. Nonetheless the atmosphere in which she raised her children remained distinctly pious without being repressive. Prayers were said morning and evening attended by family and servants alike. Benjamin Lee would hardly throw off overnight the influence of his low church childhood, now reinforced by his wife.

Like his forefathers, he believed wealth was a sacred trust. To squander money was a sin, to use it wisely for the good of others, a cardinal virtue. But although the family motto was "My Hope is in God," Benjamin Lee's reliance on a gospel of self-help appeared greater than his trust in any outside force. The "serene equipoise between God and Mammon," the very "hallmark of the family,"[31] as Bessie saw only too well, was now in jeopardy. For Benjamin Lee, Christian faith was comprised of work and duty, a concerted effort to get Ireland back on its economic feet after the famine by providing ample employment with fair remuneration. Like many Quakers of the time, he believed in providing his workforce with job security, pensions, decent housing and amenities. Wages were higher than at any other company. A job at Guinness was gold indeed.

Not surprisingly, when, on January 15th 1858, the *Daily Express* announced the imminent arrival of another, very different kind of Guinness, saying, "We understand our fellow citizens will shortly have an opportunity of hearing this now celebrated preacher," Dublin began to buzz with the news. "Is he a meteor or a star?" the newspapers asked. Dr. Urwick, minister of York St. Chapel, who had baptised the young man 23 years earlier, couldn't wait to find out. Neither, no doubt, could Bessie. Benjamin Lee might have been a little less enthusiastic at the idea of having a cousin-preacher renowned for collecting more temperance pledges than any other right on his doorstep, but no doubt he comforted himself with the reminder that his young relative had just turned down the most prestigious non-conformist pulpit in the country.

4.

Henry Grattan Guinness arrived in Ireland in February to huge acclaim. Dr. Urwick noted in his diary, "Unwonted excitement possessed all classes of what is called the religious public, and spread fast to numbers beyond it. To prevent serious disorder, admission was regulated by tickets; even so the chapel was thronged to its utmost capacity of even standing room, long before the hour for commencing the worship."

Only 22% of the population was Protestant, but Dublin was proud of her successful sons, particularly a Guinness. The pro-Catholic *Dublin Evening Post* was not going to let anyone forget the fact he was the son of D'Esterre's widow, but nonetheless showed a great deal of interest, weighing him up against other Protestant preachers like Spurgeon, as if they were professional boxers. It described him as "a modest unassuming young man...wearing a frock coat that reaches to the knees and is buttoned almost up to the neckerchief," which was really rather quaint and old-fashioned, since everyone else was wearing high collars and cravats. His shoulder-length hair framing his face, gave him "a classic or poetic grandeur, intensifying as it does every expression."

All the newspapers referred to his abstinence preaching. "Mr. Guinness is not for Guinness" said the headlines and the billboards, and it remained a popular catch phrase in Dublin for many years. By Monday February 15th, after nine sermons, he was still capturing the front page.

> Few preachers have ever addressed congregations more select. They consist of the elite of all denominations, including a considerable number of the Established Clergy. The wealth, the respectability, the cultivated intellect, as well as the evangelical piety of the city, have been represented in a measure unprecedented, we believe, on such an occasion in this country. Judges, Members of Parliament, distinguished orators, Fellows of College, the lights of the various professions, and, to a considerable extent, the rank and fashion of this gay metropolis, have been drawn out to a dissenting chapel which was thronged, even on weekdays, by this new attraction.

No mention was made of whether Benjamin Lee came to hear his cousin preach on the folly of drunkenness and riches, but there seems little doubt they met. The family remained very close. There was however a slight embarrassment on both sides beyond Henry Grattan's temperance preaching. Playing on his half-brother's acclaim, John Grattan the second, living in penury for twenty years since he bankrupted the Bristol brewery his Uncle Arthur had given him, picked this particular moment to sue Benjamin Lee for wrongful dismissal.

The reception Henry Grattan received in Northern Ireland was even more euphoric. In Belfast the classic signs of religious revival broke out, thousands lying prostrate on the ground for hours after he had preached. The large Catholic community found it disturbing, scoffing loudly at first, then shunning the Protestants in terror, in case they should catch, "the thing that's going."[32] Priests distributed holy water and consecrated medallions as protective measures, but Dr. Urwick noted, "Altogether, nothing to compare with it had been known in Ireland within living memory. An announcement that he was to preach was enough to put the population on the move." The largest buildings available were too small to accommodate the masses who wanted to hear him. "A tidal wave of popularity bore him along day after day," and the press quoted him as if he were a celebrity.

There is no doubt that in an era before the cinema and television, a handsome young preacher was wonderful entertainment, happily fulfilling the later role of screen heros. But that alone cannot explain Henry Grattan Guinness' popularity. The *Daily Express* admitted there was no "cunning exhibition of oratorical fireworks, a dazzling stage effect or theatrical contrivances to work up a "galvanic" revival." In fact, his sermons were almost child-like in their simplicity.

The industrial revolution, overturning the old ways, intensifying the divide between rich and poor, had created the right climate for religious revival, and it came, sweeping through England, Scotland and Wales, affecting every rank and class of person, giving birth years later to some of the greatest pioneering movements for social reform. Henry Grattan would say in later years, "it was hardly a matter of preaching." There was no need for "hanging back," for taking care over what he said lest he gave offense. "Everyone wanted to hear."

Ireland, for sectarian reasons, had always been resistant to Protestant-style religious expression, but 1858 heralded a new dawn. Guinness was bold enough to criticise Protestants for denouncing Romanism when they were manifestly in darkness themselves. A gratified *Dublin Evening Post* said, "The Rev Grattan Guinness will however have accomplished a great deal for society and religion, if his disinterested advice be followed...Before Protestants seek to convert Roman Catholics, let them seek to convert themselves."

He left Ireland for a few months in the summer of 1858. While he was away his half-brother's claim for compensation was dismissed. The press had conveniently forgotten this difficult little episode by the time Henry made his triumphant return the following year. This time he dispensed with chapels and ticket systems altogether. They limited his hearers to the well-healed, so he preached in the open air instead, so that no one was turned away.

In Ulster he had to be hoisted onto the roof of a cab, so that the 20,000 who had turned out could all see him. Some English newspapers including *The Times* and the *Lancet* were highly indignant that the streets of Belfast should be filled with prostitutes and drunken revellers, proving the phenomenon was nothing more than "a moral epidemic and contagious hysteria."

At the end of 1859 he set off for the United States, where a similar "moral epidemic" was about to occur. In Philadelphia he preached on average thirteen times a week for several weeks—to firemen, sailors, medical students, to 700 boys and girls from a House of Refuge, to violent prisoners in the County Gaol.

He spent seven weeks in New York, preaching a minimum of nine sermons a week, then travelled across America and Canada, stopping in many towns along the way. Everywhere he went the crowds turned out to hear him. Some of his converts would become the leaders of the American church. Henry had never known anything like it, nor would he again in his lifetime. Looking back at those days, remembering the deep hush which would fall upon his listeners, their rapt attention, and tears of repentance, he would say wistfully, "I can almost listen to him, that evangelist of other days, and wonder, WAS IT I?"

Returning to Ireland in June 1860 he expected to continue where he had left off but was by now utterly exhausted and on the verge of a breakdown. A holiday was imperative. The inveterate traveller decided upon Norway, but when plans fell through, settled reluctantly for Ilfracombe. It was one of the most fortuitous disappointments of his life.

CHAPTER FIVE
1860-1864

1

On an Ilfracombe down one sultry summer afternoon in 1860, three sisters in wide-brimmed hats are lazing on a grassy cliff top, that falls away sharply in a sheer rocky drop to the sea below, shimmering in the August sun. Mabel, the eldest, is engrossed in a book, while Laura the youngest, very self-conscious in the new muslin dress she has bought specially for the holiday, is unable to settle to anything and determined to distract the other two. Fanny, the plainest of the three, gives up and puts her sketch pad down with a sigh.

She and her sisters have not been raised in the same household, and compared to them she is insipid, a slight, sallow-faced woman, well past the first bloom of youth, wearing a dark, unfashionable dress, buttoned to the neck in the plain, simple style of the Quakers. Her dark hair is parted in the middle and dragged austerely into a bunch of ringlets on either side of a face, almost permanently creased by the difficulties life has forced upon her. Ilfracombe is a very poor second-best after the holiday in Paris she was hoping for, but it will do.

She has been vaguely aware that Laura is enthusing—again—about the dynamic Mr. Guinness, (she has talked of little else since she heard him preach on their first Sunday), and smiles to herself as she picks up her sketch pad and starts drawing again.

Laura notices the smile, and says, with a slight edge in her voice, "Well you missed something, Fanny. Why on earth didn't you come?"

Fanny felt like saying there was hardly any point since she had been given such a detailed, blow by blow account, but thought better of it. The humour would have been lost on Laura. "Such speaking, such a voice, such a manner! You never heard anything like it in your life, I am certain. And you didn't even care enough to go." Fanny laughed and shook her head, "Oh, I've no doubt I shall hear him one day," and then, teasing her younger sister, added, "and after all, it doesn't much matter whether I hear him or not."

Fanny was so busy sketching, she didn't notice Laura's sudden silence, or see the way the colour had drained from her face. Directly below them a boat had suddenly shot into view around the corner of the cliff, close enough for Laura to identify the lone rower at once. "It's him!" she whispered to Mabel, aghast, "Do you think he heard her?"

The oarsman didn't look up, and the irrepressible pair studied him with interest as he vigorously pulled his way past them through the silvery water.

"Do look, Fanny," Laura squealed , "there he is!"

"Who?" Fanny asked, without looking up, obtuse to the end.

"Mr. Guinness!"

With a sigh of resignation, Fanny glanced down at the sea and caught a fleeting glimpse of a slight, dark-haired young man disappearing round the far side of the cliff. "That youth!" she said dismissively, and got on with her sketching.

Years later, that was how Fanny would describe to her children the first sight of her future husband.

Born in 1831, Fanny Fitzgerald was descended from one of most distinguished families of the Irish Protestant ascendancy, dating back to the time of Henry II, when they had played a leading part in the conquest of the country. In recent years they had not been unsympathetic to Catholic emancipation, but marrying a Catholic was another matter, and Fanny's father, Edward Marlborough Fitzgerald, had been disowned when he took a wife from the Catholic lower middle classes. Even after an early divorce, a distinguished military career, and a prestigious second marriage to Mabel, daughter of Admiral Stopford, he was refused any reconciliation.

The second, very happy marriage was cut short by Mabel's tragic early death from tuberculosis, leaving her grief-stricken husband to raise a son and four daughters alone. Fitzgerald never got over the death of his wife and rarely socialised. Nonetheless, he made a name for himself as a journalist and reviewer, writing from home so that he could care for his young family. Fanny remembered the large front room at their home in Buchanan Street in Glasgow, lit by dozens of tiny, twinkling candles on a big square dining table, and "Papa writing, always writing."[33] But journalism did not pay well and there were financial difficulties.

A smallpox epidemic broke out and Fanny was desperately ill for weeks. In the haze of a high fever she was aware of a loud pealing of bells, and of some stiff object being carried out of the room. When she was well enough to ask for her brother, her father took her into his arms and told her that ten-year old Gerald had died the day the bells rang out for the wedding of Queen Victoria.

The pain of losing his only son so soon after the death of his wife was more than Fitzgerald could bear. Some months later, as Arthur West, actuary and Quaker, was reading in his morning paper the sad story of a military man who had taken a one-way ticket on a Channel steamer, and had thrown himself overboard, leaving four orphaned little girls without any financial provision, his partner came into the room waving a letter. Addressed from a Channel steamer, it was from Fitzgerald, begging the solicitors to see to the needs of his children.

West took the letter home and showed it to his wife, Mary. Sadly, the couple had never had children to enjoy their pleasant home and garden in Stamford Hill. Mary West put on her bonnet and paid a series of calls on leading members of the Tottenham Friends Meeting House. Before the day was out homes had been found for three of the girls. Eight-year old Fanny would live with them.

The Wests were kindly, though reserved and old-fashioned as many Quakers were, and young Fanny, raised in a freer kind of environment, often balked at their strange, rather narrow ways. Fortunately, however, the Friends were also cultured and well-read, enjoying open debate and discussion on a wide range of contemporary issues which fed and satisfied the literary and intellectual abilities Fanny had inherited from her father.

In the 1840s the family moved to Exmouth, where they became involved with a new religious movement known as "The Brethren" from its emphasis on the equality or brotherhood of all believers. Brethrenism, like Methodism, was started by a group of dissatisfied evangelical Anglicans who set up their own denomination. Based in Plymouth, it dispensed with the hierarchical divide between priest and people, and had a simple communion service, where everyone could participate on an equal footing.

Twenty years later, riven by disagreement over rules and regulations, with no central leadership, the Brethren movement split into "open" and "exclusive" factions, but in the early days it seemed to herald a new social order, breaking down the divide between rich and poor, profoundly influencing the embryonic Trade Union movement. Fanny found it dynamic and exciting, offering a faith which would sustain her through a very difficult time in her life.

When she was in her late teens, Arthur West, exhausted by years of over-exertion in the Quaker struggle against slavery, had a stroke which left him severely disabled. Mary and Fanny nursed him devotedly but there was no money coming into the house, and Fanny, refusing to make contact with her wealthy Fitzgerald relatives, was forced to combine her studies with a teaching job.

Eventually Mary West's emotional health broke down under the strain. The family moved to Bath where Fanny held a class for young ladies, earning a modest £200 a year, while taking care of both her adoptive parents. It was a terrible blow, when, like her real father, Arthur West ended his own life.

By the time she was 29, hard work, slender means and sorrow had taken their toll. A bright, vivacious personality was hidden behind a wan, rather sober appearance, but that inner warmth was still enough to put the stiffest people at their ease.

Henry Grattan Guinness felt completely comfortable with Fanny Fitzgerald from the moment they were introduced by a mutual Brethren friend in Ilfracombe. She blushed remembering her comments on the cliff top a few days before, but he gave no sign of recognising her, and asked if he could call on the sisters one evening before he left. Fanny was convinced he was interested in Laura who stood next to her, trembling with excitement. She herself had long abandoned any hope of marriage, but at 25, Laura was his age, beautifully dressed and lovely to look at. Laura's adoptive parents were wealthy enough to have provided her with every accomplishment necessary for the wife of a man like Grattan Guinness.

But when the young preacher did call, it was obviously Fanny who was the centre of his attention. His criteria for a future wife, like his attitude to money, did not conform to the usual expectations, but Fanny, intelligent, capable and devout, more than fulfilled them. After that one evening with her he could say with simple joy rather than great passion, "I felt that I had found, for the first time in my life, a woman with a mind and soul that answered to my own. With her I no longer felt alone."

When she received his proposal within a day of returning home it came as a complete shock. It was hardly the most romantic of letters, for he made no secret of the fact that his calling must come first, and marriage to a man in his position, with no home, no official employment, and no financial security, would not be easy. But Fanny's life had never been easy, and that, she now realised, had prepared her for what lay ahead. "It is a life worth living, worth suffering for, a life worth resigning all else for," she replied, almost at once. "Were it to cost a hundredfold more than in all probability it will, I would not resign the prospect or exchange it for the brightest lot earth could offer."

On October 2nd 1860, a mere two months later, they were married at the Princes Meeting House in Bath. At home that morning Fanny rose early and supervised the preparation of the wedding breakfast herself. Mary West was too frail and in a state of some distress at the thought of losing her daughter.

The meeting house was packed to capacity, crowds filling every available space on the plain, unpolished benches. The women sat expectantly in their shawls and poke bonnets, their tightly curled ringlets nestling neatly beneath the wide brims. This was to be a simple Quaker ceremony. There were no flowers, no decorations, no organ, no platform, pulpit, or minister, no bridesmaids, nothing except a table in the centre of the room and two vacant chairs for the bride and groom.

A hush descended as they walked in together, Fanny radiant in a plain white gown. They took their seats in silence. Someone suggested a hymn, and after it had been sung, unaccompanied, the bridegroom rose to his feet and began the service with prayer. Other hymns and readings were selected by various members of the congregation, and then, with a quick nod at each other, the couple rose to their feet. Henry took Fanny's hand and placed a gold ring on her wedding finger, announcing in his resonant voice that this was to signify that hereafter she would be his wife. Fanny, in turn, made her promises, then the couple knelt down together, while the meeting united them with prayer.

"Did no-one marry you? Nobody at all?" her children and grandchildren would ask incredulously, as they gathered round her lap, begging to be told the story of their wedding once again. And Fanny would reply with a radiant smile, pointing to heaven, "Father married us, darlings. Father did everything—except the registrar's work. We didn't need anybody else."

2.

The honeymoon in Clevedon on the pretty north Somerset coast was a short, blissful interlude in a tumultuous period in Henry's life. By day the couple wandered hand in hand along the sandy beach at the entrance to the Bristol Channel watching the vast expanse of churning sea stretching to the distant, grey horizon, wondering where it would carry them. At night, in their very basic lodgings, they shared the few simple provisions they had bought, revelling in the cosiness of being alone together in the gathering autumn twilight.

It was as well they had no glimpse into what lay ahead, the years of incessant wandering, of scrimping and scrounging, of raising children with all their childhood ailments in a variety of temporary, damp and inadequate, lodgings, of never owning their own home. Their lifestyle was such a stark contrast with the serene, comfortable existence of their brewing and banking cousins that it is hard to believe they were part of the same family. It developed inevitably from a sense of calling rather than deliberate choice, and eventually brought its own rewards—though they took some time in coming. Immense acclaim of the kind Henry enjoyed could not last indefinitely, and though neither of them knew it, the tide was beginning to turn.

Henry himself underwent a profound change of direction in the early days of their marriage. Fanny introduced him to the Plymouth Brethren. He had always been impressed by their zeal and earnestness, but it was their fascination for analysing political history in the light of biblical prophecy which fired his imagination.

This was not an entirely new departure for Protestants. As early as the Middle Ages, and particularly at the Reformation, Christians breaking away from the Catholicism had interpreted the "Great Beast" in the book of Daniel as the Church of Rome. The preface of the King James version of the Bible in 1611 clearly stated that "the Man of Sin" in the book of Revelation was none other than the Pope. Indeed, the world had witnessed a succession of popes more corrupt and cruel than any temporal power. Prophecies of "the Beast's" ultimate downfall enabled persecuted Protestants to stand firm in the face of martyrdom.

An Irish Protestant, who had experienced first-hand the superstition and fury of the Roman Catholic Church, Henry was predisposed to take an interest in the prophetic books. He now lamented his lack of formal theological education, and taught himself history, Greek and ancient Hebrew. Early in 1861 he produced his first pamphlet on biblical prophecy and world history, then set off immediately for a preaching tour of America, scene a few months earlier of some of his greatest triumphs.

But there too a social earthquake had began to rock the country to its very foundations. As a consequence of the religious awakening, the American government was in the process of banning slavery, as Britain had done in 1833. Eleven southern states refused to accept the legislation and revival fire had given way to war fever.

The change of moral climate was not the only reason for the more restrained reception he received on his second visit. Though the people responded as warmly as ever, crowding into church halls to hear him, the church ministers did not. Rumours had filtered across the Atlantic that Henry Grattan had become a member of an exclusive sect. After all, he had taken a Brethren wife. When he began to baptise his own converts it confirmed ministers' worst fears, and they slammed their doors in his face. Of the 30 churches in Philadelphia which had welcomed him so warmly months before, only three allowed him to preach. Henry was mystified. Certainly he admired aspects of Brethrenism, but he was also aware of their shortcomings and had never allowed himself to be associated with any one denomination.

But his Brethren contacts had influenced him more than he cared to admit, even to himself. They had told him his great gift of oratory was not divinely inspired. It stemmed from a need for popularity and attention. Young, naive, terrified of human pride, and desperate for real holiness of character, Henry believed them. He would trim away any suggestion of histrionics, assuming it would lend his words more, not less impact. But he was wrong. Like Samson after his hair was shorn, he had been deprived of his power. His style was cramped, and to some of his American audiences it seemed that all that was left of the fire in his belly were a few last desperate sparks.

In years to come he would realise he had been misled, but for the time, his confidence had been eroded and the quality of his preaching seriously undermined. It was a loss he would lament for the rest of his life.

Sensitivity to the prevailing climate would never be one of Henry's strengths. Unaware of his waning popularity he launched into a full-scale defence of pacifism. Of course the abolition of slavery was just. His own preaching had stoked the cause. But in an open letter published by the Peace Society, entitled, "The Duty of Christians in the Present Crisis," he stated that whatever the provocation, Christians should never fight and should disobey any government which ordered them to use the sword.

Such a stance, from a foreigner and an Irishman to boot, was greeted with howls of derision from the entire American press. They called him "a cowardly poltroon," and suggested he be tried by Court Martial before the chaplain of the Brooklyn phalanx. *The World* demanded a public retraction or his enforced removal.

No one had ever publicly questioned Henry Grattan's integrity before. He was devastated by such a bitter personal attack, realising, too late, that he had grossly overestimated his own influence. He had as much hope of altering public opinion as turning, "the current of Niagara with a pitch-fork." It was time to leave. Fanny was pregnant and must not be further upset.

In America, with a great deal of reluctance, she had begun to accept speaking invitations, at first to groups of women. Initially the prospect terrified her and Henry had to use all his powers of persuasion to get her into the pulpit. Preaching was not a gift she ever anticipated or desired. In fact a woman preacher was a novelty and Fanny wasn't sure it was acceptable at all. But she was such a success that Henry encouraged her to preach at his side wherever he went, even as her pregnancy became increasingly evident.

Now that they were no longer welcome in America they needed a safe haven for the birth of their baby and accepted an invitation from Toronto. On their way to Canada news reached them that war had been declared. As Henry had foreseen, America tore itself apart in a futile conflagration for four years.

3.

On Henry and Fanny's first wedding anniversary, October 2nd 1861, young Henry Grattan, known as Harry, was born in Toronto. To Fanny's relief he was a healthy baby, not adding to the burdens she already had to bear. Canada had greeted Henry with little more enthusiasm than America, and he was beginning to show signs of serious depression, disappointment and exhaustion, compounded by the rigours of a freezing Canadian winter.

With their new baby they crossed the frozen St. Lawrence River by boat to Quebec. "I was terrified, expecting each moment to be swallowed in the surging ice," Fanny recalled in her diary. Now, for the sake of Henry's mental health she knew she had to get him home to England as quickly as possible. The nearest embarkation point was Portland in America which would mean recrossing the treacherous St. Lawrence and braving a country riven by civil war with a three-month old baby. In the end she felt she had no choice. Travelling conditions would become more hazardous in the next few months as a thaw set in and the river flooded its banks. She wrapped up her tiny baby and they set off, reaching England safely in early January 1862.

Any hopes she had that Henry's spirits would be restored once he was back on familiar territory were soon dashed. A prolonged period of rest was essential and made possible by a financial gift from a generous friend. Leaving Harry behind in an English nursery, they set off for the Middle East.

Henry was overcome with awe at seeing so many sacred places. He had an overwhelming sense of walking on hallowed ground, particularly in the Judean desert. It would have a profound effect on his later ministry, though initially, when they returned to England at the end of April, his emotional health seemed little better. He still couldn't face addressing large meetings. Yet how could he support his family? Fanny was pregnant again.

When a small chapel in the run-down Waterloo area of Liverpool offered him a temporary pastorate, it seemed the ideal provision. In Liverpool on Christmas Day 1862 Mary Geraldine was born. Her father always called her Minnie and felt that her conception in the Holy Land had endowed her with a heightened spiritual awareness in preparation for a sacred destiny.

The warm, loving acceptance of the simple working class congregation at Byrom Hall helped to restore Henry's confidence and after seven months he took to the road again, preaching all over England, Ireland, and Scotland, taking cheap lodgings for his family wherever he went.

But neither his preaching, nor the response, were what they had been in the old days. Any preacher of reputation was invited by the Earl of Shaftesbury to preach on a Sunday evening to the packed Exeter Hall in London. The man hailed nationally as Spurgeon's rival a mere four years earlier received no such invitation.

In Edinburgh in the bleak November of 1863 his preaching tour came to a sudden standstill. A distinguished Irish politician accused him publicly of bribing his converts with money from the Guinness brewery. Most of the newspapers reported the story and all further speaking engagements were cancelled forthwith.

It was a bitter and cruelly ironic attack on someone who deplored alcohol and had given away his own Guinness legacy. Henry was stunned by the vilification of his character, and even more that a flagrant untruth should receive unquestioning acceptance. The shock made him ill again. He had no home, no money, no means of defending himself or now, of earning an income. Fanny did her best to comfort him, but she went into labour prematurely and gave birth to a stillborn little girl.

These undoubtedly were some of the worst months of his life. One day in March 1864, he found himself in Dundee with his wife and two small children crammed into damp, freezing cold lodgings, the cheapest available, "strangers amongst strangers, with only seventeen shillings in hand." But many of his supporters did not desert him, and a month later the family were offered no less than three country homes free of expense for as long as they liked.

Fanny chose Mount Catherine, a beautiful house in glorious surroundings three miles from Limerick. Here at last she could create a measure of normal family life and a proper Christmas. Nonetheless, she was forced to concede that their extraordinary upbringing would mean her children could be rather quaint. At a local party she was bemused by Harry who marched up to a boy teasing a little girl and said, "I'll tell you what sir, if you tease that fair lady, I'll put you in prison or shoot you dead." Where the three year old had heard such an expression she had no idea. But Harry was already a knight errant and defender of the weak, and the child would be father to the man. Each of her children reflected aspects of the circumstances of their birth and early childhood. Son of their Canadian adventure, Harry would always be the most audacious and extrovert.

Life for Fanny was never really settled at Mount Catherine. Henry was risking life and limb preaching to the Catholic community of Limerick. It was a matter of time before the tolerance of the church authorities was pushed beyond its limit. One day she was called out of the women's meeting she was addressing and sent home to find Henry had been badly beaten. Apparently, a large crowd had gathered to hear him as they usually did, but this time one or two planted ring-leaders urged the people to hustle and stone him. He tried to get away, but two burly men, one a butcher, hit him repeatedly on the head. Providentially he had fallen into a low cart. Had he not, the police informed her, Henry would have almost certainly been trampled to death. At that very moment an army officer rode past, his uniform covered in medals for gallantry in the Crimean War. He leapt down, collared the butcher, and harangued the crowd for their cowardice in attacking one defenceless man, giving Henry a chance to make his escape. According to *The Times*, which reported the incident on May 6th 1864, Mr. Guinness had been saved from the vengeance of the populace by a Captain Jones of the depot battalion.

Henry began to wonder if he were not on the wrong track. He was almost thirty, and for some time now doors had slammed shut in his face. The great religious revival had past its peak, some of its ardour dampened by the publication in 1859 of Charles Darwin's *On the Origin of the Species*. Henry was concerned that the book appeared to be rocking the moral and religious foundations of society, undermining those too weak in faith to marshal their theological arguments. What was needed to fight off an enemy invasion was an army of young men adequately equipped to proclaim the evidence for Christian truth. Instead of preaching himself, perhaps the time had come to train others to do it.

Fanny's heart sank. She knew what that would mean. They could hardly set up a training class for would-be preachers in the heart of the Irish countryside, miles from civilisation. There was no option but to give up Mount Catherine and head for Dublin.

CHAPTER SIX
1865-1870

1.

Dublin had changed very little in the seven years since the young evangelist had caused such a stir. The wealthy, largely Protestant minority, lived in elegant mansions and country houses in the suburbs, the poor, largely Catholic majority was subject to grinding poverty. Henry's first student, Tom Barnado, a young man of Italian extraction whose orphanages would eventually make his name a household word, said the whisky drinking and, "the vicious tendencies of the people who dwell in these wretched hovels, have demoralised them to the lowest degree."[34]

Benjamin Lee Guinness began to realise that to succeed, he needed to capture the whisky drinking market and turn Guinness beer into its natural heritage. The committed Unionist achieved his goal with a stroke of pure genius, exploiting nationalist pride by appropriating as his logo the symbol of the most enduring folklore of the people—the harp of the legendary Irish hero and chieftain, Brian Boru. It enabled Guinness to become a national institution.

But beer was not the only burgeoning Guinness enterprise in the Dublin of the 1860s. His cousins the banking Guinnesses, descended from Samuel, the first Arthur's younger brother, who had gave up brewing after his marriage to Sarah Jago, a goldsmith's niece, were also in the ascendancy. Guinness, Mahon and Co, bank and land agency, was about to expand its operations to London. The long line of Guinness financiers adopted the middle name of "Rundell," just as "Lee" began to identify the brewers, and "Grattan" the missionary branch of the family. More than in many family trees, the lines began to overlap and cross. Early generations of brewers, bankers and ministers remained fairly close, united by a strong sense of family, a love of Ireland and their Christian faith.

But Ben and Bessie's four children also began to reflect the "worldliness" of an upbringing that reflected their new status. Bessie wrote to Arthur Edward, her eldest son, "All tho' the Lord has given me peace and joy in believing...if I were well assured that my darling children were safe in Jesus, oh how happy I should be—well, I think they are the Lord's, but I want to SEE it."[35] Evidently there was a great deal of room for doubt. She wrote to Arthur again a little later, "I do hope you do not smoke, and that if Lee must smoke sometimes, which I wish he would not, it is not vile tobacco or cigars."[36]

Anne Lee, their only daughter, had brought the first title into the brewing line of the family when she married William Conyngham, Treasurer of St. Patrick's Cathedral, who would become the fourth Baron Plunkett on the death of his father. She, like many Guinness women, had opted for a clergyman, only this one would become the Archbishop of Dublin.

In 1865, while Henry Grattan opened his first bible school down town, Benjamin Lee personally supervised and financed the renovation of St. Patrick's Cathedral at a cost of £150,000. It was characteristic of a man whose faith was becoming more formal to express it in the grand gesture. One of Ireland's greatest monuments had been saved for the nation. Lord Wodehouse, Lord Lieutenant of Ireland enthused, "work... which the Irish Parliament had refused to undertake and which the British parliament never entertained the thought of executing, has been accomplished within four years by a single merchant." [37]

For "services to his country," Benjamin Lee was made a baronet. One particular cathedral window would become the most fitting tribute to the wealthy benefactor. Known as the Guinness window and inscribed with the text, "I was thirsty and ye gave me drink," it never failed to amuse successive generations of visitors.

2

Bessie died in September, a few weeks before Henry and Fanny arrived back in Dublin with no fanfare or publicity, but with a new baby, Lucy Evangeline. "We called her Lucy—from lux, lumiere, light," Henry explained, for she was a symbol of their own hopeful new beginning, a pinprick of light at the end of a very dark tunnel. She was a frail, fretful baby, causing her parents a great deal of anxiety. Henry, a very un-Edwardian father, carried her everywhere. "When she was a child there was no place she loved better than her father's arms," he wrote, "and to him, the delicacy of her frame and sensitiveness of her mind were no mystery, for trials which preceded her birth seemed their explanation."[38]

Lucy was something of a child prodigy, inheriting the brilliant musical flair of the Cramers, mastering complex Chopin and Mendelssohn piano pieces at an unusually early age. Emotionally she was always finely tuned, unusually sensitive, capable of such intensity of feeling that as she grew, Henry would worry for her emotional health, an anxiety which would not prove unfounded.

Though his cousin Benjamin Lee, saviour of St. Patrick's, was now the undisputed defender of the established church, Henry accepted the position of elder at Merrion Hall, a newly built, socially unfashionable Brethren Chapel. He rented 31 Upper Baggot Street, a large Georgian house just beyond the eminently fashionable Lower Baggot Street, in a more run-down part of the town, as his, "Training Home for Evangelists and Missionaries." Living in the same town, the cousins' paths had so diverged that it was hard to believe their fathers were brothers, and close.

About eight men gathered at Henry and Fanny's home to study Paley's *Evidences of Christianity* four evenings a week. There were Charles and Edward Fishe, the dashing sons of a retired colonel of the East India Company's Horse Artillery, and John McCarthy, a thoughtful older man, married with three children, all of whom would make pioneer missionary explorers one day. The Guinness children's favourite was Tom Barnado, their Sunday School teacher at Merrion Hall. He was a small, bespectacled, almost monkey-like little man whose unprepossessing appearance hid an irrepressible sense of fun. He was a great talker, waving his arms around energetically as he held forth on the subjects filling him with righteous indignation—usually the injustices suffered by the poor. The house on Baggot Street became his second home.

The evening of February 19th 1866 was a turning point. During a visit to Liverpool Henry Grattan had heard and met the renowned missionary explorer, Hudson Taylor, who had accepted an invitation to talk to the Dublin Bible class about his adventures in China before his tour of Limerick, Cork and Belfast. In exchange Henry Grattan promised to escort Taylor to his other meetings, "being better known in Ireland at present than you are." It was a genuine offer of support, not a put-down, but Henry was always immune to the subtleties of language.[39]

Hudson Taylor had sailed to China in 1853, spent ten years there, and since his return had enthralled the British public with his tales of that exotic faraway land. Throughout the 1860s the world map altered almost daily. Voyages of exploration expanded geographical horizons and revealed unknown, mysterious parts of the globe. It was a source of immense fascination. All travel was an adventure, but China, with its ancient dynasties, strange traditions and colourful culture had an almost fairy-tale mystique.

Taylor was also radical in his opposition to British expansionism in the Far East. Preaching the Gospel was not an excuse for colonialism. Missionaries must lay down their creature comforts, accept no salary, and identify with the people, as far as they were able, in lifestyle, customs, diet and dress. It was a hard and difficult path to tread, but true Christianity demanded a total rejection of the twin scourges of imperialism and denominationalism with all the self-interest they implied.

That evening, inside the large drawing room on Upper Baggot Street, Barnado, McCarthy, and the Fishe brothers, sitting stiffly in their sombre, tight-fitting frock-coats, waited in anticipation for Guinness to return from the Kingston Ferry with his special guest, whom he had arranged to meet at "half past six Irish time, seven o'clock English." The door flung open. Framed in the doorway, filling it in fact, was Guinness' magnificent figure. There was no sign of Taylor.

"Where is the great man?" Barnado whispered to McCarthy with a twinge of disappointment.

"I suppose he hasn't come," McCarthy whispered back.

But when Henry Grattan stood to one side, they all saw a slight, slim, fair-haired man in a dress-coat with an abundant white kerchief knotted at his neck. Bemused at is quaint, outdated clothing, they ogled him for some time. As he took stock of Taylor's height, or the lack of it, Barnado broke the ice, "There's hope for me yet!" he guffawed.

He was the first to volunteer for China almost before Taylor had finished speaking. Taylor loved Barnado's ebullience, but wondered whether he wasn't a little impetuous. He suggested a course of study at one of the London Hospitals to improve the student's medical knowledge. If then, he still felt called to China he could join a party leaving on the Lammermuir later in the year.

There were no such qualms about McCarthy, whose only stipulation was that his wife should be safely past her fourth confinement by the time they sailed. Nor about Charles Fishe, who, still very young, promised to go as soon as he had his father's permission. Taylor's greatest surprise was reserved for the journey to Cork, when Henry told him that he and Fanny were intending to sail on the Lammermuir. Taylor promised to give the matter serious consideration as he travelled on alone to Belfast and by the time he called in at Baggot Street on his return, had reached a decision. As gently as possible he tried to explain to them that since they were past thirty they were too old. They would find language study too difficult. "Stay here," he said to Henry, "and train me the men and women."

While Henry and Fanny were struggling to come to terms with their disappointment, Hudson Taylor noticed a little girl standing at his side staring up at him with her enormous, almond-shaped eyes. He bent down, picked her up and sat her on his knee.

"And how old are you?"

"Three," Minnie said.

"I have a three-year old," he told her, "a boy, called Howard."

A bond was sealed that day between Taylor and the Grattan Guinness family, and especially with the little girl who sat on his knee, who forty years later would become his best-known biographer and greatest comfort at a time of almost unbearable trial.

Fanny couldn't simply set aside her newly inspired passion for China and days after his departure wrote to Hudson Taylor, "We see our way clearly now, I think, to aid the work not *directly* but indirectly...*Here* we may do much and be the means of sending you more efficient labourers than ourselves."[40] She went on to propose the immediate establishment of an Irish Auxiliary of the China Inland Mission, "to disseminate information and stir up interest....to promote prayer and liberality on its behalf....and provide funds for passage and outfit money." She enclosed a notice they intended to disseminate throughout Ireland.

Taylor was seriously alarmed at the proposition and wrote back to say so. Such formidable supporters could damage his cause. Taylor's policy was never to ask for money, and he explained this as gently as he knew how. To her credit, Fanny graciously took the point, and learned a lesson which would prove invaluable in her own missionary enterprises in the years ahead.

Nonetheless, Taylor needed a substantial amount of money before the sailing of the Lammermuir, and invited the Guinnesses to share in the limelight at a special reception given for him at the home of Lord and Lady Radstock at 30 Bryanston Square in London. The Radstocks were inveterate supporters of all kinds of missionary work, using their influential position to relieve many of their social circle of their extraneous income and guilt. They would one day prove invaluable friends to Henry and Fanny.

This was Fanny's introduction to the upper-class London elite, and she felt gauche and faded. She couldn't get over the revealing décolletès of the ladies, or decide whether covering her neck and shoulders in true Quaker fashion made more of a statement about her modesty or her provinciality. Henry, however, was in great form, exuding his usual magnetic charm, speaking about the work with what Taylor referred to as "marvellous power," in contrast to Taylor's own measured presentation of the facts.

3.

The Taylors finally sailed for China in May,[41] leaving Henry and Fanny feeling so bereft and out-of-sorts that they gave up the house in Baggot Street, and set off on their travels again. One evening, as he wandered through the streets of Keighley in Yorkshire, he noticed a poster on the wall of a house announcing a series of lectures by a Mrs. Harriet Law, a well-known exponent of Darwinism, who would prove beyond doubt that the Bible and its claims were false. He tilted back his high crowned hat and stared at the poster with mounting indignation. Up to that moment he had presumed the new scepticism was limited to academia. If the intelligentsia chose the path to spiritual destruction so be it, but they had no right to drag down those whose limited education left them without argument.

When Mrs. Law delivered her first address Henry Grattan Guinness, expert in fossils and future fellow of the Royal Geological Society, was in the front row, ready for the first round of a mighty battle of minds. By the second night most of the town turned out to watch the sport. Keighley had never had such entertainment. Mrs. Law was no match for a man of Henry Grattan's verbal genius. The people loved him and she bowed to his popularity, if not to his theology.

Henry noted in his journal that in 1866 he preached 230 times and was ill only twice. By the following year, which included a very successful mission in Sunderland, Fanny was longing for a base for herself and the children, and persuaded Henry to let her buy their own home, their first in seven years of marriage. They opted for Bath so that she could take care of her mother. It was also near enough to Cheltenham for Henry to spend time with Jane Lucretia who was becoming very frail.

Influenced by the example of Catherine Booth, Mother of the Salvation Army, Fanny began to preach again regularly —to both genders, still feeling very ambivalent about it. She later wrote that from around 1858, "women (the daring of it!), *women* began to take part in the revival meetings, with trepidation at first, and after long searchings of heart and much anguished prayer. There was an outcry, of course, but the broader minded among the revivalists soon came to see that resistance to such compelling sincerity would be in vain."[42]

Her children were her greatest fans. Returning from one meeting to which Harry had accompanied his mother, he said to the maid, "Ah, Susan, if you were to go with Mamma like me, then you'd know what *preaching* means."

Fanny however maintained that, "the *rule* is men—the *exception* only, women; and that, as always, the exception only proves the rule." But in 1867, in Bath, she went to hear the extraordinary Geraldine Hooper. Hooper, daughter of a well-to-do family, was elegant and fashionable, and only 27. "It was at eight o clock on a Sunday morning in a low back street where tramps, sweeps and costermongers live. She stood on a chair, surrounded by a rabble of the lowest kind, but who formed a most attentive and respectful audience. Wretched women sat at the widows of the surrounding houses, and the tears rolled down many a black and hardened face as she sweetly commended to them from the story of the prodigal the free and boundless love of God."[43]

When Geraldine Hooper died in childbirth four years later at the age of 31 after her marriage to Henry Dening, Fanny was devastated. She had lost a close friend and inspiration. But never again did she question a woman's right to preach.

In September 1867, Henry and Fanny's fifth child, Henrietta, was born and lived only a few months. Fanny blamed herself for Henrietta's death and though she never said so openly, felt she was being punished for her materialism. The three children deprived of a cosseted existence had thrived, while the only baby born in the security of their own home had died. It could mean only one thing—time to uproot again. What did it matter that China was denied them when just across the Channel was a continent gripped by a spiritual darkness as dense in the great Eastern Empire?

4.

On May 19th 1868, Sir Benjamin Lee Guinness caught a chill and died, enjoying his title and parliamentary seat for only a few months.

Although he had only had complete control of the brewery for the last ten years of his life, had made it the most successful in the country, becoming the most prominent figure in Irish business life. His estate was valued at £1.1 million, making his will the largest in Ireland to date. There were bequests for his daughter, Anne, and for Lee, his middle son, who was only 26 and a captain in the Royal Horse Guards, but the bulk of the estate went to his eldest and youngest sons, Arthur Edward and Edward Cecil, who were both working at the brewery.

With his usual far-sightedness, Sir Benjamin Lee managed to do what many a rich man longed to do and failed—to control the future of his fortune from beyond the grave, ensuring it would be neither dissipated nor dispersed, but remain in the family business. The brewery was to be divided equally between the two young men, with the proviso that if one of them should ever withdraw from the partnership he would receive not the value of his share, but a mere honorarium of £30,000. Ben remembered only too well the family trauma provoked by his elder brother, Arthur Lee, whose preference for artistic pursuits put the brewery in jeopardy and almost cost him his livelihood. The capital must be left in the business so that the surviving partner could continue without fear of liquidation.

In an uncanny way he appears to have foreseen the future. Perhaps he knew that history tends to repeat itself in genealogical lines. Perhaps he simply knew and understood his sons better than his own father. He certainly seems to have had a shrewd idea which of the two most closely reflected him in character. Educated at Eton, 27-year old Arthur Edward was a grave, rather serious young man, old before his time, fond of his creature comforts, conservative in his opinions, a politician, not a visionary. He inherited St. Anne's Clontarf, the gracious Ashford Estate—and his father's parliamentary seat. Edward Cecil, on the other hand, though only 21, was apprenticed to the brewery at the age of fifteen, educated himself at Trinity in his spare time and had already shown instinctive business flair. His father left him 80 St. Stephen's Green, the real symbol of status and prosperity.

The funeral was described in *The Times* as, "one of the most impressive demonstrations of public feeling ever seen in this city." 500 Guinness employees, dressed in black, marched at the front of the cortege. Behind the hearse and family coaches, in 239 private carriages, were the Lord Lieutenant, the Lord Mayor, representatives of the gentry and of every aspect of the civic and professional life of Dublin. All along the route from St. Anne's to the family vault at the Mount Jerome Cemetery shops were closed and the streets lined with silent mourners. It was a remarkable tribute to an avowed Unionist, yet Sir Ben was also known for his courtesy and kindliness. Despite wealth and status, he remained, like his father, unassuming and approachable, sensitive to the needs of his employees and his family. The bronze statue by Foley erected in his honour within the precincts of St. Patrick's is of a merchant prince, dignified yet benevolent.

Sir Benjamin's death marked the end of an era for the entire Guinness family whose lives would never be quite so closely entwined with the city of Dublin again. For brewers, bankers and missionaries the great metropolis beckoned. London would increasingly become the hub of the wheel. But while brewers and bankers maintained their links with Ireland, gravitating between their Irish and English homes, depending on the social season, Henry Grattan simply went wherever he felt called, wherever he was provided with a house.

There were other family deaths in the year 1868. In September, at the age of 69, weeks before Henry and Fanny were due to sail to France, Jane Lucretia died suddenly in Lyme Grove in Manchester while visiting Fred, her youngest son, who was a curate there. Unlike Bessie, Jane Lucretia had no qualms about the eternal destiny of her three boys. Both of Henry's brothers, Fred and Wyndham, were Anglican clergymen, and she gave thanks to God for such an answer to her prayers.

5

Henry and Fanny settled in Paris where Napoleon III and his beautiful wife, the Empress Eugenie held court in the glittering splendour of the

Palace of Versailles. As ever, it was the challenge, not the sophistication of life in Paris which attracted Henry. There had been no religious revival in France. Resistance was nationally ingrained. Home of the philosopher Voltaire, France was the centre of rational scepticism. Like Ireland, it was also a stronghold of Romanist superstition, but the Protestantism, without a Wesley or a Whitfield, was turgid and dreary. This was pioneer work and though he barely spoke a word of French, Henry threw himself into it with his usual gusto, preaching in the market place to Catholics as they came out of Mass. The French had never known anyone foolhardy enough do that before, but then, they said, Grattan Guinness was a "true Englishman," (even if he was Irish), and used to free speech.[44]

In a few months he addressed around 700 meetings, and soon a combination of exhaustion and a recurrent eye infection brought on the familiar black depression. Fanny sent him off to Switzerland to rest. During his journey back through Spain he had a bizarre experience which would prove very formative.

While he was in Madrid he heard that workmen constructing a new road on the outskirts of the city, had cut through the top of a hill and discovered, sandwiched between the usual layers of red gravel, an unfamiliar stratum of soft black dust. On examining the dust more closely, they had found, to their horror, bits of bone and hair. Suddenly the realisation dawned that this was the site of a vast human grave—the legendary Quemadero, where the Spanish Inquisition had tortured and burned thousands of Protestant heretics.

Henry couldn't resist a chance to see the site for himself. As the workmen went on digging they unearthed more gruesome remains, evidence of the most barbaric form of cruelty—rusty chains, two hands clasped tightly in prayer transfixed by a huge iron nail, a ribcage penetrated by a spear.

Henry stood watching, unable to hold back the tears. So many martyrs! Never had the history of the church touched him so profoundly, or filled him with such a mixture of grief and revulsion. He collected a heap of ashes, folded them in a Spanish newspaper and took them home.

Minnie always felt in awe of the pile of human ashes which sat on his desk from that day on. In years to come, whenever Henry was tempted to feel depressed and downhearted, they would be a constant reminder of the need to fulfil the aspirations of those who had laid down their lives for their faith.

The spring of 1869 was a happy one. Paris was breath-takingly beautiful, the tree-lined avenues heavy with almond blossom. There was no presage of the disastrous political events which threatened its serenity. On April 25th Gershom Whitfield was born—Gershom meaning "stranger in a strange land," though Paris hardly seemed strange. The family loved the accommodation they had been given at the Chateau Foicy and even Fanny addressing meetings with a fair degree of fluency. "Love reigned in our home," Minnie wrote, looking back at those early years, "Life seemed free and generous. All the changes didn't matter, there was home and happiness everywhere as long as we were together."

That sense of security was mainly Fanny's influence. Neither beautiful nor particularly creative, she nonetheless had some indefinable charm which made people notice her. She was calm and capable, essential for the wife of a man with as passionate a nature as Grattan Guinness. One visitor described how she had once waited for Fanny in the nursery. Whitfield began to scream and neither she nor the nanny had been able to placate him. Fanny swept into the room, picked up her son, carried him to the window and showing him a glorious Parisian sunset, simply said, "look!" He was only a few weeks old but he did as she said. "It was not a vacant stare but a look of beautiful intelligence which lit up his eyes as he gazed at the glowing sky." Mother and baby stood bathed in the sunset glow for at least three minutes, "Then, without a word, she handed the quieted child back to the nurse and turned to me to speak of other things, not at all aware that she had given me one of the finest object-lessons of my life." [45]

By the time Phoebe Canfield was born, a year after her brother, the halcyon interlude in Paris was almost over. Day after day the city was filled with ugly demonstrations, angry workmen in their caps and overalls demanding war with Prussia. Harry, Minnie and Lucy were returning from a walk one day with their nanny who was carrying fifteen month old Whitfield in her arms, when their way was blocked by a noisy procession. As they tried to squeeze past, the nanny and Whitfield were thrown to the ground in the path of an oncoming carriage and dragged to safety just in time.

The children were extremely upset and Fanny decided there and then that they had no choice but to return to the safety of England. With a heavy heart Henry handed over responsibility for the chapel he had founded in the Rue Royale between the Madeleine and the Place de la Concorde to Pastor Armand Delille. Throughout the war with Prussia, and the terrible months of the siege of Paris which followed, the chapel doors would stay open, making it a refuge for thousands of suffering soldiers and civilians.

By then the Guinnesses were back in Bath, following the harrowing accounts in the newspapers. They could hardly believe the photographs of the city they loved, surrounded by the Prussian army, an ever-advancing ring of artillery fire, and Napoleon III and his empress fleeing for their lives.

From Henry's perspective events began to take on apocalyptic significance. The day before France had declared war on Prussia, the Pope decreed his infallibility. This wasn't simply heresy, it was blasphemy. The pile of ashes on his desk cried out for justice, and vindication was swift. The French troops in Rome, sorely needed at home, evacuated the Vatican, leaving it at the mercy of King Victor Emmanuel who intended being the sole monarch of a united Italy. By the end of 1870, in a matter of months, the balance of power in Europe had shifted radically. The temporal authority of the Pope had been destroyed forever, France was in ruins, and Bismarck's Germany was a force to be reckoned with. Henry was convinced this was significant for the history of civilisation. There must be an overall plan, but what was it?

When Fanny broke her leg badly and was confined to a couch, pregnant again and unable to care for her five children, travelling was out of the question. This proved an invaluable opportunity for Henry to study biblical prophecy and begin the successful writing career which would exercise a profound influence on government policy in the Middle East even after his death.

Every night Harry, Minnie and Lucy would climb into his arms as he sat in the huge armchair in his study, and in the firelight glow he would read what he had written that day, excerpts from what was to become *The Approaching End of the Age* which would sell in thousands. He told them not to be afraid of what was happening in Europe. It all pointed to the certainty that Christ would soon return, "perhaps not in my lifetime, but in yours." The idea fired the children's imagination. It would become a driving force in their lives.

Subtly, the dawn of a new era in Europe had heralded a new beginning for Henry Grattan Guinness. The preacher was becoming a teacher and would influence the nation in a more far-reaching way than he had ever done before.

CHAPTER SEVEN
1871-1878

1

In 1872, after years of spiritual fog, "the cloud moves," Henry wrote in his diary, "may I have grace to follow."

His vision was to set up the world's first interdenominational missionary training college run on the same principles as Hudson Taylor's China Inland Mission. The few theological colleges that existed were denominational, reserved for those who had access to paid education. Attendance at Henry's college would not depend on denomination, gender or financial wherewithal. There would be no fees. God would provide the location, the staff, the students—and the food to feed them.

After twelve years of marriage, Fanny understood her part in her husband's grand schemes. There was no question of Henry's ability to inspire and teach, but the practicalities of running such an institution would be left to her—in addition to raising six children, Agnes having been born in 1871.

One cold December evening she found herself alighting from a horse-drawn tram into East London's teaming Mile End Road to look for a suitable property. The road itself, a broad thoroughfare, was thronged with weary, work-grimy labourers manoeuvring their way around cabs and horse dung as they headed home. Every tenth building was an alluring public house, its garish lighting holding out the promise of warmth and solace. Cocky factory girls in jaunty feathered hats dallied in the doorways.

The squalor and deprivation described by Charles Dickens was painfully evident. Huddling in doorways, shivering women drew threadbare shawls around their shoulders, some clutching babies, little more than filthy bundles of rags, to their shrunken breasts. Starving-looking children dressed in tatters played in the gutters. Fanny was appalled. They stopped to stare at her as she passed, but then, she reflected, she and Henry must have made an interesting sight—the funny little woman on the arm of a large, striking man.

They turned into a narrow, ugly street with brick houses on either side, semi-hidden by rows of tall spiked iron palings. Number 29 was the shabbiest of them all. Henry's excitement failed to raise Fanny's sinking spirits. This was a major test of her faith. "I felt just like a would-be swimmer longing to strike out and feel the water up-bearing him, yet fearing to trust himself to do it," she wrote in her diary later, adding with her usual determination, "But I shall swim yet."

She moved her family from Bath to London at the end of 1872 under a siege of criticism from friends and acquaintances. How could she take her children to such an unhealthy, unsavoury neighbourhood? Fanny replied tartly that the noise was trying, the dirt and dust disagreeable, that they gasped for a breath of fresh air and sighed for sights other than a never-ending succession of omnibuses and market carts, and for sounds other than the shriek of the railway-whistle. "But when we recall the lot of our missionary friends in the narrow lanes and streets of undrained Chinese cities, unable to secure in their comfortless dwellings even privacy from rude and curious crowds, or freedom from fever-breeding odours... we feel that we have good reason to be content with such things as we have."

Henry had chosen the East End because he believed no man or woman could possibly cope with the rigours of missionary life if they could not live amongst their own poor. Tom Barnado, who had given up any idea of going to China, had alerted him to the appalling deprivation of people in the London slums. Conditions were far worse than anything Barnado had seen in Dublin Bay. Children were starved, kicked and brutalised as if they were animals. So many died during the cholera epidemic of 1866 that their bodies were taken in barrow loads outside the city and shovelled into mass graves. The demands of political crusaders like Lord Shaftesbury for legislation to protect child chimney sweeps, mine and factory workers, appeared to fall on deaf ears.

Like Grattan Guinness, Barnardo thought up grandiose schemes by the minute and always managed to carry them off. In 1872, without a penny in his pocket, he attended the auction of one of London's largest gin palaces and bawdiest music halls—and bought it. When the day came to pay the bill he handed over the entire amount, and the Edinburgh Castle Public House was converted into the Edinburgh Castle People's Mission Church with a congregation of over 3,000, including the Guinnesses. Barnado could say with some satisfaction that "those who tell us that the working classes are inimical to Christianity are wholly misinformed." [46]

He still, however, needed somewhere to live, and Henry needed a college supervisor. The Stepney Institute, as Henry called their first training establishment, was a stone's throw from the Edinburgh Castle, so Barnado moved in, enabling Henry to take a house for his family in nearby Clapton. It meant the Guinnesses could fill the institute with students rather than their children.

Accommodation at the Institute was basic, though adequate enough, claimed Fanny. "In the first place, it is roomy;" she wrote in her diary, "and as we want to pack a good many people into it, that is one great point. Why, it has a hall twenty three feet long by ten feet broad! There are not many houses in London at £63 a year of which as much can be said." The dining-room was big enough to seat twenty, and there were ten bedrooms, even if nine of them were only the size of a ship's cabin. "But each contains a bed and a chair and a gaslight, if not a candle, so they answer their purpose as prophets' chambers. The beds only measure two feet six in width; but as the Duke of Wellington said to the young officer, who, on seeing his Grace's camp bed, exclaimed, "Why, dear me! your Grace, there's no room to turn round in it!" "Turn, Sir, turn? When a man wants to turn, its time he turned out." So we think. We provide beds, not to soothe the restlessness of the slothful, but only to give rest to the weary, and two feet six is enough for that."[47]

Number 29 also had its own garden at the front, "a square of sufficient dimensions to admit a fair amount of exercise," and a timber yard at the back, which, compared to dreary slated roofs and blank walls, was, Fanny declared, the next best thing to a view. It was furnished sensibly according to their limited budget, with strong chairs, well-stocked bookcases, warm coconut matting and serge curtains. Fanny couldn't abide extravagance.

The first theological student arrived from India at the beginning of 1873. Joshua Chowriappah spoke so little English that the Guinnesses decided he should live with them at Clapton. The children loved his sparkling dark eyes and mischievous toothy grin and he quickly became part of the family. When he left them several years later Chowriappah would become an outstanding pioneer missionary in his own country.

As Henry travelled and news of the Institute spread, potential students began to arrive. Along with the British were French, German, Russian, Armenian, Spanish and Kaffir applicants, a hundred in the first year. Each served a month's probation and was subjected to rigorous examination. Thirty two were finally accepted, which meant the college was full.

£1,500 was received in donations, just enough, Fanny calculated. She wrote to their supporters, "Deeming it wise that intending missionaries be trained to independent and active habits, we keep no servants." This was revolutionary in a Victorian household. Men were never expected to do housework. But Henry and Fanny deplored the tendency of British expatriates to turn the natives into servants. The missionary himself should be the servant of those to whom he was called. If he could not respect the integrity of local people, better he did not go at all.

The Institute schedule reflected the Guinness' radical attitude to theological training. It was practical and spiritual, as well as academic and intellectual. The rising bell sounded at six. There was housework at six thirty for an hour, then prayer until breakfast at eight. Classes began at nine, and ended at one thirty with lunch at the Edinburgh Castle to save cooking meals at the house. During the afternoon students learned a variety of crafts, including mechanics, building, carpentry, basic medicine, cookery, botany, and reading the compass and sundial. At seven in the evening they were out in the streets learning to field the physical and verbal brickbats hurled at any open air preacher, "to counter the deadening influence of study on their souls." Henry never forgot the lessons he learned at New College. Local brewers, more paranoid than Arthur or Benjamin Lee Guinness about possible losses caused by intemperance preaching, hired rabble rousers to disrupt the meetings. Letting students loose on the Mile End Waste would make or break them. The long day ended with prayers at nine.

Grattan Guinness was criticised by the academic institutions of the time for offering amateur, "short-cut" theological education. But the Institute provided first-rate missionary preparation, and applications poured in from all over the world. It became abundantly clear that the house at Stepney Green was far too small. Fanny felt increasingly that she should be on hand to mother the students, particularly after Barnado left to get married in the summer of 1873, so one year after opening the Institute the Guinnesses also acquired Harley House in Bow. The ground floor would provide class rooms, a dining-room, and a study for Fanny, where she could do the accounts and administration, and the upper floor, the Guinnesses own accommodation. 29 Stepney Green became a student residence.

A few days before they left Clapton, the doorbell rang, and ten-year old Minnie ran to answer it. Howard Taylor was standing on the doorstep with a letter from his father for Henry. Hudson Taylor had arrived from China to look after his children after the untimely death of his wife, Maria and was living nearby. At eleven Howard felt very grown up to be entrusted with such an important errand, but his confidence dissolved at the first sight of the solemn little face, framed by two long blond pigtails, slowly appearing around the open door. The children stared at each other for some time before Howard finally found his tongue and explained why he had come. Minnie invited him in and as far as she was concerned, that was the end of the episode. Howard, however, would maintain for the rest of his life that from that moment there would never be any other woman in his life.

The whole family was thrilled with their new home. Although Harley House faced the Bow Road with its constant din, there was about an acre of land at the back, filled with shrubs and choice trees, separated from a spacious lawn by a bridge over a grassy ditch. It gave a sense of seclusion and tranquillity to Fanny, and freedom for the children who quickly converted a large, gnarled pear tree into a tree-house. Best of all, in the middle of the lawn stood a small fountain. Stopping to admire the garden, one local visitor said to Fanny, "Shouldn't think Miss, as 'ow you'd ever want to go to 'eaven with that there waterspout."

Harley College was ideally situated for student training. Bryant and May's match factory was nearby. So was the London Hospital where many patients died alone and abandoned, the Tower with its garrisons of soldiers, and the docks with bewildered immigrants arrived daily. Directly opposite was the most imposing building in the area—the workhouse. Opportunity for practical pastoral care was virtually limitless here where thousands lived in hopelessness and despair.

The house was large and old-fashioned, dating back to the time when Bow had been a pleasant London suburb. "Sounds that never disturb the echoes of the West End squares are paining our ears," wrote Fanny wryly, but, "The noise is endurable when the windows are shut." Fanny's ability to look on the bright side of any situation enabled her and the family to cope with the strange lifestyle imposed by her husband's visionary schemes. "We would sooner live in the broad, cheerful, airy Bow Road than in many a dull, confined and built-up West End square, or in many an elevated cage-like apartment on the palace-lined Boulevards of Paris," she wrote, but at that time she had no idea just how much the decision to take her family into such a confined, disease-ridden corner would cost her.

2.

In the year that Fanny and Henry moved into Harley House, Edward Cecil Guinness, youngest son of Sir Benjamin Lee, and the real power behind the brewery, married his cousin Adelaide Mary, uniting the brewing and the banking lines of the family. Although "Dodo," as she was known, was three years older than her groom, and at 29, well on the way to confirmed spinsterhood, her mother was not at all pleased with the match. Dodo had been "finished" at the court of her brother-in-law, the Duc de Montebello, with the intention of enticing a title into the family, but she went and picked a tradesman instead. That he was Deputy Lieutenant of Dublin and one of the richest men in the country seems to have counted for little.

The couple met in Fanny's "dull, confined" West End. Edward Cecil had been spending an increasing amount of time at 5, Berkeley Square, particularly during the season. The dashing young bachelor had earned quite a reputation as a charming and entertaining host, but socialising never distracted him from his duties at the brewery. He expected to be kept informed about the daily running of affairs, however practical or mundane, and to be consulted on all matters of policy. Throughout his life he maintained ultimate control of the business.

While most of his managers appreciated the flexibility they were given, within the limits of Edward Cecil's absolute authority, his elder brother and partner, Arthur Edward resented being told what to do. He, it seems, regarded the brewery primarily as a source of income. His real love was politics. Sir Arthur retained his father's Dublin seat in the General Election of 1868, but was divested of it the following year when it emerged that his agents had been bribing the electorate. He was never personally incriminated, but five long years would pass before he successfully climbed his way back into political favour.

Meanwhile, in 1871, he married the formidable Lady Olivia Charlotte White, daughter of the third Earl of Bantry, converted St. Anne's, Clontarf into an Italian palazzo and upgraded his property at Ashford by planting an extravagant larch forest to make it the best woodcock shoot in Britain—appreciated in time by no less than the Prince of Wales himself.

Edward Cecil too had social aspirations, hence his choice of a wife. Dodo was the ideal spouse for a man who needed manners not money. Her cultured ways acquired in France and her innate intelligence, made her the perfect hostess. The Edward Cecil Guinnesses quickly earned a reputation for their beautiful homes, lavish hospitality and the glamour of their entourage.

They were, naturally, leading lights in Dublin, where it was easy to be an exceptionally large fish in a relatively small pond. Dodo converted their home at 80 St. Stephen's Green into the most fashionable house in town, throwing sumptuous parties in the London style, making her rivals pale by comparison.

In 1874 they bought and renovated Farmleigh, a substantial property overlooking Phoenix Park, so that when they were in town for the season, as they invariably were, Edward Cecil could take a daily constitutional across the park to the brewery. At Farmleigh they established a family tradition for jolly house parties, when, like the rest of their set, they opened their house for the Punchestown Races, the leading event in the Irish social calendar. After Dublin there was the London season and Cowes, then back to Dublin for the Horse Show, Scotland for the shooting, and a trip to the continent, if it could be fitted in. The arrival of their first child on 29th March 1874 at 5 Berkeley Square doesn't seem to have disrupted Dodo's social life in any noticeable way. She noted in her diary with an extraordinary lack of emotion, "Baby born at quarter to six. Boy." One month later he was christened Edward Cecil Lee Rupert.

Two more sons followed, Ernest born in 1876, and Walter in 1880. The upbringing of the three boys could not have been more different from their Grattan cousins. Although Henry and Fanny employed a nanny, normal practice for most middle or upper class families, they were constant visitors to the nursery, and easily distracted from their work. Edward Cecil and Dodo's boys, however, were not allowed to impinge upon their parents' whirlwind social routine, and might not see their parents for weeks, even months at a time.

Though not the best of fathers, Edward Cecil was not a hard man. He had become increasingly appalled by the slum conditions he saw every day on his way to work. If the Corporation wouldn't do anything to improve the living standards of the poor, he would. Partly out of altruism, partly out of shrewd common sense—a healthy worker was a more efficient worker after all—in 1872 he began building homes for Guinness employees. This was the first step of a radical programme of social reform which would affect the lives of thousands of Dublin citizens.

Meanwhile, his relationship with his elder brother over the running of the brewery grew ever more strained. When Sir Arthur won back his Dublin seat in 1874, it sounded the final death-knell as far as his interest in the business was concerned. The powerful Lady Olive was no more keen on trade than her sister-in-law's mother, and appears to have exerted a great deal of influence over her husband. Rumour had it that one evening she and her husband were taking a walk in Dublin, when a labourer, disgusted to find his bottle of Guinness had gone off, slung it over a wall and landed it at their feet. The following morning Sir Arthur resigned. But since Lady Olive never went anywhere, other than in her carriage, the connection hardly seems likely.

Edward, who never felt any tension between his aristocratic aspirations and the means that made them possible, had balked for some time at the way, in theory, responsibility was shared, while in practice, he did most of the work. But his father's will imposed heavy penalties on a partner who withdrew. Edward, however, was more than able to be generous. He had a new deed drawn up allowing a retiring partner to draw out compensation of almost £480,000, and under pressure from his wife, Sir Arthur snapped up the bait. The intent of the will had been honoured and the brewery remained firmly in family hands.

3.

Edward Cecil's cousin, Henry Grattan, lived in relative squalor at the other end of town, "unnoticed by the world of fashion, business or pleasure," Lucy would write years later. The prophetic and scientific writings that would bring him the attention of government leaders were as yet unwritten. There was no organisation, denomination or society to fall back on, and nothing in hand for the running of the college.

Henry had determined never to take a salary from the college funds. "Never, as far as I remember, in the course of a long ministry, have I made any bargain for fee or reward. £400 had been left me as a legacy by my uncle Arthur Guinness of Beaumont, and when my mother needed pecuniary help, I gave her this sum, and went down to Birmingham to preach the gospel with half a crown in my pocket...and from that day I have never lacked a home to shelter in, or provision for daily needs."

Fanny always found it difficult to rise to her husband's heroic heights of faith. Feeding fifty young men with healthy appetites taxed her to the limit. Henry often set off on preaching tours leaving her with an empty cash box. She would write to him in desperation, "In these days of high prices money rapidly melts away," and he would reply with maddening confidence, "Let us go without meat in the Institute for another week, and give ourselves to prayer and searching of heart." And Fanny would stand before the students, account book in hand, and explain why even more stringent economies were necessary.

Being of a more practical turn of mind than Henry she did not see prayer and effort as mutually exclusive. "We cannot expect God to do by a miracle that which we can do for ourselves," she stated firmly. That meant writing endless, time-consuming bulletins and reports to the Institute's supporters. Yet time and time again, Henry was right. Provisions would simply appear, just as they were most needed.

Harley House began to attract its own share of high profile visitors, Harry Moorhouse, Ireland's most notorious pick-pocket until he was converted in the Irish revival, Richard Weaver and his wife, rough diamonds but celebrated preachers, George Holland the wealthy businessman who gave up his comfortable existence to open in ragged school in Whitechapel in the George Yard Mission, Amy McPherson who opened the first home for destitute children. Charles Haddon Spurgeon, pastor of the Metropolitan Tabernacle, the most well-known British preacher of the century and William and Catherine Booth, founders of the Salvation Army. Occasionally, the gracious, elderly Earl of Shaftesbury himself would take time away from the demands of the House to sit on a bench in the shade of the gnarled pear tree.

One visitor, unknown in Britain when Henry first befriended him and created preaching opportunities for him, would soon become their most famous guest of all. The American evangelist, Dwight L Moody arrived in London in 1873, initially for a few weeks, but stayed two years. In that time almost three million people heard him preach. His influence on the Guinness family was immense. He introduced them to the Holiness Movement, and encouraged them to ask God to revitalise their ministry with the power of his Holy Spirit.

The family environment was stimulating. Social history, economics, politics and geography were everyday topics of conversation around the meal table. Stanley had just published his illustrated and rather glamorised account of finding the pioneer missionary, David Livingstone. Lucy wrote later, "Foreign missions were as real as Guy Fawkes and quite as interesting. Curled up in a big armchair one can feel oneself fascinated still by the spell of Stanley's journey through the dark continent. He was only Hans Anderson with bigger print and a little more ponderous to hold. Truth, Henry would say to them, is always more wonderful than fiction.

Fanny was forever at her desk. There was always one last story with her two little ones before bed, but then she returned to her work. It seemed to Lucy that all people, children, nurses, governess, servants, men and women should go to bed at night, "but that mothers should stay up and start at about half past ten their hardest writing. I believed with a perfect faith that all mothers did this; that they worked on till one or two a.m. and came down to breakfast at eight o' clock the next morning as regularly as the sun went round the earth."

Shortly before Harry left to go to school at Tettenhall College in Wolverhampton, Harry, Minnie and Lucy were baptised at the Edinburgh Castle by their father. Rubens Saillens, a French student at the college said it was one of the most moving occasions he had ever witnessed. "He did it in so touching a way, speaking to them with such tenderness and depth of meaning, in tones so vibrant, yet so calm, that there were few present who were not moved to tears." For Minnie it was the most important day in her life. She had found the courage to demonstrate her convictions in public.

Fanny decided the girls needed a governess and hired a genteel Miss Gardner, who was unnerved on her first morning to be confronted at breakfast by two swarthy-looking Syrians, one of whom was blind. But Fanny put Miss Gardner at ease and with her usual charm, quickly made her feel part of the family.

At mealtimes the parents emerged from their respective studies, Fanny to listen to their children's progress, Henry, "radiant with the light of heaven, absorbed in some fresh thought connected with the Second Advent."[48] According to Miss Gardner, he was writing *The Approaching End of the Age*, and Mrs. Guinness was "putting it into more simple, popular form."

Miss Gardner became an indispensable part of the Guinness household, helping Fanny with her correspondence, the students with their English, presiding at the meal table when Henry and Fanny were away. Encouraged by Fanny, an increasing number of match girls from the Bryant and May factory dropped in on their way home from work, and if the children were toffee-making, joined in. Poor Miss Gardner was all but turned to toffee, and Henry was roused from his meditations by the hilarity in the kitchen.

In 1875 he acquired his own stately home and country residence. In Derbyshire there lived a couple by the name of Hulme, devout Congregationalists who owned a large, elegant country house, a farm, and many outbuildings, to which they had added a small chapel, all set in twenty one acres of rolling Peak District overlooking the River Derwent. The Hulmes were elderly and there were no children to inherit the home they loved so much. Driving home from the station one day, as he watched the house come into view, James Hulme had the strongest feeling that Cliff House should become a missionary training college, though he had no idea how that might be possible, and died before he could see the fulfilment of his dream.

Shortly after her bereavement Mrs. Hulme happened to visit Harley College, and knew at once what she must do. The lease on Cliff House, then in the hands of a group of trustees, was offered to Henry Grattan so that he could set up a northern branch of the Institute.

The Hulmes however had not been able to manage the property for some time. The floors were riddled with dry rot, most of the window frames had disintegrated, the plumbing had ceased to function and the roof was full of holes. Fanny groaned at the thought of taking on a white elephant, but Henry was adamant. Apart from a principal's salary the college would be self-supporting. Enthralled by news of recent exploration in Africa, an increasing number of students were feeling a sense of call to the great lost continent. But life there was utterly primitive. To survive they would need to understand the rudiments of subsistence farming. Where better to do so than in the wilds of Derbyshire?

The lease became theirs in December 1875, and Henry set off immediately with a working party of students, blessing the Almighty that amongst this year's intake were several carpenters, joiners, painters and glaziers. They camped in the empty shell of the house in freezing conditions, working from morning to night, breaking off only to eat and for chapel services. Once the basic repairs were complete, alterations began, the conversion of barns into dormitories, the building of additional staircases, windows, bathrooms and a large number of lavatories. Then there was the wallpapering, whitewashing and painting to do, all accompanied by the loud singing of the popular new hymns by the American, Ira Sankey.

The quiet, rural village of Calver had never experienced such an invasion before, and local people turned out to watch. Word got round that these were theological students and they were soon in great demand in the surrounding chapels. "The people expected us to be great guns, coming from a college in London and having attended Moody's meetings," wrote one of the students, "so we try not to disappoint them!" [49] That meant sitting up half Saturday night after an exhausting day of hard physical work to put a decent sermon together.

While Henry acted as supervisor of works, Fanny in London had the task of justifying the expense to their supporters. Funds were urgently needed. The work of the Institute was expanding rapidly in many different directions. As well as buying two more East End houses as student residences, Fanny had publicly committed herself to creating ten new congregations in the area. She was appalled at the way established churches, Anglican and even Methodist, were moving out of the slums into more salubrious neighbourhoods at a time when hundreds of the growing East End population were turning out night after night, sometimes in pouring rain, to hear the students preach.

For weeks, while Henry was in Derbyshire, she trailed the streets looking for possible venues for new congregations, but none of the abandoned churches and chapels she visited fulfilled her requirements. They were largely "cheerless, desolate, dirty-looking structures...with their high-backed pews and their formal religious associations sure most effectively to repel the very class we want to attract." How could such dismal, sepulchral buildings compete with gaudy, brilliant gin palaces?

Fanny eventually found several possible mission halls, a sign-painter's shed in Old Ford, a little disused chapel in Bow, a Presbyterian iron church which she uprooted and moved to Stratford. She rented a local school on Sunday evenings for 300 rough, uneducated children who poured off the streets into the established churches to keep warm and were ejected on the spot for being disruptive. Two oxy-hydrogen lanterns were bought so that the students could hold the children's attention by illustrating their talks with slides, or "dissolving views" as they were called. "Our men make the oxygen gas and work the apparatus themselves," Fanny explained to supporters, "so the expense is trifling, while the benefit and enjoyment they afford is great."

One of their students, a former sailor who intended working among seamen, managed to persuade Fanny that one of her mission halls should be afloat. It could sail up and down the Thames, round the coast among British and foreign shipping, and anchor in the summer at seaside resorts. Early in 1876 a thirteen-ton cutter came on the market at the incredibly low price of £120 and was bought with the help of a single donation. The students lovingly repaired and repainted her, and launched "The Evangelist" the following spring with a captain and three students on board.

It wasn't difficult for Fanny to justify missionary work among London's poor, but how could she explain the acquisition of a property, not in squalid Bow, but in the lush countryside of Derbyshire? It was, she wrote, an unimaginable release to escape from the noise and filth, to see a sky unobscured by a leaden pall of smoke, to hear the birdsong and see the distant hills. "Night brings real silence. Your whole being seems to expand with a sense of relief."

Furthermore, learning experimental farming was providing an invaluable tool not only for the students, but for some of Tom Barnado's boys, who were acquiring useful skills in a restorative environment for the first time in their lives. Altogether, Fanny concluded, despite her original misgivings, Cliff College was a gift from God not to be refused.

From that first summer Cliff was not only home to the Guinness family, it was an idyllic paradise, a summer retreat and a refuge at other crucial times from the pressures they would all face in the years ahead. But the expenditure exceeded her worst fears. While Henry became embroiled in the protest against the Bulgarian atrocities, speaking up and down the country in support of Bosnian Christians facing barbaric persecution at the hands of Muslim Turks and Bulgars, Fanny was absorbed in the mammoth task of finding carpets and curtains for Cliff. "No funds came in today, only bills. We have never been so low before," she wrote in her diary "*May 2nd.* Nothing again this morning, save tidings they have the measles at Cliff!"

The situation eased a little over the summer, but by December Fanny was urging both houses to give up meat for the foreseeable future. Henry, never willing to ask his students to do what he was not prepared to do himself, wrote from his preaching tour in Cornwall to say he would join them in their fast. But how, Fanny lamented, could they be vegetarians on Christmas Day? She so badly wanted to treat her Sunday School children to their first turkey dinner. "Feeling cast down and tried," she noted in her diary. On Christmas Eve a cheque for £50 was delivered to the door of Harley House, enough to provide Christmas dinner for the Guinness family, the Sunday School children, and any overseas students unable to return home for the festive season, not to mention a special Christmas tea for Fanny's mothers' group.

Despite financial constraints, Fanny and Henry were forced to recognise that Harley House was too small and began a major building project in the East End. Harley College, the East London Institute for Home and Foreign Missions, was opened without debt on a biting autumnal day in 1878. It was an imposing red-brick building with a grey roof and large sash windows. The Venetian blinds were Fanny's pride and joy. Nothing could have prepared her for the cruel blow that was about to come.

4.

In 1875 the first twelve students went out from Harley House, Joshua Chowriappah to India, the two kaffirs to South Africa, one to Burma, one to Japan, four to China, Arthur Douthwaite leaving his fiancee behind because he thought he could be more useful without a wife, and Rubens Saillens to Paris, where he founded a theological college at Nogent which exists to this day. On the day of their departure the "Mother of Harley" delivered her last words of advice. Aware of the solemnity of the occasion, for who knew what destiny awaited, one of the students sharpened a pencil and opened his note-book in readiness. She said, "I have one piece of advice to give to you which I hope you will remember all your life. Whatever part of the mission field you may be in, always be sure to keep your hair tidy." There was, he decided, an unmistakable twinkle in her eye, masking the terrible wrench she felt at parting. After all, they had become *her* children, and she would never see some of them again.

"Our first twelve" always had a special place in her affections. She hung a photograph of them over the chimney piece in the dining-room and at mealtimes, allowed her vivid imagination to carry her to the countries they represented. Letters were read aloud to the children, who were enthralled with the descriptions of lively Japanese towns, of Chinese waters crossed in dozens of little boats known as junks, of scorching plains in India or Burma, of back-breaking work on Caribbean plantations.

The family also followed the daily descriptions of Stanley's discoveries in the unknown continent of Africa in the *Daily Telegraph*. For years Africa had exerted an almost magnetic charm over a succession of explorers like David Livingstone, commissioned by the Royal Geographical Society to discover the sources of the Nile. After Livingstone's death in 1873, Stanley went back to Africa, determined to take up where the doctor had left off, finally managing to reach the mouth of the Congo.

Shortly before his death Livingstone had written, "All I can add in my solitude is may Heaven's richest blessings come down on everyone, American, English or Turk, who will help to heal this open sore of the world." Dying on his knees, stretched out across his bed in an agony of prayer for Africa, he had thrown down the gauntlet to the enthusiastic students of the Harley Institute.

In 1878 Henry and Fanny set up the Livingstone Inland Mission. The aim was to establish missionary stations all the way down the swift-flowing Congo River to Stanley Pool, where it contracted to an unnavigable torrent, hurtling its way in a series of cataracts to the lower Congo and Atlantic Sea. Many Harley students rose to the challenge. They knew the risks involved. Stanley had made it clear that the African waterways, the only real means of access into the continent, were treacherous, the climate unbearable, disease rife and the natives not only hostile, but cannibalistic. Hardly any of his own or Livingstone's party had survived. Africa meant almost certain death.

Nonetheless, a small party at Harley, led by an ideal candidate, Adam M'Call, no stranger to Africa for he had spent seven years as a government official big game hunting on the Upper Zambezi, was preparing to go. Fanny felt deeply ambivalent about encouraging "her children" to make sacrifices she would never make, safe in England. But before the little group sailed, events she could never have foreseen, seemed to put her on an equal footing.

The Easter holidays of 1879 were fast approaching. Fanny planned to take her family to their Uncle Wyndham's rambling old vicarage overlooking the sea at Rathdrum for a good long rest. Some ten days before they were due to leave for Ireland, Henry set off for a series of meetings in Torquay taking Whitfield with him. Fanny was loathe to let the child go, but he was not a robust little nine-year-old, and she thought the sea air would do him good. With Phoebe and Agnes, she stood on the porch at Harley waving them off until the carriage was out of sight.

The following morning, Wednesday, Agnes complained of a headache. Fanny thought little of it and made her stay in bed. She seemed better by the afternoon, got up and played as usual. By early evening she had a pain in her neck and ear and it hurt when she moved her mouth. Fanny, who was about to go out to speak at a meeting, thought she must have caught a cold and instructed Minnie to make sure Agnes had an early night.

But Agnes deteriorated, and in the morning Fanny sent for the family physician, Dr. Dixon, who diagnosed tonsillitis, a condition unknown to Fanny, but apparently not serious. As the next two, endless days went by and Agnes showed no sign of improvement, a terrible, sickening fear began to take hold of Fanny. What if her little girl had diphtheria? How could she have contracted it? She suddenly remembered the meeting that evening before Henry left for Torquay, 150 Sunday school teachers and seven-year old Agnes handing out tea and cake. Her friends and relatives, so critical of her for taking her children into the disease-ridden East End, were probably right.

By Saturday Agnes' throat was so sore it took her ten minutes to find the courage to swallow her medicine. There could no longer be any doubt about the nature of the illness. Dr. Dixon urged Fanny not to worry about the students, but to get the other children out of the house. Meanwhile, he sent for a throat specialist who managed to scrape away some of the membrane, leaving the tissue raw and bleeding. Fanny held Agnes and sang to her, and when she finally slept, scribbled a note to Henry begging him to leave Whitfield with her cousin in Torquay and come home.

Harry, mercifully, was still away at school, Lucy was dispatched to relations, but on the Sunday, before Fanny could finalise arrangements for the other two girls, it became clear that eight-year old Phoebe was ill too.

That was a night to end all nights. Agnes was desperately ill, Phoebe was incessantly and violently sick and Minnie, an invaluable source of support, began to develop the dreaded symptoms and was too unwell to help. Fanny struggled on, but by Monday morning her own throat was extremely painful. She told herself she was simply suffering from strain, and telegraphed Henry again. By the time he arrived home on Monday evening Dr. Dixon had seen the characteristic membrane across her throat and sent her to bed.

Henry was in enforced quarantine downstairs with the students. Even if she couldn't see him it was a relief to Fanny to have him in the house. They communicated by notes, and on Tuesday, decided to send the students home for a prolonged vacation. The house stank of carbolic, but that was hardly a guaranteed protection against the spread of infection. Agnes was a little improved, Phoebe holding her own, and at seventeen, Minnie was old enough to fight the disease. Fanny was beginning to let herself believe the worst was over.

By Wednesday, however, Phoebe had deteriorated so rapidly that the two doctors held out little hope for her survival. Fanny begged them to let her go to her child, but they refused. Finally, in the evening, she could bear it no longer, and dragged herself to the nursery. Phoebe was labouring for breath. Her hand was cold and clammy. Fanny sat on the edge of the bed, sponging her brow. She opened her eyes and seeing her mother said, "you shouldn't take that trouble. You'll make yourself worse."

The following morning Dr. Dixon performed an emergency tracheotomy, opening the windpipe and inserting a tube below the obstructive tissue. Phoebe's relief was instantaneous. She began to breathe freely. Fanny sent a message to Henry to say she had regained consciousness, and he was allowed to come and stand in her room, just inside the door. It was the first time they had seen each other since his return from Torquay, and they knew they must not go near or touch each other. All Henry could do was watch from the doorway while his little girl died in Fanny's arms. Fanny sat for some time without moving, too stunned at that stage even to cry. She kissed her daughter one last time, then went to look after Agnes.

The disease had spread to Agnes' chest. For several hours Fanny fought on, filling her with medicines, willing her to live. Life was inconceivable without her bright, giggly baby dancing around the house like a sunbeam. But by late evening Agnes breathing slowed and her pulse weakened. Henry came and stood just in the room again. Agnes could not see him, but recognised her father's voice. She died at ten o'clock, ten hours after her sister.

Fanny was distraught with grief and weakened by the disease. She longed for Henry, for the comfort of his arms, to share in his pain, but it would have been madness to take such a risk. Instead, she and Minnie cried the night away together.

The following day she wrote to Harry, Lucy and Whitfield, the hardest letters she ever had to write. To Wyndham and his wife, Dora, she wrote that in the last years Institute work had left her little time for recreation. Her only relaxation had been brief moments snatched with her two little girls. They had been such merry, considerate, undemanding children. She couldn't believe they wouldn't run in from the nursery or garden at any moment. She couldn't bear to think of the treats she would never be able to give them. Heaven had better treats—that was her only consolation. She thanked God they were in his presence, and that one day they would be joyously reunited. "But oh, dear brother and sister, need I say, for the present, it is not joyous, but very, very grievous."

The funeral took place without Fanny or Minnie on Wednesday April 2nd at the Abney Hall Cemetery, Stoke Newington, where Fanny's sister, Madeline and her four children were buried. Fanny was bewildered, full of questions about why God seemed to answer certain prayers but not others. Why had she and Minnie been spared? Why had Lucy not succumbed? Why was Whitfield providentially out of the way? Perhaps it meant God had some special work for them to do. A tiny ray of light penetrated the darkness threatening to engulf her. Perhaps, one day, there would be meaning in this apparently pointless bereavement. But for the time being it was a case of surviving each day at a time, when every ounce of her being seemed to scream, "How can I ever go on without them?"

CHAPTER EIGHT
1879-1882

1.

Henry and Fanny coped with their bereavement by submerging themselves in their work. They had just set up the North Africa Mission, sending Jane Pearse, formerly Jane Bonnycastle, and her husband, George, to Algeria. Jane had been converted in Paris under Henry's preaching. Now, with the establishment of the North Africa mission, the Guinnesses had the oversight of three missions, two colleges, and ten mission halls. A budget of £1,500 in 1873 had risen to £11,000 by 1878, and even that barely covered the running costs and salaries for missionaries, teaching staff, and pastors. The college courses were still free and applications poured in—over a thousand in the first six years.

One day in 1879, five young Jewish immigrants turned up at Harley College. Like most of their fellow Eastern Europeans who had sought refuge in Britain from the pogroms of Eastern Europe, they had no money and little command of English. But they had been recently converted to Christianity through the work of Christian relief organisations and were determined to study under Henry Grattan Guinness because of his reputation as an expert in Biblical Zionism. There were no vacancies at Harley, but Fanny took the men in all the same. One of them, David Baron, would later play an important part in the first international Zionist congress.

By the beginning of 1880 sales of *The Approaching End of the Age* had exceeded all Henry's expectations. Lord Shaftesbury said he was "so struck and moved by its contents...that I cannot resist the desire I feel to bring it under the immediate and serious attention of the public."[50]

From his studies in the Old Testament Shaftesbury himself had long been convinced that the return of the Jews to their homeland in Palestine was a crucial part of God's plan. As early as 1839 he had convinced the Foreign Secretary, Lord Palmerston, that Palestine under Turkish rule and British protection could become a national homeland with Jerusalem as its capital.

Henry Grattan Guinness was not alone in making the connection between biblical prophecy and world history, but his distinctive contribution grew out of a recently acquired interest in astronomy. T.R. Birks, Professor of Theology at Cambridge University, had introduced him to the discoveries of a Swiss astronomer called Jean Philippe Loys de Cheseaux, who was determined to establish, from his studies of the book of Daniel, the exact date of the crucifixion . Medieval astronomers had always maintained there was no correlation between the orbits of the earth, the sun, and the moon, but in 1754 De Cheseaux inadvertently discovered that 315 years constitute a soli-lunar cycle, at the end of which the sun and moon come within three hours and twenty-four seconds of their relative positions in space. To his excitement he then realised that 315 was a quarter of 1260, the number of "days" stipulated in the books of Daniel and Revelation as significant for the end of the age. De Cheseaux realised that 1260 years, as a multiple of 315 years, must also constitute a soli-lunar cycle, but when he went back to his calculations he made an even more extraordinary discovery. Twelve-hundred sixty years was the time it took for the sun and moon to complete a cycle in space to within one hour of each other. In other words, 1260 years was the key cycle in time that brought the solar and lunar calendars into almost total harmony. This discovery was the key that opened the door to understanding biblical prophecy.

Henry Grattan was so enthralled by De Cheseaux's deductions that he acquired an eight-inch telescope for himself so that he could continue the astronomer's work. Serious academic study and painstaking research in these matters, and in his beloved fossils, eventually earned him fellowships of both the Royal College of Astronomers and the Royal Geological Society. Ultimately, he earned the title Doctor of Divinity for the connections he made between these studies and theological study.

For some months the telescope occupied pride of place in the Guinnesses' overcrowded dining room at Harley House, until the scope was equatorially mounted at a purposely built observatory at Cliff. It was Henry's most treasured possession. At some stage in their training most of the students were invited to admire and use it. David Baron went back to the observatory time and time again, noticing on one occasion the Hebrew words "Holiness to the Lord," scratched onto the telescope's side.

Henry would explain to students that just as the earth had its own cycles—the minute hand on a clock measuring an hour, the hour hand marking a cycle of twelve hours, light and dark denoting a day, and four seasons encompassing a year—so there were other cycles known to astronomers which measured huge periods of time. Henry was convinced that unlike human beings with their limited concept of time, God measured time by these vast astronomical clocks. Daniel and Revelation, the apocalyptic books, were subject to an astronomical code. Indeed, the writers spoke of the books' being "sealed up" until an appointed time. De Cheseaux had unwittingly cracked the code; the appointed time had come. References in the text to days, weeks, years, and "times" were "natural astronomic cycles of singular accuracy and beauty, unknown to mankind until discovered by means of these very prophecies."

It was now relatively easy for Henry to establish the fact that biblical time was often measured, not in solar years as was the western calendar, but in lunar years. Many scholars of prophecy had long realised that a biblical "day" symbolised a year, and a "week" a multiple of seven, but when Henry used lunar years to calculate Daniel's figure for the end times, his "week of years" or "seven times," Henry arrived at a figure of 2520 years—twice de Cheseaux's figure of 1260!

Henry believed that the "end times" of the apocalyptic books were the years referred to by Jesus Christ as "the times of the Gentiles"—an era of Jewish degradation and dispersion, dating from the destruction of the great temple in Jerusalem in AD 70. If this period were to last 2520 years, the "end times" were fast running out.

But Henry Grattan Guinness was no crank presaging the end of the world.[51] He rejected any attempt to foretell the second coming of Christ, or to turn the Scriptures into little more than an almanac. Historical facts, not speculation on the future, would point to the truth. The prophet Daniel, in his own futuristic vision, had seen the world dominated by four terrible beasts for "a time, two times and a half a time." These beasts were the four great pagan empires of antiquity: Babylon, Persia, Greece, and Rome. The period of time beginning with the accession of Nabonassar, the first King of Babylon, and ending with the fall of Romulus Augustus, last emperor of Rome, was a period of 1260 lunar years. That was fact.

Daniel's fourth beast, Rome, had ten horns. Once they were destroyed the beast would sprout another horn, very different in kind from those it followed. Henry believed that this horn represented the political and very corrupt power of the Vatican. From the moment it began to exercise a powerful influence in European affairs until its sudden collapse in 1870, witnessed personally by Henry and Fanny, there was another period of 1260 years. That, too, was fact.

That fact meant that the year 1870, marking the end of "seven times" and a cycle of 2520 years, must have been a turning point in world history. The main indication that the "times of the Gentiles" really were drawing to a close would be the end of the diaspora following the establishment of a Jewish homeland in Palestine.

Before 1870 no sensible person would have deemed that event possible. Palestine had been controlled by the all-powerful Ottoman Empire for hundreds of years. But Henry had also calculated that a cycle of 1260 years of Muslim occupation of the holy city would soon be complete, and by 1870, it looked as if the Turkish stranglehold in the Middle East was beginning to fail.

Many politicians like Lord Shaftesbury believed that Jewish restoration was the obvious solution to the power vacuum in the Holy Land. But millions of Jews were living in Eastern Europe in relative tranquillity with no desire to uproot—until March 1st, 1881, when Tsar Alexander II was assassinated, and they found they had become scapegoats overnight. Jewish refugees fled by the thousands, some to Palestine, some to America, but most to Britain, particularly to the East End of London. Now Henry's analysis of biblical prophesy began to be significant. Along with several other early Christian Zionists, he and Fanny bought land in Palestine, intending to hand it back to its historic owners as the opportunity arose. Neither knew it would never arise in their lifetime.

In a 600-page volume supplementary to *The Approaching End of the Age,* Henry included his meticulous astronomical and historical charts, charts which even Fanny, in her popular precis of the book, was forced to admit looked rather daunting. Nonetheless, she said, they showed how every important world event fitted into an astronomical cycle in such a way that "any person of ordinary education and intelligence, reading [the book] with attention will find no difficulty whatever in understanding and following its statements." In this volume, she concluded triumphantly, the Christian student had found "a new weapon wherewith to defend the Book of God against the oppositions of science falsely so called—a weapon with which, indeed, he may assume the aggressive, and challenge opposers to account for a fact which nothing but the Divine inspiration of the Bible can account for."

2.

Sometime in the late 70s, the Grattans renewed their links with their brewing and banking relatives. Sir Arthur and Lady Olive were particularly kind to the young people, offering them the benefits of "society." Their sister-in-law Dodo's full cousin, Richard Seymour Guinness, had recently moved to London to expand the Guinness Mahon banking business, taking up residence in St. George's Square, and establishing himself at the Carlton Club in St. Swithin's Lane, where he carried out business without a clerk or an account book. Richard Seymour had ten children around the same age as Henry's, so the various branches of the family played tennis together and went on boating expeditions and picnics.

But Dodo's legendary parties and balls were out of the question—largely because dancing was an evangelical taboo. Dodo found the taboo hard to understand. After all, she was devout, although in the high church tradition. She took the sacrament as often as possible and dressed in a sensible, dignified manner. Her bustle was restrained, her neckline modest, her dark hair drawn neatly back into a bun at the nape of her neck.

But when it came to entertaining, she showed no restraint. An onyx-studded ballroom at St. Stephen's Green and one in Carrera marble at Farmleigh cost approximately £30,000 each. They were lit by an array of massive wax candles and decorated with live parrots. Augustus Hare, a professional socialite who published a diary containing startling revelations about the private lives of the rich and famous, recorded his observations of Dodo's entertainment on June 18th, 1879. "In the evening I was with the Prince at Mrs. E Guinness' ball on which £6,000 are said to have been wasted. It was a perfect fairy land, ice pillars up to the ceiling, an avenue of palms, a veil of stephanotis from the staircase, and you pushed your way through a brake of papyrus to the cloakroom."

But every morning and evening, the servants filed into the library in their distinctive uniforms—the parlourmaids in high, white, frilly collars, the footmen in red velvet breeches and white stockings, silver buckles on their black polished shoes—and sat in rows while Edward Cecil led the family in prayers.

The gentlemanly Sir Arthur was a favourite of Harry, Geraldine, and Lucy. He seemed to have a permanent twinkle in his eye—except when he was discussing Irish politics. The children had all grown up with a strong sense of their Irish identity, but it was Sir Arthur, with his determined and often unreasoned opposition to Home Rule, who fired their indignation with his tales of that instigator of all trouble, the leader of the Land League, Charles Stewart Parnell.

To help protect tenant farmers from eviction and destitution at time of worsening economic conditions, Parnell had urged that any man taking on another's farm be shunned in the streets and in the shops, in the marketplace and at the fair, and even at the place of worship. That man was to be a leper. The first victim of this ostracization was an English land agent called Captain Boycott. He was shunned completely. He couldn't even hire a workforce. The Irish had discovered that passive resistance was a deadly weapon in the fight with their landlords to gain much needed reforms.

At boarding school in Hastings, Lucy was anxious about her uncle, Sir Arthur, at his estate in County Galway. She was infuriated that no one, not even her form teacher, even knew what Boycotting meant. That ignorance was remarkable, since the newspapers were full of little else! On January 30th, 1881, she wrote in her diary, "I wonder really what has happened there since I left and how Sir Arthur has been, and if his tenants have risen against him as they were expected to do; and if Parnell is imprisoned or punished in any way for rousing the people as he has, but no one can tell me." Papa was coming soon on his way to take some meetings. He would tell her, because he knew all there was to know about Ireland.

Since his retirement from the brewery Sir Arthur had devoted himself to a career in benevolent philanthropy. As a boy he had always enjoyed access to the large private park overlooked by his home in St. Stephen's Green. It seemed a pity it should be fenced off from the public. Sir Arthur bought the twenty-two-acre site from local householders, had it landscaped with walks, flower beds, and an ornamental lake, and presented it to the city. This particular gift earned him a great deal of gratitude in Dublin, countering some of the unpopularity of his diehard politics.

In 1880, after he lost his Commons seat, Disraeli made Sir Arthur the first Guinness peer of the realm as Baron Ardilaun of Ashford.

Unlike many of his class Sir Arthur was an enlightened, caring landlord, continually developing imaginative plans to stimulate industry for the tenants on his country estate in County Galway, determined to prove that a manifest and confirmed Unionist could still love and serve the Irish people. His tenants did not arrange a boycott. Indeed, considering the advantages they enjoyed, it would have been very strange if they had.

In society, the Ardilauns so established themselves as the arbiters of good taste that when a family member committed a social gaffe, others would gasp in mock horror, "What would the Ardilauns say?"[52]

Lady Olive wanted to present Harry and Geraldine at court. Fanny insisted that Lady Olive ask them, and not her, since they were old enough to decide for themselves. Enlightened in comparison to many Victorian parents, Fanny and Henry did not believe in over-burdening their children with prohibitions. Some prohibitions, such as those against alcohol and dancing, were inherent in their religious tradition, but too many could be counter-productive. "There are parents who in their desire to keep their children right," Henry preached, "are perpetually forbidding this and that. The word most commonly in the lips of those who have to do with children is DON'T....They are constantly repressing, forbidding, prohibiting. Now there is another, far better, more useful word—that is DO."

None of the Grattan children appear to have given Lady Olive's offer serious consideration. High social life simply wasn't their scene. Geraldine dismissed the social whirlwind as "the unsatisfying round of amusements." And Harry had just won a coveted place at the London Hospital to study medicine.

3.

Harry and Howard Taylor began their medical training together. Their professor, Sir Frederick Treves, was one of the foremost physicians of the time. His reputation was to be established for posterity some years later when he gave sanctuary to the famous "elephant man," protecting him from the lurid fascination of the British public. Harry and Howard felt privileged to sit at the great man's feet.

Whereas Howard Taylor was quiet and retiring, Harry was an extrovert, a born leader and a brilliant sportsman—tall, dynamic, and handsome, with his father's magnetic eyes and a hearty laugh that was his alone. He was the kind of young man who inspired both envy and admiration in his fellow males. Nothing fazed him.

On his first day of medical study, for instance, a fellow student canvassed the fresher for the Debating Society. "We like to get new men," the student said, adding, "You needn't be a bit afraid—there's nothing religious about it. In fact, one of our rules is that no one is allowed to allude to a religious thing."

Amused, Harry decided to go along. Sir Frederick himself was in the chair. The subject for debate was some medical matter which Harry as yet knew little about. He listened in silence, until, for no apparent reason, one of the speakers made an offensive remark about Jesus Christ. "I wondered what ought to be done," he wrote, recalling the experience. "I think, as far as I know, that my brain had not made up its mind, but my legs had automatically, and I found myself standing on my feet."

After asking whether a first-year was allowed to speak, Henry said, "Well, I may be out of order, but I was informed when I came up here by the gentleman who invited me that it is against the laws of your society to allude to religious matters. Is that so?" They agreed it was.

"If that be so, Mr. President, then I beg to protest against the words of the gentleman who has just sat down. He has spoken against one who is my Lord, my Saviour and my King in a way that has made my blood boil."

Harry sat down waiting for the laughter and the jeers, but what he heard, after a moment's stunned silence, to his utter astonishment, was thunderous applause.

As he was leaving the hall he felt a hand on his shoulder, turned, and found himself face to face with Sir Frederick himself. He asked Harry his name, then said, "Now look here Guinness, I'm glad to know you. You come back to these meetings, and if ever a man does what that man did tonight, you do what you did."

From that day on Sir Frederick Treves became a personal friend, as well as a wise and brilliant tutor.

Harry went on to found the Hospital Athletic Club. On June 10th, 1881, at the Crystal Palace, cheered on by a large crowd of supporters from Harley, he won the world record for slow bicycling—a real feat given the fashion for high bicycles, almost impossible to ride at any other than top speed.

In any free moments after medical studies and sporting activities, Harry helped out at the College. The East End population was growing steadily, spreading from Bow to Limehouse, Stratford and Hackney. There were no educational facilities other than the few ragged schools set up by charities; there was little health or social care; and there was no entertainment other than the gin palaces. Harley College tried to fill the gap. Whatever the time of day it was always a hive of activity, with night schools of one kind or another, lantern lectures in the winter, and in the summer, garden parties for women, cabmen, or policemen. Harry could play the cornet and the piano, sing, organise games and even manage a passable conjuring or ventriloquist act. When he wasn't involved in cabaret he taught local men to read and write.

Howard Taylor went with him, ostensibly to help, in reality to catch a glimpse of Geraldine who was too absorbed in running the night school to notice.

Fanny had planned to open a night school from the moment she moved to Bow. She and Geraldine would watch the girls pouring out of Bryant and May at seven each night, and occasionally invite them in. In dark skirts and dark shawls, the plumage of their hats the only splash of colour in their wardrobe, they looked for all the world like birds let loose from a cage. Clearly exhausted, they were hungry for any distraction from the terrible monotony of work which would start again at six the next morning. "Their often wretched homes afford nothing," Fanny wrote to her supporters; "they cannot get a country walk or a stroll on the sea shore;

they are shut up to crowded, noisy streets, all aglow with gin palaces, and thronged with young men who are only too glad to take them into these hell-traps, or into the penny gaffs and dancing-saloons, or even to the cheap theatres. Small wonder they are led astray or end up on the streets."

Fanny understood the power of education to liberate vulnerable young women. She bought a little chapel down the road from Harley College next door to Bryant and May, and issued an open invitation to her new school, the free "Working Girls' Improvement Association." There would be classes on Tuesdays and Thursdays in reading, writing, dress-making, book-keeping, and music. Since the girls would be coming straight from work, tea would be provided. If they behaved nicely, were quiet, gentle, and polite, they might talk and ask questions, for "we quite understand that what you want, after a hard day's work, is a pleasant evening, 'a good time' (as the girls in America say), and that is what we will try to give you."

From the very first evening Harley Hall was packed to capacity. Two evenings a week were clearly insufficient, and once Geraldine joined the teacher, Mrs. Cole, classes were extended to every night. In 1880 the night school moved into larger premises at the brand new Berger Hall, called after William Berger, who was as generous to Henry and Fanny as he was to Hudson Taylor and the China Inland Mission.

For Geraldine, being face to face with factory girls was an eye opener. Fourteen-year-old Matilda spent one evening trying to shield a black eye from her teacher's hawkish attention—to no avail. "I knocked it," she said, when Geraldine asked her how she had got it.

"It's a lie, Miss Guinness," her neighbour shouted; "Her father give 'er it."

Geraldine invited Matilda to tell her more about her home life. The story appalled her.

Unused to such attention, Matilda took advantage. She disrupted Geraldine's Sunday Bible class completely, winking at her friends and making faces behind Geraldine's back.

"Close your Bible, Matilda, and see me after class," Geraldine snapped.

At the end of the lesson Matilda decided to make a quick getaway. She had heard that naughty girls were invited to take a walk around the garden at Harley House, where Geraldine would pick them a button-hole and attempt to "civilise" them. Matilda slipped downstairs and was amazed to find her teacher waiting for her in the street.

Matilda found herself taking the inevitable turn around the garden. She was asked to explain why she was being so difficult. "Well, Miss, you know I can't read," Matilda answered.

Geraldine hadn't known. She leant forward and kissed the girl apologetically on the cheek. Matilda, expecting to be hit, shrank away in terror. No one had ever kissed her before.

The incident left a deep impression on both women, and, within a short space of time, Geraldine had found Matilda a place in service in the country with kind family friends. Years later, Matilda would more than repay her benefactress when she became her devoted housekeeper.

To free her mother who was increasingly absorbed in promoting missionary work in the Congo, Geraldine also took over the domestic reins at Harley College, acting as hostess to a number of influential guests. The society she had spurned came to her—not only Lord Shaftesbury and his friends Lord and Lady Radstock, but also Lord Poleworth, a member of the Congo Mission Committee, Lady Louisa Asburton, and Dr. Karl Baedecker, the celebrated travel writer whose name had become synonymous with his indispensable European travel guide.

When Charles Spurgeon brought the students of his Pastors' College to Harley for an athletics competition, Harry was in his element. So was Lucy, who had developed a sudden interest in male theological students. In December of 1880 Spurgeon's College returned the invitation in the form of a pre-Christmas dinner, stipulating that Fanny should be the only female member of the Harley party. Spurgeon did not believe in exposing his students to the temptations of the opposite sex. Fanny, to Lucy's great glee, ignored him and took along five female companions, including her two daughters.

Even on Christmas Day the family was surrounded by students. There were presents bought on a shopping expedition by omnibus to Whiteley's Universal Emporium, the first department store in London. "After tea, Papa brought down some of his experiments, microscopes and electric machines, besides lots of others.... It was great fun watching some of the students trying to get a sixpence out of the water. Of course, none of them could." Harry then did a few conjuring tricks; Lucy organised charades; and Henry Grattan read from Byron, Cowper, and Milton. Sadly, however, "Darling Mother" spent the day in bed, thanks to a very bad headache brought on by riding in the omnibus.

4.

On March 8th, 1881, Harley students and Congo Mission supporters gathered at Forrest's ship-building yard to launch their first Congo steamer. It was one of the earliest and most ingenious examples of flat-pack, self-assembly goods. The idea was that the steamer would be carried in pieces by Adam M'Call's expedition up 230 miles of treacherous cataracts in the lower Congo to Stanley Pool. At Stanley Pool the steamer would be re-assembled, taking the missionaries along a thousand-mile stretch of navigable river into the heart of Africa. The only problem was that so far, no one, not even the explorer Craven who had been struggling in appalling conditions in the Lower Congo, had managed to reach Stanley Pool.

There had been pressure at Harley to name the steamer the *Fanny Guinness*, but Fanny and Henry felt that the name *Livingstone* was more appropriate. Minnie and Lucy, who had been chosen to perform the launching ceremony, stood on a wooden jetty and shouted, "God speed the Livingstone." Cheers rent the air, but the boat refused to budge. "This part of the performance," Lucy commented drily in her diary, "was rather ignominious because the tide was too low for her to slide off gracefully in the correct manner and it took rather a long time to shove her into the water."

The call to Africa was suddenly and cruelly stripped of its romance when news reached England of the death of Mary Richards, the first woman missionary to the Congo. She had recently married one of the Harley students, and they had been gone only a few weeks. Her husband buried her and sent a drawing home of her grave. Lucy copied it into her diary. She was devastated by the young woman's death. It brought home to her the inescapable reality of missionary life in Africa. Beside the picture she wrote simply, "How could M'Call?"

Meanwhile, her own overseas adventure loomed large. Lady Olive, with some encouragement from Lucy, had managed to persuade Fanny to send her younger daughter to a proper finishing school in Paris where she could acquire a good command of a foreign language and develop her special musical ability. At the end of December, 1881, Henry Grattan Guinness deposited his youngest daughter at The Miss Ellerby's Finishing School for Young Ladies on the elegant Boulevard Malesherbes.

Lucy loved Paris from the first—the taste, the chic, the charm of the pretty shops. But the school was disappointingly dreary. Tucked away on the top two floors of a six-storey building, its elegant facade hid a penny-pinching, rigid, regimented routine which lacked imagination and real creativity.

The months in Paris represented that strange adolescent no-man's land between childhood and maturity, when the former slips sadly out of our grasp while the latter is still a frightening substitute. Her "bodily troubles" caused Lucy a great deal of angst. Womanhood both beckoned and repelled her. One of her friends had just had a baby. "A BABY! Florrie, who used to do lessons with Minnie and me only yesterday as it seems. How dreadfully old I must be getting. How happy Florrie must be to have a baby all of her own! But how CAN people do such things! I can't understand."

In the summer, Geraldine, who was recovering from a broken romance with a young medical student, was sent to Paris to bring her sister home. Lucy ran out to meet her sister, looking very chic in a new emerald Parisian dress. When Geraldine heard Lucy's superficial, catty conversations with her friends, however, she feared school had done Lucy no good at all. Lucy was scolded; she duly repented, and harmony was restored.

In Paris, Geraldine appeared more alive than Lucy had ever seen her, "coiffing herself with a little bow of bright red ribbon in the middle of her arrangement behind, and singing "Suppose, and suppose that your highland lad, etc.," in such a loud voice that Lucy couldn't concentrate on finishing her work.

Two of Lucy's closest school friends were the Dreyfus sisters. They lived in a flat on the ground floor of the finishing school with their brother, a colonel in the French Army. Lucy and Geraldine passed him on several occasions on their way up the stairs and developed a little more than just a nodding acquaintance. A decade later, when "the Dreyfus affair" was emblazoned on the front of every French and English newspaper, Geraldine would remember a quiet, gracious man. She would marvel at the curious irony that she and Lucy, daughters of a leading Zionist thinker, had known the French army officer court-martialled for treason because he was a Jew. With the support of the writer Emile Zola, Dreyfus would become the cause celebre to highlight nineteenth-century anti-semitism, and justify the Zionist cause.

5.

No summer was complete for Henry Grattan and his family without a month's houseparty at Cliff. Lord Ardilaun and Edward Cecil had their country estates where they entertained royalty; Henry Grattan shared his estate with a motley collection of friends and ever-increasing family.

Geraldine had the responsibility of supervising an advance party which transformed the college into a comfortable holiday home. The task was a mammoth one. The main classroom was converted into a drawing-room. Desks were removed to make way for the summer furniture, kept in store from year to year. The piano was transported from the other end of the house, and vast arrangements of fresh flowers were brought in from the garden.

The sleeping and catering arrangements were particularly complex, since visitors came and went. In the summer of 1882, all forty bedrooms were in use. One evening Lucy counted fifty-three people sitting down to dinner. She didn't mind the quantity, "if they are select...which unhappily they are not always!"

Henry would have brought the entire world to Cliff, if he could. He never ceased to marvel that such a wonderful place could be his, and he was too generous to keep it all to himself. For Lucy, surrounded on every side by perpendicular gritstone cliffs falling away to miles of moorland, rocky gullies, and verdant valleys, with the "glittering Derwent...filling the air with the sound of ever-falling waters," Cliff was the next best thing to heaven, an oasis of calm and tranquillity. "We call this our Galilee—our refuge from close, crowded, noisy, dusty, ill-favoured, enormous London."

Unlike his cousins at Ashford and Farmleigh, Henry Grattan may not have offered a decent shoot, but his house parties were every bit as companionable as were those of his relatives. There were tennis and chess competitions; picnic expeditions to Haddon Hall in Castleton, with its famous caves; boating parties on the Derwent; and hikes up Eagle Rock, led by Henry himself, hammer in hand, in search of interesting fossils.

The evenings were filled with music. Most years Grattan and his guests could muster a full orchestra. In 1882 there were eight violins alone. If there wasn't a concert, or organised games, there might be a lecture from Fanny on Central Africa, or from Henry on prophecy and Zionism. The older members of the party would groan if Henry happened to choose astronomy as his subject, for he would march the young people out to the observatory to spend half a night with the telescope. Harry, who often disrupted the proceedings with ghost stories so terrifying that no one would go to bed, later claimed he grew up knowing more about the mountains on the moon than the geography of his native land.

In the summer of 1883 Lucy counted sixty or so visitors to Cliff. Among them was a commanding, regal-looking widow called Mrs. Henry Reed. The Reeds were a wealthy Christian family, pioneers and founding fathers of Tasmania. Mrs. Reed suggested to Fanny that Lucy and Whitfield accompany her home. Fanny was very much against the idea at first, but Mrs. Reed was used to getting her own way. Lucy would go to school with her daughter, Mary, and Whitfield would go with her son, Henry. The experience would broaden their minds, the climate do wonders for their constitutions. Lucy and Whitfield said farewell to their family, and on Saturday, September 8th, they set sail for the new world.

CHAPTER NINE
1882-1886

1.

In the 1880s the Edward Guinnesses were the undisputed leaders of the Dublin social jet set. The glamour of their social life gave no indication of the hard work Edward put into making the brewery one of the most profitable and highly respected companies in the world. He had set his heart on a peerage, to be achieved not by means of the usual philanthropic route which had served his brother well, but through recognition of his own contribution to industry. Edward intended to take the social stigma out of trade and establish a tradition for acknowledging the value of enlightened capitalism in increasing national prosperity.

Many of Edward's political machinations in the early 1880s were concentrated on that particular goal. In 1885 he resisted the offer to stand for a parliamentary seat because of pressure at work. "To sit would be most distasteful to me in every way; the unpleasantness of it would be very great, for I was always to be found by anyone at St. James' Gate."[53] Edward finally acquiesced, but did not win the seat, nor did he stand again at a bye-election. It could not bring him the coveted peerage, and in the end he asked the Prime Minister outright. Gladstone made him Baron Iveagh, "in recognition not only of your high position in Ireland, but especially of the marked services rendered by you on the important occasion of the visit recently paid to that country by the Prince and Princess of Wales."[54]

Assuring the future Edward VII of England and his Queen not only protection, but also a warm welcome was no mean achievement. Anti-

British feelings were running high. Three years earlier two high-ranking government officials had been killed by terrorists in Phoenix Park. In the recent General Election, Charles Parnell's Irish Party had taken eighty-five seats. The Chamber of Commerce did not think it was the best time for a royal visit. But as High Sheriff of Dublin and the most respected member of the Council, Edward Cecil used all his powers of diplomacy to rally the city dignitaries to a fairly convincing show of goodwill.

Their parents' social whirl meant constant upheaval for the three children. Rupert's earliest memories consisted of endless journeys from house to house along with a retinue of nannies and governesses. Winston Churchill's grandfather was Viceroy for a time, and the two boys, Rupert and Winston, shared a governess. On one occasion they were given a toy harness and coachman's whip and told to go and play together. "You be the horse," Winston commanded Rupert. When Rupert refused, Winston, who had the whip in his hand, lashed him across the face, catching his eye. A leading Dublin eye specialist applied ice and a caustic solution which burned off Rupert's eyelashes and brows and left him with permanent scarring. Years later when the two men, both in their eighties, met again at a rehearsal for the new Knights of the Garter at St. James's Palace, Winston asked the second Earl of Iveagh if he remembered their boyhood fight in Dublin.[55]

Rupert was a shy, retiring boy, and his apparent lack of academic ability was a source of bitter disappointment to his parents. Dyslexia was not a recognised condition. Had they stopped to consider it, Edward and Dodo should have known their eldest son was not unintelligent. When Rupert was seven Edward Cecil acquired a microscope to study the effects of the yeast culture on brewing. Rupert begged his father for a microscope of his own. It was his favourite toy, and it heralded the beginning of a lifelong fascination in the sciences, compensating for the attention his parents gave to Ernest because he was obviously clever, and to Walter, their favourite.

The children admired rather than loved their parents. Rupert's letters home from Eton contain no reference to his feelings. Growing up was a hard and lonely process, but a combination of public-school stoicism and genetic determination buoyed up his spirit, and in the end, adversity revealed the true mettle in the man.

2

Unlike Rupert, Lucy was raised in a loving, sheltered environment which had ill prepared her for ship-board life on the P and O Line's HMS Ballarat. From Lucy's perspective, the poor classes of the East End could be expected to indulge in worldly pleasures; they had little else to relieve the misery of their daily existence. But the well-heeled passengers of the Ballarat were another matter. Lucy found their smoking, drinking, dancing, playing cards, flirting, gossiping, and falling out profoundly distasteful.

The truth was that she felt very alone in the rather frightening, hostile adult environment. Mrs. Reed, so charming at Cliff, turned out to be autocratic, never explaining her motives for any command. Used to Fanny's sensible reasoning, Lucy was not surprised that the two younger Reed daughters, Maggie and Mary, were almost out of control, flirting with every officer in sight. Mrs. Reed's constant haranguing drove them to it, and they had daily "rowings-up" with her.

Her late husband, dead three years, had been an immensely wealthy businessman. Henry Reed was also extremely devout, a preacher and philanthropist, ruthlessly honest and totally inflexible, one of the foremost supporters of the newly formed Salvation Army. He had married Margaret Frith, daughter of a well-to-do Anglo-Irish family, when he was 57 and she 35. Despite their maturity in years the Reeds produced three daughters and a son, raising them alternately in Tasmania and at Dunorlan in Tunbridge Wells, their English holiday home. They counted the Guinnesses as their closest friends. The two families had many interests in common and their children were of a similar age. In 1880 when Henry Reed died, Margaret Reed made an extremely generous donation to the Livingstone Inland Mission: a second steamer for the Upper Congo, a ship which would be called the *Henry Reed* in his memory.

In 1883 the eldest of the Reeds' three daughters, Annie, joined the Booths' daughter, Katie, in Paris, where she was trying to establish a Salvation Army base. "La Marechale," as she was known, was a genius at handling crowds of lewd, drunken men, but Annie was not. News of the innuendos and cat-calls Annie attracted reached her mother at Dunorlan who set off for Paris and sent her daughter back to Tasmania forthwith. It was Fanny, thoughtful and practical as ever, who wondered whether a summer at Cliff might not be a way of calming Mrs. Reed and defusing family tensions.

The Reeds were seasoned travellers, blasé about the journey home. Lucy was homesick and profoundly disturbed by some of the sightseeing trips. A trip to a Capuchin Monastery on Malta left her with nightmares for a week. In the freezing cellars, propped up in niches gouged into the stone walls, were the skeletons of dead monks, still covered in bits of rotting flesh, their tongues hanging out, their eyes glaring in the torchlight. The visit was a terrifying ordeal for any youngster, let alone one who had not long since experienced a painful bereavement, and it confirmed her worst prejudices against Roman Catholicism. She was equally intolerant of the boring Sunday Church of England services in the Captain's cabin, with their "weary, meaningless hymns and prayers."

Occasionally, in the evening, Lucy was called on to give a virtuoso piano performance, accompanied by Whitfield on the violin, but, to her acute embarrassment, when there was dancing in the lounge, Mrs. Reed, made her and her girls sit in the stern singing stirring hymns.

The barriers Lucy had so carefully constructed around herself had begun to crack. She even felt the first flutters of romance. Her sense of superiority was shattered. Now, like any other young girl, she longed to dress up in beautiful clothes, to dance, to shine, to go to the fancy dress ball. But it was out of the question for a Christian young woman. So was her romance, especially as she stood before the entire ship's company accused of stealing someone else's young man.

She cut off the relationship as the ship docked in Melbourne, and it almost broke her heart. The whole business left her feeling older, wiser, and somewhat chastened. "One cannot live in this world and do it good without understanding some of its evil—but oh—I would like to be as trustful and pure and innocent as I was before I came on shipboard."

Farewell to her first love had been a farewell to childhood.

3.

Mount Pleasant, the Reed family home, stood in a perfect setting against the Blue Mountains, high above the town of Launceston, commanding a magnificent view of the Esk Valley. The house was in its glory in the late Australian spring, the gardens a riot of colour, lush crops of cherries and strawberries waiting to be picked, apricots and peaches ripening slowly in their turn.

Whitfield was in his element. He threw himself with gusto into the Reeds quasi-colonial life in the outback, learned to ride, pole vault, shoot rabbits, and drive the pony and trap bought to take him and young Henry Reed to school in Launceston. Any local pupils who thought the white-skinned pommy with the plummy accent fair game regretted their thoughts when they discovered he had been having lessons in ju-jitsu and could toss them over his shoulder.

Lucy, however, missed the sophistication of Paris. Reed family life was as Spartan emotionally as it was physically. Mrs. Reed seemed unable to show affection. Only Annie, nicknamed "Cull," showed Lucy any attention, and she was totally matter-of-fact and devoid of sentimentality. It was a relief to accompany Mary Reed across the Straits to the Presbyterian Ladies' College in Melbourne, Dame Nellie Melba's old school with a fine reputation for its music teaching.

For the first time in her life Lucy was a triumph. She excelled at English and composition. The other girls adored her. Years later Mary Reed was asked whether Lucy was pretty. "Pretty?" Mary replied. "No! She was more than pretty, she was interesting to the last degree. She was small and dark with a clear, pale face and with something vivid about her.

She had a way of getting herself up in the evening—a rose in her hair—a scrap of lace maybe—and the result would be charming."

Her musical brilliance was recognised and given every encouragement. She won the Senior Pianoforte Scholarship with little competition. "It is a fine thing to get," Whitfield wrote proudly to his parents; "they have to play before a lot of swell Melbourne musicians." The scholarship provided her with an opportunity to play a solo at the Athenaeum Concert Hall. The music critic from *The Age*, a popular Australian newspaper, hailed her as a talent with a great future. "Miss Guinness' tempo was at times a little faulty, no doubt owing to nervousness in the young performer." When she re-read the cutting years later, Mary Reed laughed out loud. "Lucy Guinness was never nervous. Her tempo was often faulty, but it was because she preferred her own tempo to that of the composer! She was after all a great granddaughter of Cramer, the composer, the first pianist of his day." [56]

So impressed was the school with Lucy's musical ability that the great violinist, Remenyi, was invited to hear her play. He concluded that she was "on the very threshold of the inner temple of classical music," and that a career as a concert pianist was indeed within her reach.

Mrs. Reed quickly put a stop to such nonsense, deciding, after a year, that two marriageable young women needed no further formal education and should fill their time instead with domestic pursuits. Lucy tried her hand at jam-making, baking bread, and saffroning lace, but had no aptitude for any kind of home-making. She promised herself she would keep up with her piano practice, but boredom and discouragement made her lethargic, and she soon lost the will to press for further lessons.

In January 1885 news reached them that Harry was coming to take Whitfield and Lucy home. It was March before he actually sailed on the Lusitania, since Fanny had suffered an attack of Bell's Palsy in the intervening month. It left her with a distressing facial paralysis.

Harry made light of the palsy in April when he finally arrived in Tasmania, not wanting to worry Lucy and Whitfield unduly. Mrs. Reed was delighted to have such a personable young man around, a budding young preacher with all the charisma and promise of his father. She put him to work and he was soon in demand all over Tasmania. To Lucy's dismay he consented to stay on another few months. It gradually became very plain to her that her hostess's motives were not altogether disinterested. Mrs. Reed was in the business of "throwing her daughters at Harry's head."

Meanwhile they all set off for a sight-seeing tour of Australia, Harry preaching in Brisbane, Melbourne, Adelaide, and Sydney—often giving talks for men on subjects such as "Social Purity," or "The Temptations of Men in the City." As a newly qualified doctor he was concerned at the widespread masculine ignorance on sexual matters.

In England men had fainted and were carried out of Harry's lectures. The Australians found it rather novel. No one had ever spoken in public about such matters before, and they admired his courage. "The Admirable Crichton must have been such a man," claimed one Melbourne newspaper. "He has revelation in his right hand and science in his left, and can use both weapons freely."

By the end of 1885 Harry was still in such demand that Mrs. Reed would not hear of his returning to England. Lucy and Whitfield arranged to go on ahead without him, accompanied by Henry and Annie Reed. If Mrs. Reed did not "effectually catch him now, she ought to!" Lucy noted cryptically. But she had already. On January 29th, 1886, he announced his engagement to Annie Reed. Lucy described in her diary what she felt was a very unsatisfactory proposal.

That Friday night everyone had arrived home late from a church meeting and gone straight to bed—except Harry and Annie. Annie was on her way upstairs when Harry called her to ask if she was coming back down.

> She came into the dining-room and Harry evidently wanted to say something to her but could not. So they two stood there (Harry describes his own experience at that moment as that of having his tongue glued to the roof of his mouth—unusual for him!) and at last Harry said, "Cull—I want a great many things," and she answered, "So do we all" (in her blunt tone!) and Harry said nothing more, so

she said goodnight and went out into the hall and had got up two of the stairs when she turned round and Harry was behind her. So they two stood again and then he said, "You will soon be leaving the old home, Cull," to which she answered, "Yes—it was very soon," and he said, "I should like to make a home for you in the old country, Cull, if you will let me,"—and Cull stood still feeling like a stone, and knowing now, until she said, "I will—if Mother will." And the two turned and went into the little room—and I don't know what happened there exactly.

Lucy commented dismissively, "I think they did it very badly myself!"

Of the three sisters Annie was the least pretty and the most devout. Her features were heavy, her nose long and thin. But she was sensible and practical, very like Fanny. Unknown to Lucy, Annie had caught Harry's eye from the first. "Annie is just splendid," he had written to his parents after he had watched her organise tea for 1500 people without the slightest sign of fatigue or strain. Harry the charmer, the incurable romantic, who could have had any one of a large number of beautiful women in Australia or England, had common sense enough to see that this woman, plain as she was, had all the qualities he wanted in a wife.

Lucy was stunned. How had she been so blind to Harry's interest? Even Whitfield seemed to have known that Annie was "the real nugget." But as the initial shock wore off she was forced to admit that if Harry had to have one of the Reed sisters, Annie was the best option. The two were, Lucy decided, eminently well-suited—"Harry poetically inclined—Cull absolutely matter-of-fact. Cull a businesswoman—Harry not very practical." The strong resemblance to her parents' relationship does not seem to have occurred to her.

3.

While Lucy and Whitfield were away in Tasmania, Henry, Fanny, and Geraldine, like everyone else at Harley College, had been following M'Call's progress, step by painful step up the 230 miles of cataracts in the

Lower Congo. His progress was recorded with tiny markers on a huge map of Africa as it was then presumed to be, hung on the wall at Harley. The markers were moved every time news of the little party arrived. Stanley Pool, gateway to a vast, unexplored continent, lay just beyond their reach. They struggled on in desperate conditions, with inadequate supplies, no map or guide except Stanley's diagrams, no drugs, and no understanding of the causes of malaria, dysentery or the fatal Blackwater Fever.

The arrival of the *Livingstone* in Africa in 1881 enabled M'Call to press on as never before, establishing mission stations all the way up the cataracts—at Banana, Mattadi, Minkanda, Pallaballa, Banza Manteki, Bembi, and Manyenga. Each station was consecrated with a grave. Husbands buried their wives and wives their husbands. Others sailed out for Africa, some dying faster than those they had gone to replace. At Harley each loss was a personal bereavement. But there was still no shortage of volunteers.

Stanley Pool was finally reached in 1883—but M'Call didn't live to see it. The new steamer, the *Henry Reed*, arrived in Africa in five hundred pieces and was transported up the cataract region, as Stanley's boat had been, on the heads of a thousand carriers, to be reconstructed at Stanley Pool. Sixteen thousand rivets were required to fasten the vessel's one hundred sixty plates. The men worked beneath a blazing African sun with no access to spare parts. Some died, some were invalided home. But at last the *Henry Reed* was afloat on the upper river. The new adventure could begin.

The major development at home was the purchase of Doric Lodge, a large house opposite Harley College, as the first missionary training institute for women. Within the social culture of the time this was a radical step and largely due to Fanny's insistence. Unlike the denominational missions, the faith missions had always taken on female missionaries, and, if they were single, accepted them in their own right. In 1878 Harley student, Henry Craven, was accompanied to the Lower Congo by his fiancee, Miss Bossom, the first white woman the natives had ever seen. The North Africa Mission had been set up with Henry's encouragement by Jane Pearce, and many of its stations manned by women only. The Algiers Missionary Band was led by Lilias Trotter, a woman whose courage was universally admired.

Fanny was convinced it was time to offer women proper training. She and her fellow female preachers, like Catherine Booth, had begun to see there were no limits to a woman's ministry. They constituted a great "neglected force." No army goes to war, Catherine Booth said, with half its forces left behind in the kitchen. "We are increasingly convinced of the importance of well-trained female agents among the heathen," Fanny wrote, appealing for her first students, "and of the fact that multitudes of women who have the natural and spiritual qualifications...are wasting their time at home here in England. [57]

The extra administrative work took its toll on her health. She was fifty-four and tired more easily since her stroke. The facial paralysis made her feel uncomfortable about accepting speaking engagements on behalf of the Livingstone Inland Mission. When Fanny heard that Adoniram Judson Gordon, Director of the American Baptist Missionary Union, wanted to absorb the fledgling North Africa Mission, she saw a way forward. Edward Glenny, leader of the small North Africa Mission, resented the attempted American takeover, but Fanny saw there were obvious advantages in Gordon's having the Livingstone Inland Mission instead. It was unusual for a Bible College to have its own mission. Though students were told they were free to join the mission of their choice, it put pressure on their loyalties. Fanny also believed that new, more appropriate missionaries might be found for the future Zaire amongst America's black congregations. It was not an easy decision to make, but Henry and Fanny were never possessive about their work.

Meanwhile, Geraldine tried to shoulder as much of the Institute work as she could. Before he left for Tasmania Harry had begged her to take over his men's night classes. Geraldine thought it irresponsible of him to think she could she cope with loud, rough working men, many of them the worse for drink. But one Sunday afternoon he sent a message to the Berger Hall to say he had been unavoidably detained at the hospital. The men were waiting for their class. She could hardly disappoint them, and discovered it wasn't such a trial after all. They were stunned into good behaviour by her appearance. "I can see her now, standing on the platform with her white handkerchief on the rostrum," one of them said in later years, "She was like an angel." None of them knew how frightened she was.

From that day the men's classes were taken by women. Edith Fookes, more academically minded than Geraldine, taught Latin, Logic, and Mathematics to the advanced class, while Geraldine's special responsibility was the beginners and the drunks. Howard Taylor supplied her with some medicine which was supposed to sober up any miscreant she was forced to drag out of the classroom for causing disruption.

One night Geraldine was feverish and Edith went to Berger Hall unaccompanied. Despite her protestations, Henry insisted she mustn't walk home alone. He would collect her at the end of her class. She waited and waited, but there was no sign of her uncle. Eventually she set off. As she walked down Devons Road she noticed a small crowd underneath the flaring lights of a public house. Intrigued, she went to see the source of the curiosity, and standing on tiptoes, caught sight of her uncle, so absorbed in scribbling down astronomical notes, he was totally unaware of being the centre of attention. Edith pushed her way to him and touched his arm to bring him back to reality. He apologised profusely. He was writing *Light for the Last Days*, and could think of little else. Edith forgave him, but never waited for him again. Like Harry she had learned that for her uncle, "sustained reflection on high themes was a necessity of life." Harry had once travelled with his father on a tramcar from Bromley to Bow without Henry Grattan's noticing he was there.

Despite Edith's insistence they take an evening off a week, remove the drab deaconess's uniform they wore and go to concerts or lectures, Geraldine suffered from complete exhaustion. She had inherited her father's intensity without his Irish expansiveness. She could never see the humour of any situation. The pain of the East End oppressed her unbearably. She drove herself and eventually developed acute back pain. The doctor ordered a surgical corset to support the spine and complete rest.

In Redhill, where she was sent to recuperate, she received a wise, loving letter from her father. She wrote on the envelope the words, "To go with me wherever I go," and carried it in her handbag for the rest of her life, eventually publishing it after her father's death. He told her she was like him and so he understood her suffering. "You have been brought face to face with sorrow, poverty, pain, death, miseries of many kinds. You see the world full of them. The problem presses upon your thoughts, it is too much for weary nerves and heart." He too had once teetered on the edge of a complete breakdown and he apologised for not recognising the signs in her, for relying on her so much and appreciating her sensitivity so little. Now it was time for her to have a complete change. "Give the brain a rest, give it sleep, give it fresh subjects. Read about other things, about natural history, and whatever interests and pleases you... Go out; let the sweet influences of Nature refresh your tired physical frame and mental nature too. Let sunshine and breezes, singing of birds, flowers and springtime, do their work."

4

Geraldine arrived back at Harley in the summer of 1886 fit and well and ready to help Fanny with preparations for the arrival of Whitfield, Lucy, Henry Reed and their new sister-to-be. When it became apparent that Annie Reed was at least as competent at supervising the domestic routine, if not a great deal more, she handed over the reins willingly. House management had been a necessity for Geraldine, not a pleasure.

In the autumn Whitfield and Henry Reed set off for the Leys School in Cambridge; Lucy accompanied her parents to Cliff where Henry could write in peace; and Annie was left in charge of the London house. At a loose end, Geraldine happened to pick up a pamphlet called *The Bitter Cry of Outcast London*, written by a crusading social reformer. The pamphlet affected her deeply. She thought she knew all there was to know about conditions in the East End, but it was one thing to see them from the safe confines of Harley, it was another to experience them first-hand. How could she understand what it felt like to be poor when she was so sheltered and comfortable? Gradually the idea took root that the only way to get inside the skin of local people was to become one herself.

She saw no necessity to consult her parents. She was twenty-three after all, and what they did not know could not worry them. But she did need an ally. Annie Reed was the obvious choice. As a Tasmanian Annie was free from English caution and reserve, and had had her own adventures in Paris.

Annie remembered that the kitchen maid, Sarah, had once been a factory girl, one of the wildest and roughest at that. Pledging the maid to absolute secrecy, they told her the plan and asked about suitable clothing and accommodation. Sarah thought Miss Geraldine must have taken leave of her senses! Her posh accent would give her away at once. Factory girls had ways and means of dealing with people who tried to ape them. With no disrespect, Miss Guinness was such a frail-looking little thing that they could blow her over in one puff. But nothing Sarah said would deter Geraldine, and eventually the girl agreed to help, on condition that she went too. Geraldine consented. She was not as brave as she tried to pretend.

In a pawn shop Sarah found clothes for them both. Then she was sent to Colliers Rents just south of London Bridge, to hire a furnished room. Geraldine could hardly preserve her incognito in the East End where everyone knew the family. South London was unfamiliar territory and Colliers Rents in Long Lane the very street mentioned by name in the pamphlet she had read. A triumphant Sarah returned with the news that she had managed to rent a room with a bed, table and a chair.

Factory hours were seven in the morning to seven at night, so Geraldine decided to move to Bermondsey on a Saturday evening. That would give her all day Sunday to get used to her new surroundings before she started work on Monday morning.

As the appointed Saturday drew near she was filled with an increasing sense of dread. She kept handling the strange, rough clothes, wondering why on earth she was taking such a step, yet convinced she had to do it. The moment to put on the clothes finally came. She had never felt so nervous in her life as she buttoned up the drab skirt, wrapped the ticklish woollen cross-over round her shoulders, then pinned on her apron. She stood looking at the transformation for some time in the mirror. Tentatively, she lifted up the hat with its large, gaudy, trailing feathers and put it on her head. The sight shocked her and she took it off quickly. Slipping a fur cloak around her shoulders, she ran downstairs, holding the awful hat in her hand. She couldn't bring herself to put it on until last possible moment.

Annie was waiting in the hall. For a moment their eyes met, Geraldine's as grave as ever, Annie's twinkling with unsuppressed amusement. Annie had to fight hard to stifle her laughter all the way out to the pony chaise. She was to drive Geraldine to London Bridge where Sarah would be waiting for her under a lamp by the church. They drove in silence. When they reached the bridge Annie slowed the chaise. With a rather desperate sounding, "Goodbye," Geraldine dropped the fur cloak onto the seat, slapped the hat on her head, and stepped down. Annie shook the reins and Geraldine watched the chaise speed away, fading quickly out of sight in the murky October dusk. Sarah was waiting for her and they walked down Long Lane together. As the dank chill of night began to enter her bones, the countless public houses looked increasingly inviting. She was pushed, shoved and jostled by swarming humanity out for a good time and reeking of drink. It was a relief to reach the comparative quiet of Colliers Rents.

The door of their lodgings was locked and there was no sign of the landlady. A woman poked her head out of the next door window and said she had just gone round to the "public" and would be straight back. Sarah and Geraldine sat on the doorstep for hours. Mrs. Tester appeared at last, considerably the worse for drink, yet kindly nonetheless. She showed them in and they climbed up a ladder to get to their room. Geraldine could hardly believe her eyes. It was far worse than anything she had seen in the East End. Sarah had tried to clean it up, but the dirt had defied all her attempts.

That night was the most frightening of Geraldine's life. A whole lodging-house of seventy men was involved in a fight underneath their window. Geraldine trembled so much that the bed shook. The fight was no sooner over than a window was flung open nearby and a woman started screaming, "Murder! murder!" until the police came and took her away. The drunken brawls in the street continued until the small hours of the morning.

As dawn cast a grey light over the drab little lane, a sort of uneasy, exhausted silence descended at last. Lying next to her, Sarah had managed to doze off. Beneath her Mrs. Tester was snoring loudly. She got up to think and pray, sorely tempted to give up the whole idea. Then she remembered it was Sunday; she would have to find a church. Looking at her skirt and apron it suddenly occurred to her that her presence would not be acceptable in a "respectable" place of worship. Only a mission hall would welcome her. This sudden awareness of how pernicious the class system was, how alien to true Christianity, strengthened her resolve to stick it out.

On Monday morning Geraldine and Sarah started to work at the match factory. Sarah introduced Geraldine to the other girls as her mate from the country, which was half true as Geraldine had only recently come back from Cliff. She didn't say much because life was so strange down here and she was shy. The explanation was accepted. These country bumpkins did find city life hard at first.

Geraldine was torn apart by her experience in the factory. She was terrified of opening her mouth, yet longed to get close to the girls. Her heart went out to them. She was appalled by their conditions of work and angered by the way they were treated. Constant contact with phosphorescence caused a cancer of the skin known as "phossy jaw," which eventually caused the disintegration of all the surrounding tissue. Yet no one appeared to care. A girl was of no more value than an animal. At the end of the week Geraldine and Sarah had earned a mere four shillings and fourpence-halfpenny between them. It had been a slack week. On a good week they might have earned eight shillings.

After a fortnight Geraldine began to feel unwell. The pastor of the mission church she had attended urged her to go home and reluctantly she allowed him to send for Annie. It was a dejected-looking Geraldine who climbed into the pony chaise for the return journey. She felt a failure. Those girls had to put up with their lot forever and she could barely cope with two weeks. And yet, in years to come she was to see how formative they had been. The experience taught her that if necessary she could adapt to a totally alien culture. Had she known it, there could be no better preparation for her future.

She recounted every detail to an enthralled Lucy, just back from Cliff. Lucy had been feeling listless since she came home from Tasmania and decided to write up Geraldine's adventure. But on reflection, felt that to write an honest, realistic account, she could not simply rely on her sister's version. She must experience the life of a factory girl herself. Poor Sarah was requisitioned again and repeated the whole process, this time with a determined, persevering Lucy, who in her quest for authenticity was prepared to go to greater lengths than her sister.

In her booklet *Only a Factory Girl* Lucy powerfully conveyed her impressions of life in the squalid end of London. In the streets with their piles of stinking rubbish, a middle-aged woman in shabby, torn clothing, with a red and bloated face, dances about with a drunken man to the sound of a black minstrel band, while the children look on and laugh "at the pitiful spectacle of degraded womanhood."

The door of a public house swings to and fro and a rough working lad inside, seeing Lucy standing outside in the shadows, puts his head out and speaks kindly. "'E ain't 'ere, ole gal! 'E's gorn 'ome, 'e is." Seeing she ignores him, he adds, "Never you mind 'im, 'e ain't comin' back 'ere agen tonight. You just come into the warm, ole gal, you an' yer mate!" And Lucy takes her first faltering steps into a public house.

Inside, dozens of factory girls with pretty faces, half-stupid with drink, allow themselves to be fondled in turn by various men. "We have often wondered at the language and uncontrollable wildness of factory girls. After tonight's experience, we shall never wonder again, but rather marvel that, seeing their lives are such, and that such places are open to them nightly, they should ever be content to come to our evening classes and sit and sew and spell!"

Out in the street large gangs of girls and lads lark about under the archways, shouting, swearing, and singing music-hall songs. What is there to go home to? A wretched tumble-down tenement, cold, damp, and overcrowded? Whom is there to go home to?

Lucy had never felt so invisible in her life. As a factory girl she simply did not exist. No one cared that she was cold and wet through, the rain beating down on her bare head. There was one way of keeping warm, the girls told her! "If we listen to their suggestions, we shall never go home again—! Pardon, gentle reader! We did not mean to shock you. We only wanted to tell you of things as they are."

The booklet did shock its polite readership for all the reasons Lucy hoped it would. Its immense popularity led to the formation of the Shaftesbury Society, an organisation still committed, more than a hundred years later, to improving conditions among the poor.

In 1888, two years after the booklet's publication, the match girls went on strike demanding better treatment and protective measures against "phossy jaw." They won their fight, but Lucy had prepared the way. Her first success with the power of the pen ensured she would never be less than outspoken.

5

In 1886, while Geraldine and Lucy were absorbed in the plight of factory girls, news broke in the city that Arthur Guinness and Sons was to go public. Since most businesses were private partnerships this was an unusual event. Edward Cecil received £6 million—a sixth in shares, the rest in cash. The new chairman could afford to be generous. The workmen received four weeks pay, there were cheques for the clerks and three months salary-worth of shares for the brewers. To brother Lee of the Royal

Horse Guards, who had enjoyed none of the benefits of the family firm, he gave £150,000. Only John Tertius Purser, General Manager, who had worked for the brewery for sixty two years refused a hand-out. The old family retainer wanted nothing to do with a public company. He feared it would compromise his Moravian values. He was probably right.

The demand for shares had been underestimated. The Chairman used his cash to make a killing, and by February 1888 had acquired more than 50%. Their value rocketed. In those days "insider dealing" was not a criminal offence. Edward Cecil had no qualms about the integrity of his dealings. He had said all along he intended to retain ultimate control of the company.

As Bessie had foreseen, Edward Cecil's rejection of the evangelical teaching he received as a child and his reading Darwin to prove it, affected his morality more than he cared to admit. All that was left of his religion was a sense of duty to humanity. His was not the only company to renounce exploitation of the workforce. Firms like Cadbury's and Rowntrees were equally committed to applying Christian values to industrial practice. Where the first Lord Iveagh excelled was the scope and scale of the welfare he provided.

Unlike a factory girl in London, a Guinness employee in Dublin was a someone. His wages were the highest in Ireland. In 1860 pensions and holiday pay were introduced. Free medical services and midwifery, a dispensary and sick pay were added in 1869. There was security of employment, and misdemeanours such as drunkenness, smoking on duty, late arrival, carelessness and wilful neglect, which would earn a man the sack elsewhere, incurred a fine instead. Edward Cecil is supposed to have said, "You can't expect to make money out of people, unless you are prepared to let them make money out of you"—a fairly radical statement for a Victorian employer, let alone an Irish Protestant with a largely Roman Catholic workforce.

Like his Grattan cousins in Bow, Edward Cecil's social conscience was not immune to the slum conditions he saw every morning on his way to work. While education was their solution, decent housing was his. "A man living in a well-ventilated, clean and sanitary dwelling is healthier, happier and capable of performing double the work of one who resides in an over-crowded house, not to mention the liability of the latter to contract disease, draw sick money, or perhaps die prematurely, leaving a widow and family to be supported by the firm."

By the time he wrote that report in 1884 he had provided housing for a seventh of his workforce, with the Belview Building in 1872, and the Rialto Buildings in 1882. In 1885, in evidence to the Royal Commission on the Housing of the Working Classes, he described how he had provided one hundred eighty dwellings, mostly one- or two-bedroom flats, with living-room, scullery, running water, and lavatory. Tenants were regularly inspected to ensure they were complying with basic hygiene regulations.

After the firm went public, Edward Cecil felt less inclined to give his time to business commitments and more disposed to pursuing his philanthropic dreams. But securing the succession was a problem. Rupert was only sixteen and still at Eton along with Ernest. Edward's two nephews, Benjamin Lee's sons, Algernon Lee and Kenelm Lee, were younger than his own.

Instinctively Edward felt his heir should be a member of his side of the family, a direct descendant of the first Arthur Guinness. Loyalty to the family was paramount, but he had no full cousins. All five sons of his father's only brother, the Reverend William Smythe Lee Grattan Guinness had died without issue. One, Frederick Darley Guinness, had taken "poison by accident" in 1869, making him the first member of the family to die in mysterious circumstances. Edward would have to look further afield.

The first Arthur's eldest son, Hosea the clergyman, had thirteen children, but only two of his sons produced any issue. The younger and more dynamic of the two, Francis Hart Vicesimus Guinness, went to India, then settled in New Zealand and started a branch of the family there. His eldest son, Sir Arthur Robert Guinness, KCB, had embarked on a brilliant political career and was about to become Speaker in the New Zealand parliament.

Of the first Arthur's other sons, both Edward and Benjamin conceived daughters only, and William Lunell's only son, William Newton, not only became a clergyman, but emigrated to Melbourne.

Edward was left with the line descended from Captain John—the Grattan Guinnesses—and Sir Edward had to admit that their teetotalism made them unlikely candidates for the Brewery Board. Although Henry Grattan was responsible for a large international company of his own, he had little practical business sense. Harry, who certainly had the qualities needed, appeared committed to a career in medicine. There was no doubt he and his brother and sisters had inherited the Guinness drive, but they had decided to use it for an altogether different purpose. They believed that all that was needed to change the world was not wealth, but one man or woman totally given into God's hands.

Edward Cecil had no choice but to turn to his wife's side of the family—the banking line. In 1881 he took on Claude, his wife's younger brother, with a view to grooming him to succeed John Tertius Purser as General Manager, installing him in Knockmaroon off Phoenix Park, a house which remains in the family to this day. Claude Guinness was intelligent and loyal, exceptionally astute in business matters, a man after Edward's own heart. When the role of Chairman became available, Edward had no qualms about turning to Claude's elder brother, Reginald. And so the descendants of Samuel Guinness, the goldbeater, found their way onto the Brewery Board.

The Grattan Guinnesses had had their chance, and made their choice. Their vision was made of a different kind of spirit.

CHAPTER TEN
1886-1890

1

The Grattans had their own problems of inheritance. The empire was increasing as Fanny's strength diminished, but her four children had their own lives to lead. Shortly before he left for home at the end of 1886, Harry received a letter from his mother that made his heart sink. She was "son-sick," she said. "How glad I shall be to have you to talk to. A man of action, of sociable disposition and popular sympathies." Marriage to a man who lived as much in heaven as he did on earth, rich as it was, could be a lonely business. But it was not simply companionship Fanny had in mind. "Darling Father, you inherit from him all your best gifts, but you also have a touch of your mother in you that will make you doubly useful, I hope." This was Fanny's way of suggesting her son might take over her work when he came home.

It was the last thing Harry wanted. Treves had predicted a brilliant medical career. Or perhaps, after his success in Australia, he should become an itinerant preacher. Marriage into the wealthy Reed family would release him from ever having to earn his living. But sitting at a desk piled high with paper played no part in his dreams. Then who else would carry on his mother's work? Henry needed her to help him with his writing. He struggled without her, unable to convey the great concepts in his head onto paper, in readable form.

Reluctantly, Harry conceded. His future was as carved in concrete as that of his brewing cousin, Rupert. It was the duty of the eldest son to take over the family business.

When he saw his mother again, so small, tired and shrunken, he knew he had made the right decision. Annie had already taken a great deal of practical responsibility for the daily running of the Institute onto her own capable shoulders. He would have the right woman at his side.

They were married on March 17th, 1887, at the East London Tabernacle, followed by a reception in Charrington's Great Assembly Hall, the only room in the East End large enough to accommodate all their friends and family. The guest list was the oddest mix of rich and poor. Wealthy Institute supporters, elegantly and tastefully dressed, rubbed shoulders with the night class students, a motley group of barrow boys, labourers and factory girls, all got up for the occasion in their gaudiest array.

The honeymoon was a trip to Egypt and the Holy Land. Annie's generous allowance was a novelty for Harry who couldn't resist buying his bride expensive gifts. But never did a woman appreciate them less. Annie Guinness began a practice she continued throughout their married life, of selling the jewellery and china he gave her and using the money for missionary work. Harry, blessed with little memory in these matters, was never any the wiser.

His impetuosity was a constant source of irritation to her. On the day after their wedding he left her in the Metropole Hotel and went off to conduct some "business," presumably fund-raising for the Institute, although he never offered any explanation. The following morning he disappeared again on yet another venture, and they only just managed to catch the Paris train. Life with Harry would test her patience, but it would never be dull.

Geraldine, meanwhile, was still struggling with acute back pain. Howard Taylor had watched her suffering from a distance for years. It grieved him he could do so little to help. Seeing his distress, his aunt, Mrs. Broomhall suggested Geraldine might be pining because he had not declared his love. Howard was unsure. She had given him no sign, and in her present state was hardly likely to receive a proposal with any degree of enthusiasm. Still, he knew little about the ways of women and bowed to his aunt's superior wisdom.

One beautiful June day when the sun was streaming through the windows of the dining-room at Harley House, Howard found Geraldine there alone. He told her quite simply that he loved her, that he had always loved her since he was a boy, and that there was no other woman with whom he would ever want to share his life.

Geraldine was appalled. She loved Howard as a brother, not in any romantic light... The pain in his eyes as she declined his offer distressed her unutterably. The last thing she wanted was to hurt this dear, gentle man who had always been such a loyal and faithful friend. She tried to soften the blow by saying she and Edith had decided not to marry. They were going to consecrate themselves to serving the poor. But that robbed him of any hope and distressed him all the more. Summoning every ounce of dignity he possessed, he apologised for having embarrassed her and let himself quietly out of the house.

When Geraldine told her mother she had refused Howard Taylor's proposal, on the grounds that she intended never to marry, Fanny decided her daughter was becoming too pious for her own good and packed her off to her Uncle Wyndham's in Rathdrum.

The tranquil atmosphere of Rathdrum Rectory was exactly what Geraldine needed. Daily rides on the long stretch of firm, white sand, the sea air filling her lungs and stinging her skin, made her feel more at one with herself than she had done for years. One morning she arose particularly early and went down to the beach to watch the sunrise. A strange orange glow gradually lit up the sky, melting the grey first light of early morning. Suddenly, she became aware of another parallel, light flooding her inner grey, and in a flash, knew with absolute certainty that she was called to go to China.

She wrote to tell her parents at once. Henry was deeply upset. Of all of his children, she was his soul-mate. He couldn't let her go without being absolutely sure she knew what she was doing. Since he had a preaching engagement in Ireland he went on to Courtdown Harbour to see her.

For two days they walked up and down the beach together, and finally, Henry was convinced. Writing poetry had become a regular outlet for his emotions, and that night, in deep anguish, he wrote a poem entitled, "I give thee up to God, my Geraldine."

Geraldine's farewell took place in a packed Exeter Hall on January 23rd, 1888. Every eye was fastened on the slim, pale, serious young woman in close-fitting black dress and black bonnet. Her long fair hair, parted in the middle and drawn neatly back from her forehead, hung loosely down her back. She looked much younger than her twenty five years. Dr. Barnado described how he had watched her grow from a babe in arms to a fine young woman. Then Henry Grattan rose to his feet and said that this was one of the gladdest yet saddest occasions he had ever attended. As he looked at her he said, "It is one thing to send out other people's children, but quite another to send out your own." Their was hardly a dry eye in the hall.

Outside, in the cold winter rain, the men and women of the night school were waiting to say goodbye. When Geraldine finally emerged from the hall, one old man, a tall, rough-looking pedlar, was too overcome to speak. He took her hands in his, work-toughened and calloused as they were, and with as much dignity as a prince, stooped and kissed them as tenderly as he knew how, sobbing all the while. It was only then that Geraldine let go of the control she had fought so hard to maintain and allowed the tears to come.

On her last morning the family gathered in the dining-room at Harley. Henry read Psalm 121 from his large, familiar, black Bible. "The Lord shall preserve thy going out and thy coming in from this day forth and for evermore." Lucy noticed the wintry sunshine playing on the coloured glass of the window, painting mysterious patches on the floor. "Details are noticed in the presence of a great, overwhelming pain," she wrote.

A huge crowd gathered at the docks to wave Geraldine off. She could still hear the sound of their singing floating after her on the wind as she sailed down the Thames.

The boat docked at Naples to give passengers the chance to visit the Pozzuoli Palace. As Geraldine bent to sign the visitors' book, she noticed, with a mixture of horror and amusement, the name of the last entry: F. Howard Taylor. Howard had been to Pozzuoli the previous summer. No one had signed the book again until she came. It was an extraordinary coincidence, but she made no mention of it in her letters home.

At Penang she made her first acquaintance with the people she felt called to serve, when a crowd of Chinese came aboard with boxes, bedding and household goods. She felt excited and nervous all at once. "Real Chinese they are, with shaven heads, long pigtails and yellow skins—so strange!"

The *HMS Deccan* sailed round the Malay Peninsula to the beautiful tropical island of Singapore where it made an unintentional, extended stay when it became stuck in the mud. Geraldine couldn't resist going ashore, and was enchanted by the silent, moonlit, tropical jungle. The vegetation was so luxurious. Singapore town was five miles away and the only means of transport a jinricksha, the human-pony drawn "hansom cab of China." Nothing would induce her at first to climb into this baby's perambulator or bathchair, but if she wanted to see the town, there was no alternative. A jinricksha came to a standstill beside her. The coolie invited her and her companion to climb in. They stepped gingerly inside, convinced they were going to be tipped out backwards the moment they sat down. To their amazement they stayed upright—until the coolie lifted the shafts and they landed on their backs with their legs in the air in a most indecorous manner. Helpless with laughter they clung to each other as the coolie tore off at a terrific pace through the banana forest. Many times in the future, crossing China in a wheelbarrow, Geraldine would long for the comfort of a jinricksha.

The orient released rather than inhibited Geraldine. Thousands of miles from home the reserve which hounded her melted away and she felt ready for any adventure. At the China Inland Mission home in Shanghai she put on Chinese dress for the first time. Some of the missionaries obviously found it amusing, but to Geraldine, unaware of how like a nun she sounded, it was "a sacred and serious exchange—a sacrament." She still refused to go out in her new clothes until it was dark.

On the steamer to the language school at Yang-chou, two days journey up the Yangtze River, she saw the effects of opium for the first time. Drowsy and apathetic, Chinese women lay out smoking in the hot sun all day. When she finally arrived at Yang-chou the school was so overcrowded there was no bed for her. She would have to make do with the table until one became available. It was a very short wait. That night she sat with a young missionary woman who had been in China five weeks and was dying of typhoid fever. Geraldine marvelled at her radiant acceptance of God's will and promised herself she would never give any room to self-pity again.

But then language study almost defeated her and she cried so much with sheer frustration that her eyes began to trouble her. Nor, as ever, could she cope with the misery around her.

One afternoon a loud hammering at the door announced yet another urgent demand for the missionaries to come and save an opium suicide. There were several every week, usually women seeking to escape their terrible lot. They belonged to whatever man had bought them and were utterly dependent on his whims and moods. When he died they were as much value as refuse.

On that particular day the missionaries experienced in overdoses had dealt with two cases already and were too exhausted to go out again. Geraldine would have to stand in for them, with Lottie MacFarlane as interpreter. A guide led them through a maze of streets to a respectable looking house in a quiet courtyard. The darkened living room was crammed with excited women, shouting at the tops of their voices. As she pushed her way into the room and her eyes became accustomed to the light, she saw to her horror, that the moaning she could hear was coming from a child of around fourteen who was struggling to free herself from those who held her down on the bed. Geraldine and Lottie tried to cam the crowds, and prepared a strong emetic which the girl refused to take, swearing she would throw herself down a well if the overdose didn't work. It was obvious they could do little for her while she was the centre of attention. Gently, Geraldine led her to a cubicle at the back of the room and managed to persuade her to take the medicine.

In between bouts of vomiting she told them she had been sold at six to a cruel family to be the wife of one of the sons. Her mother-in-law had beaten her regularly for eight years. The only reason she had sent for the missionaries was because she didn't want to have to buy another wife for her son.

Whenever a man's face appeared at the window or in the doorway the girl shrunk back in terror. Geraldine covered it with a makeshift paper curtain, but they tore it away and continued to leer at her and giggle. Eventually she lay quiet, her face a picture of utter despair. Lottie was in the living-room, trying to tell the women about the great God who loved the people he had made, but the man of the house appeared and sent the missionaries on their way.

Geraldine wondered exactly what they had achieved and was horrified back at the mission house to discover that the girl's story could be repeated thousands of times, throughout the entire empire. She ran up to her room, threw herself down on her bed and wept. "Oh, God—China! The whole vast empire, million-peopled—all its suffering, sinning, anguished hearts; its women, its little children! The long years of darkness, the few to bring them light!"

2.

The 1880s saw Henry Grattan Guinness established as one of the foremost authorities in the world on history, astronomy and biblical prophecy. His books, which sold in their thousands and had to reprinted almost at once, were devoured by a public hungry for a pre-planned purpose in the historical events of their time. In *Light for the Last Days*, published in 1887, and *The Divine Programme of the World's History* in 1888, Henry Grattan claimed for the first time that all the evidence pointed to 1917 as a key year for Jewish restoration to the Holy Land. His astronomical tables, the third of the three volumes which made up *Light For the Last Days*, became standard reference in observatories throughout the world, earning him a fellowship of the Royal Astronomical Society.

Inexplicably, the more successful his writing, the more his preaching appeared to suffer. For Henry preaching was an art, and like any artist he relied on the spark of inspiration to kindle the dry wood of discipline. But inspiration began to escape him with increasing, yet arbitrary, regularity. At some insignificant gathering he would enthral his audience with his message, but when a particularly memorable address was required, could be suddenly lost for words. Harry accompanied him one Sunday to a small church near Victoria Park where he preached a marvellous sermon to a sparse congregation. The same evening, in a packed East London Tabernacle, he stood in the pulpit stuttering and stammering, unable to marshal his thoughts. For months after, whenever he thought about it, Harry would feel the sweat pricking the back of his neck.

The doctor prescribed complete rest—preferably in a milder climate. For Henry this seemed the perfect opportunity for a prolonged trip to the USA. His books had been published there to great acclaim, earning him an honorary doctorate from Browns University which he wanted to receive in person. He also wanted to see his old friend, Moody, and, with his help, to share with the wider church the lessons they had learned at Harley College.

Many influential American ministers attributed their own conversion and calling to his preaching in the 1850s, among them A.B. Simpson, Pastor of the New York Tabernacle, and founder of the Christian Missionary Alliance. In 1882, Simpson had called for the establishing of an American Bible College, based on the principles of the East London Training Institute. There were established theological seminaries in the States, but a large number of potential missionary candidates were denied access to them because they came from a background which couldn't supply them with the necessary education or funding.

There were several attempts to form non-denominational colleges in the States in the 1870s, but Simpson's New York Missionary Training College was the first formal US Bible School, a pattern for many others throughout America and Canada, including the Prairie Bible Institute in Alberta. Even the later Pentecostal schools were based on Simpson's model, and Simpson was inspired by Harley College.[58]

But Simpson had some ideas which Grattan Guinness found rather worrying. In a rush of pietism, his first students had set off for Africa without adequate medical supplies in the naive expectation that God would protect them from harm. They died like flies. Guinness was appalled, and said so. Not only that, but in an attempt to reduce costs, the Americans were also committed to the idea of establishing "agricultural missions" in the Congo, small farms which would make their missionaries self-supporting as quickly as possible. The Guinnesses knew from experience that it was impracticable. African labourers had to be paid with goods, and that proved more, not less expensive.

By the time Henry Grattan Guinness arrived in the States in 1889 these problems were being resolved. At least Simpson had missionary candidates, unlike the American Baptist Missionary Society. Henry and Fanny were desperately disappointed with its inability to advance any further into Zaire. When he met the Director, Adoniram Judson Gordon, Henry suggested he train his own missionaries, and by the time he returned to England, Gordon had opened the Boston Missionary Training Institute.

In Minneapolis Henry encouraged Dr. Henry Mabie to start a similar college there. It only lasted a few years, but Lucy, who had accompanied her father, took on speaking engagements of her own at a number of women's colleges, and founded many new branches of the Student Volunteer Movement.

The new wave Bible Schools attracted a fair amount of criticism in the press. Surely they could only detract from the first rate theological education provided by the "higher schools." Gordon defended himself so well that he turned the attacks into free advertising, producing a fresh burst of applications.

The most influential Bible School in the history of faith missions was yet to be founded, and Henry had a hand in that too. In 1873, before he left for England, Moody had asked Emma Dryer to organise some follow-up to his missions. He forgot about the commission, but Emma Dryer did not. In 1886 she tried to persuade Moody to let her extend the two-month summer courses she had set up into a full-blown college. It was another three years before Moody decided to buy a plot of land for a residential college, with money given to him by CT Studd for missionary work in India. He left Emma Dryer to sort out the practical arrangements of setting up the "Bible Institute for Home and Foreign Missions of the Chicago Evangelisation Society." Emma had spent some time in England and seen the work of Harley College. Discovering Henry Grattan Guinness was in the USA she invited him to come and give her the benefit of his wisdom. The new college was called the Moody Bible Institute.

3

While Henry was away Fanny remained quietly at Cliff, but was far from inactive. Whitfield, who went up to Caius College, Cambridge, known affectionately as "stinks," to study medicine, wrote to Geraldine, "Mother is writing another missionary book about the Upper Congo. How she does work! As far back as I can remember, it is always Mother writing away late at night, by the light of a green-shaded candle lamp. Darling Mother, may God keep her strong and well."

Following a well-established pattern, Harry imposed his ever-expanding vision on Harley College, while Annie took care of the practical implications. She gave birth to their first child, Annie Geraldine, known as Gene, in 1888, then John Frith Grattan in 1889, while administering a business which was rapidly expanding to include a soup kitchen, medical mission and dispensary, midwifery school, maternity hospital and children's home. When she returned home from America Lucy joined them, taking over the running of the Berger Hall Night School, but more importantly, producing a monthly magazine to keep supporters informed about the ever-burgeoning industry.

Literature was the only real means of communication on a widespread scale, a resource the Guinnesses tapped from 1874, when Henry Grattan took over as editor of the *Illustrated Missionary News*, a religious, quasi-geographic, popular version of the glossy, fashionable *Illustrated London News*. Full of anecdotes, stories, biographies and correspondence, with graphic illustrations, it had developed an interested, committed readership in the eight years of its existence.

Every month Fanny wrote a special report from the East London Training Institute. The report grew to such an extent that by March 1877, the *Illustrated Missionary News* had become an insert. Even then space for Harley news was insufficient and in 1878 Fanny decided to begin her own magazine, *The Regions Beyond*, first as an "occasional paper," then as a quarterly journal, and finally as a monthly magazine. Lucy became its editor in 1888.

In her hands *The Regions Beyond* progressed rapidly from being a means to touch the readers' hearts and purses into one of the foremost, left wing, polemical journals of its day, with a circulation beyond her wildest dreams. Eugene Stock, editorial secretary of the Church Missionary Society claimed, "Lucy Guinness is the finest Christian editor by far in the British Isles. There is none like her."

No social injustice escaped comment, from the miners whose strike left thousands homeless "under pitiless wintry skies," the 50,000 unemployed in London, or the 150 who died of alcohol poisoning every day. It was a miracle, Lucy claimed, that the working classes did not rise up and shake off the shackles of oppression.

In pre-litigious, pre-libellous England, Lucy attacked whomsoever she chose—usually the "spin" of her Majesty's government, "full of loud futilities and arguments to prove the excellence of its system."

She was most outspoken in her campaign against the opium trade. The government enquiry was a farce, as Lord Brassey, KCB, Chairman of the Commission, was the director of a company making enormous profits from the drug. Its parliamentary representative, Mr. Robert Mowbray, MP, had voted in favour of the traffic. Its Indian representative, the Maharajah of Darbhanga, had a large poppy growing business. The Commission was doomed from the start, making Queen Victoria the greatest poison seller in the world. One day, she swore, Britain would pay the price for its indefensible treatment of China. But even she could not have guessed the implications for her own family.

Under Lucy's supervision the Berger Hall now provided daily meals. She never did get used to the daily rush when she opened the doors. A meat pudding could effect a radical change, "an altered look— a human look—comes over the men."

It was essential to provide health care and midwifery as well. A doctor's visit cost a shilling, the main part of a weekly wage. The London Hospital provided free medical help, but it was three miles away, too far for a mother with a sick child and no means of transport. At two thirty every Tuesday and Thursday afternoon people pushed and shoved their way up the stone stairs to get an early place in the queue.

It was an invaluable hands-on placement for Harley students. Under close supervision they ran a dispensary, handling vast quantities of strychnine, prussic acid, arsenic and opium. The experience was a little frightening at first, but they recognised that as future missionaries they would be handing out such substances with little further training.

One Harley student had to means test the patients. It was a thankless task.

"What's your father's occupation?" one of them asked a young girl.

"A bricklayer."

"Bricklayer or bricklayer's man?" asks the student.

"I couldn't say which, Sir. I never sees 'im lay the bricks!"

Known as "them 'eternity nurses," deaconesses took three months to complete their midwifery training. Such was the wealth of their experience in that short time that all students passed the London Obstetrical Society's examination with little difficulty. Harley opened a maternity ward in 1890, and converted the Bromley Mission Hall into a nursing home in 1894. Most maternity and post-natal care was provided in peoples' homes. Of all Harley's work it was the most heart-rending. Women lay in indescribably filthy conditions, on beds of dirty rags with no blankets to cover them, in damp, freezing houses with no money for food or coal. Many were so malnourished or consumptive they produced a still-born baby. Many more did not survive the birth themselves. The deaconesses could not bring themselves to take an orphaned baby to the workhouse, so Harley opened their first children's home in 1895, Annie's particular interest for many years.

The Harley Institute's commitment to London's poor was by no means unique. It was one of many Christian charitable organisations whose work was a striking feature of the East End in the 1880s and 1890s. Political socialists accused them of dealing with the symptoms rather than the disease itself, but they believed that changing the individual was the only way to change the system. There were times, however, when aggressive political action became the only resort—as Harry was about to discover.

4.

In China Geraldine's grasp of the language did not improve, and after only a few weeks at Yang-chou, her tutors decided the only way she would ever learn to communicate was by living with the Chinese people themselves. She set off with three other women missionaries in a river boat down the Grand Imperial Canal to a mission station at Tsingkiangpu, scribbling down her impressions on the way. She knew by now that Lucy was publishing her letters in the *Regions Beyond* magazine, but did not know that in pouring out her ever-increasing passion for China, she had embarked upon her life's work.

Raised with the concept of "regions beyond," of treading where no missionary had ever trod before, Geraldine was not satisfied with staying at Tsingkiangpu where there were Chinese Christians already. She set her sights on an isolated town called Antung, persuading a Chinese man to arrange accommodation on a farm for her and faithful Lottie with her fluent Chinese. "We're going to live in a real Chinese home," she wrote to Lucy with great excitement, "and in all ways possible to conform to Chinese customs and manners. We thought we had better begin at once by taking into use Chinese chopsticks and dining in Chinese fashion."

Reality soon dampened her enthusiasm. Antung was a mere twenty five miles from Tsingkiangpu, but took ten hours by wheelbarrow. A Chinese wheelbarrow consisted of a large single wheel traversed by a horizontal crossbar with a seat on either side. Passengers clung on to their belongings while a coolie pushed for all he was worth. After ten minutes, let alone ten hours, Geraldine felt as if she would never sit down again. They stopped frequently at villages along the way. Crowds came out to gape and chatter, and demand treatment from the magical medical case.

Late in the evening they arrived at the farmhouse. To Geraldine's dismay, it was the dreariest, dirtiest house she had ever seen. Two brothers, their wives and children, lived in one large room, their sleeping quarters one corner of the room, partitioned off with a rough blue curtain. Geraldine and Lottie were shown to their own corner, where there was little more than a double bed. It was so dark they could see very little at first, but their sense of smell was not impaired. As their eyes became accustomed to the moonlight struggling through a tiny, barred window, they became aware that a small floor area at the foot of their filthy bed was the lavatory for all the women in the house.

The family was very anxious to please, but unnerved by such unusual company. Adults and children watched the two missionaries in absolute silence. They ate their first meal together, rice and hard-boiled eggs, and Lottie made one or two valiant attempts at conversation but eventually gave up. Several pairs of wide, searching eyes followed their every movement, even as they got ready for bed. Eventually Geraldine begged them to blow their candle out.

Despite the nausea caused by the stench and the filthy bedclothes, Lottie fell asleep. Geraldine waited until she heard the women retire, then balancing a lamp on Lottie's lifeless form, wrote in her journal, "A painful misgiving for a moment crosses my mind as to the advisability of prolonged residence in such a place!" Her misgivings proved correct. The following day she couldn't stop scratching. But neither woman was prepared to give up.

Their determination paid off. Not only were they accepted in town, but were soon in demand for their medical help. Geraldine, whose medical knowledge was rudimentary, was forced to treat cases which would have tested the skills of a qualified physician. She learned Chinese quickly.

On May 26th, the anniversary of the sailing of the first missionaries to China, designated a special day of prayer by the China Inland Mission, Geraldine rose early and went to a barn where she could be alone. She rededicated her life to God, promising she would go anywhere, do anything he asked.

As she remained on her knees, in the all-enveloping silence she gradually became aware of an inner voice, speaking quietly, but clearly nonetheless. "Go anywhere, Geraldine? Do anything? Even marry Howard Taylor?" She was stunned. That was the last thing she wanted to hear. The very idea repelled her. But then, as she thought about it, she wondered whether in fact she wasn't in love with her own romantic notion of the self-sacrificial missionary life. Marriage wasn't such a dreadful proposition. She had said "anything" after all, and "anything" it would be. She shelved the notion for the time being. She could do little about it, and anyway, there were few men whose pride would allow them to propose to the same woman twice. But she told Lottie that if he did, she would not be able to refuse him.

Only a few months later, at Kiangsi, sitting on the shores of the lake, an announcement in *The Regions Beyond* caught her attention.

Dr. Howard Taylor, MB, FRCS, has been assisting his father, the Revd J Hudson Taylor, in his present lecturing tour in the United States and Canada. We heartily congratulate both father and son on the entrance of the latter on that co-operation in the China Inland Mission for which he has been so long and so thoroughly preparing, and to which he so unhesitatingly devotes the superior talents, high qualifications and bright young energies which could easily raise him to eminence and fortune at home.

So, he was coming. What would it mean? She couldn't bear to think about it.

As it happened, Howard's elder brother Herbert, his wife and two little boys were taking a few weeks leave at the lake too. They got on well with Geraldine and invited her to accompany them to the province of Honan, well-known as the "unreached" centre of the Chinese empire, where fifteen million people were without access to medical, social or spiritual help of any kind. It was the sort of challenge she loved.

The journey in January 1890 across Honan to She-ki-shen, their ultimate destination, was the worse she had ever known. Snow made the roads virtually impassable. A bitter wind howled across the exposed fields, making a trip in a sedan chair unutterably miserable, especially for Herbert's small children. No foreign woman had ever been to the region before, so whenever they stopped at an inn, Geraldine and Herbert's wife were besieged by crowds trying to catch a glimpse of their unbound feet. On one occasion the landlord begged them to leave, but not before scores of leering men had fingered them from top to toe to ensure they really were women and not men in disguise.

In She-ki-shen life was difficult. She was in constant demand. Mumps, measles and whooping cough often proved fatal. A crude, unskilled and painful version of acupuncture, which involved inserting a variety of long, red hot needles under the skin, was the most common treatment for any illness. Few babies survived the cure. Etiquette forbade women to leave the house at all. Geraldine was unable to visit the women in their homes. She felt she would go mad if she was locked up within four walls any longer and tried to venture out. But large crowds of men would gather around her, poking and prodding her, and jeering as she went. She resented having her liberty curtailed because she was a woman. But this was China, not Africa, not amenable to Western influence. She had no choice but to submit.

In those tense and difficult conditions an event occurred which would haunt her for the rest of her life. Herbert Taylor's wife had given birth to a baby girl. It was not easy in their cramped living conditions, but a nurse from another station had managed to get to them in time and the delivery had gone well. Although the baby was strong and healthy, it had taken the mother a while to recover and this put an added strain on Geraldine. She ran the house, cared for the Taylor children and responded to many callers for medical help. Her eyes, once again very infected, were causing her a great deal of distress. When the baby became ill with dysentery it was almost the final straw.

One night, at utter exhaustion point, Geraldine made a fatal mistake. She went to pour out a dose of medicine for the baby and in her haste, picked up the wrong bottle. The little one quickly lost consciousness and died.

It was the most appalling shock. A funeral was out of the question. Baby girls were of no value. Herbert Taylor carried his little daughter to a quiet spot in the Honan countryside and buried her there.

Geraldine was utterly devastated, all the more because Herbert and his wife refused to apportion any blame and bore her no ill will. She didn't know where to turn for consolation and wrote to Hudson Taylor, telling him the full story, asking him whether it might not just be possible that his granddaughter had actually died of dysentery. Not a medical man himself, Hudson passed the letter on to Howard and asked him to reply.

The correspondence established a new intimacy between the pair. Howard alone knew the guilty secret which blighted her every waking moment. He seemed to understand her despair. She had forgotten what a dear friend he had always been to her, how she had always relied on his brotherly comfort in the past.

Some months later, when she went to Shanghai for treatment for her eyes, Howard was standing on the shore of the river waiting to meet her off the boat. One look at his face told her that his feelings had not altered with the passage of time. His attentions embarrassed her, but as he took over her medical care in his usual dignified, unobtrusive way, she was in no mood to resist. She was tired of being independent and brave. Howard prescribed treatment for her eyes and to her relief, left almost at once for language school.

Meanwhile, without telling her sister, Lucy had illustrated and edited Geraldine's letters, publishing them in a book called, *In the Far East*. A first print run of 5,000 sold out in weeks. It was translated into French and Swedish and the publicity about the effects of opium seriously embarrassed the British Government.

Unwittingly, however, Geraldine's vivid descriptions of China had a contradictory effect, on the one hand to raise indignation as she intended to do, on the other, to caricature the Chinese as slanty-eyed, sly and untrustworthy, which she never intended to do. With the intention of repairing some of the damage, Hudson Taylor asked her to write a history of the Mission. She agreed, reluctantly. The idea of being stuck in Shanghai and the discipline of writing was irksome. Still, she could see the value of it.

In May 1890 Howard came to see her before setting off for Honan. Before he left he asked her again to be his wife. She had sensed from the moment he arrived in Shanghai that it was inevitable and had dreaded the moment, never guessing how numb she would actually feel. She had thought that as she accepted his proposal, some emotion, a flicker of romantic love, if not the fire of grand passion, would be sparked in her heart. But she felt nothing.

Howard only heard the word yes and was overjoyed. He cabled home at once and both sets of parents were delighted with the news. Everyone was thrilled—except her. She couldn't cope with any more congratulations and begged Howard to keep their engagement a secret. He was puzzled by her request but reluctantly agreed as he set off for Honan without her.

He had only just reached his destination when her a letter arrived begging him to release her. She loved him as a sister, not a wife. She needed time. Would he continue writing to her as he always had, as a friend, not a fiancee? Howard was more pained than he had been in his entire life but conceded. He loved her too much to force her into anything so obviously abhorrent.

Fortunately, he had no means of knowing how long that wait would be. In March 1892 a cable arrived in Shanghai urging Geraldine to return home to England at once. Fanny had suffered a stroke.

5

Throughout the 1890s, while the Grattan empire continued to expand in the East End, Edward Cecil Guinness, Baron Iveagh, was building his own. He felt the time had come to find himself an English country seat, suitable for the earldom on which he had his sights and accessible to the London set. When Elveden Hall in Suffolk came onto the market following the death of the Maharajah Duleep Singh, he recognised its potential and paid £159,000 for it at once.

The house was long past its glory, and far too small for his plans, but the estate was ideal. There was stiff competition for royal patronage, and the 17,000 acres of scrubland was renowned as being one of the best shoots in England.

With her usual flair, Dodo set to work on the house. Duleep Singh had tried to create an Indian Palace, but the result was an unfortunate mix of pillared portico Italian Renaissance on the outside, and quasi-Asian temple on the inside. The overall effect was of a high class brothel—not quite Dodo's style. The sensational, round, snow-white marble ballroom was however. An attempt to recreate the Taj Mahal in miniature, it was constructed between 1870 and 1874 by 150 workmen around twenty eight, intricately hand-carved pillars, supporting three levels of galleries, and crowned with a massive copper dome. Dodo ingeniously used the room as the focal point of her new, extended country residence, by building an exact replica of Duleep's mansion on its other side, so that it formed the link between the two, a dramatic "great assembly hall" with a massive real fire on either side.

The one hundred-room stately home with en suite guest facilities, marble baths and solid silver taps, was sumptuously furnished with exquisite tapestries, Chippendale mirrors, and oriental rugs. A brand new servants' wing accommodated 1000 servants. Seventy men were employed in the game department alone. A houseparty of thirty guests would require at least as many household servants, and accommodation for maids accompanying their mistresses.

It was not an easy life for domestic staff. They worked long hours, rising before dawn to clean out the grates and re-lay the coal in the huge renaissance-style fire-places dominating the state and drawing rooms. And it was little consolation that the fireplaces were for show, for the Guinnesses had installed central heating. At 8.30 in the morning every household member, staff and guest alike, was expected to assemble in the Cedar Room on the ground floor, where Edward Cecil conducted family prayers. They worked all day, and sometimes, during a shoot, it might be 11 pm before the maids finally fell into bed. Nonetheless, watching the guests in their finery, their jewels glittering in the firelight as they danced on the mirror-smooth sprung floor to the best orchestras of the day, seemed like the stuff of fairy story. Some couldn't help but peep through the balustrades of the upstairs galleries, though the penalty for being found out was instant dismissal.[59]

To be fair to the Edward Cecils, true to their class, they were largely unaware of life below stairs, and did their best to treat their staff courteously and with respect. Another of Edward Cecil's pithy little sayings was, "It costs nothing to be polite." It also cost him little to be generous. While he feathered his own extensive nest he didn't neglect theirs and rebuilt Elveden village.

The effort and energy invested in redesigning Elveden paid off, heralding a truly golden era. The Prince of Wales was a regular visitor even after he became Edward VII. So was his son, the Duke of York. The future George V appreciated the facilities more than his father. He at least was a genuine crack-shot, whereas his father didn't appear to take any interest in the proceedings until lunchtime and the appearance of the ladies.[60] "The royal suite at Elveden, decorated in coral and green, was the last word in luxury, surpassing any comparable accommodation in the other great mansions honoured by the British monarchs." [61] Half the peers of the realm were regular Elveden guests. So were the foremost politicians, including the future foreign secretary A.J. Balfour.

Throughout their lives the first Iveaghs remained a paradox. Everyone agreed that despite their public face, the couple were actually rather reserved. Dodo had a penny-pinching childhood, Edward's was evangelical. Their lifestyle, away from the social glare, was fairly simple. Edward Cecil enjoyed the company of Mr. Blundell, the Rector of Elveden, whose fiery sermons were known to reduce the congregation to tears. Inevitably, he had built the rectory, initially within Elveden grounds. But Blundell's predecessor had been caught snooping through the ground floor windows of the Hall. Sir Edward couldn't tolerate any invasion of his privacy, and built a new one just outside the gates.

His sudden incursion into the art market between the years of 1887 and 1891 was typically anonymous. But two hundred choice paintings by artists such as Rembrandt, Millais, Vermeer, Gainsborough, Turner, Watteau, Van Dyke and Canaletto couldn't disappear for long without someone discovering their destination. One or two claimed it was undertaken for financial rather than aesthetic purposes, but younger family members remembered the quiet, obvious pleasure in Edward Cecil's face, as he took them to see his treasures. Later, the paintings were housed at Kenwood and bequeathed to the nation, so that the public could share in his enjoyment. In fact, Sir Edward Cecil had the perspicacity to see, that in warding off millionaire American competition, he would effectively preserve a collection of priceless art for the British nation.

CHAPTER ELEVEN
1890-1900

1

In 1891, when Annie was pregnant with their third child, Harry sailed for the Congo. Since the idea was planted by ex-Harley student, John McKittrick three years earlier, he had been determined to go, and no danger was going to dissuade him.

McKittrick was a genial, enthusiastic Irishman who had spent four frustrating years with the Livingstone Inland Mission in the lower cataract region, its furthest outpost on the Equator. Its parent organisation, the American Baptist Missionary Union, still had no intention of forging forwards into the unexplored upper Congo. Shortly before his leave, McKittrick asked if he could go on an exploratory journey up river by canoe to the vast horseshoe bend between Equatorville and the Stanley Falls to the Lulonga region. This was home of the Balolo, one of the most savage, blood-thirsty peoples in Africa. What McKittrick saw there made the hairs on the back of his neck stand on end.

He knew no one would believe the tales he told, so brought a native boy called Bompole back to Britain to verify his account. Bompole's plea for the white man to come and help his people touched Harry deeply, and he decided to support McKittrick's new venture, setting up the Congo and Balolo Mission—later known as the Regions Beyond Missionary Union—in 1889. Harley College was once again a base for pioneering missionary work.

McKittrick married Dora Fookes, Harry's cousin and they left for the Congo in February with a team of six other Harley students. Dora sent

Harry a detailed account of their arduous journey, made for the most part on foot. Sudden violent storms turned gentle tributary rivers into virtually impassable torrents, impeding the progress of the ladies whose respectable Victorian skirts clung limply around those potentially provocative ankles. The heat was unbearable, especially in a long-sleeved blouse, buttoned to the neck. Yet despite the discomfort, Dora was dazzled. Africa was more beautiful than she could have ever imagined. Immense flowering shrubs, a riot of colour, wafted their incredible perfume down-river on the breeze, long before the sight of them took her breath away.

Once on board the *Henry Reed*, steaming from Stanley Pool into Lulonga territory, Dora's letters expressed horror at what she saw. A naked corpse floated past them down-river, its hands and feet bound to a stake—the work of the slavers. Hours later she saw them in broad daylight, their canoes laden with their terrible human booty.

The party couldn't land at Lulonga as the river bank was lined with hostile natives, armed with knives and spears, in preparation for the next invasion of slave traders. McKittrick anchored mid-stream and made friendly overtures from a safe distance. Eventually, the jungle drums telegraphed a message of peace, and they knew they had been given permission go ashore.

The missionaries quickly earned a reputation for peace and fair-play, and in three years, established four stations at Boginda, Ikau, Lulonga, and Bogandanga—an impressive record which masked the toll on their emotional health. Dora McKittrick soon discovered that Bompole's account of the cruelty of his people had been a pale reflection of the gruesome truth. Victims of tribal warfare, or simply tribal customs, would be strung up, their arms and legs broken, and left to die. Knife throwing at a human target, throat slitting, and feeding each other to the crocodiles were commonplace. Legs, arms, and hands, boiling in a pot or dry roasted were great delicacies. The macabre reality of life in Lulongaland tore Dora's nerves to shreds. Reading between the lines of her letters, Harry knew it, and decided to see for himself. How could the secretary of the Congo Mission represent or support missionaries adequately from the safety of his own home?

There was another justification for the trip. In 1890 a young Congo Christian by the name of Mandombi arrived at Harley College suffering from sleeping sickness. He had made the long journey at his own expense in the hope that English doctors might find a cure for a condition that was destroying the life of his people. Having recently completed his MD in tropical medicine, Harry decided to conduct his own research into the disease.

Annie accompanied him part of the way, then took their children to Tasmania to visit her mother, while Harry went on to Boginda to meet up with the McKittricks. He and John began to prepare their feasibility study into setting up new mission stations almost at once, planning two exploratory journeys, one north and one south. The north was inhabited by the fierce N'gombe tribe, given to a particularly nasty form of cannibalism. They would go there first, double back, pick up Dora and continue south. But nothing turned out as planned.

The two men set off by boat in good heart, Harry with his treasured tripod and large box camera with heavy metal plates. Photography was still in its infancy, and photos were an invaluable means of arousing interest in the audiences at home. They carried guns as a protection against wild animals, never to be used on human beings—not even in self-defence.

Initially, the beauty and tranquillity of his surroundings lulled Harry into a false sense of security. He began to wonder whether some of the tales he had heard were not a little exaggerated. One evening however, taking shelter in a wood, they came upon the burnt-out ruins of a village recently raided by the N'gombe. Harry was confronted with the sight of the decapitated, frightfully mutilated corpse of a young boy. He managed to overcome his nausea enough to take a few photographs. Anyone at home who doubted his account would be forced to see what he had seen.

On August 22nd, 1891, they arrived at a village called Bosi Dikolo. The natives were extremely friendly and appeared to like very close contact. They ushered the white men into their meeting place, a low-roofed contraption on posts, and kept pressing in on them until the perspiration poured down Harry's face. A "palaver" was arranged for the following morning.

It began with the presentation of the ritual goodwill offering—plantains, fowls and a goat. The chief's first minister than expressed the hope that the white men would act as arbitrators in their dispute with a neighbouring N'gombe village, Bongwonga. Bateko, Harry's interpreter, said they would be delighted to try and re-establish peace between the two villages but would not accept the goat until they had succeeded. He then offered their "dash" to the chief—two tin plates, two tin spoons, some blue beads, cowrie shells and two pieces of cloth.

Harry, naively, expected a similar warm welcome in Bongwonga, but the natives, warned by a scout that they were coming, thought they were representatives of the Belgian State authorities and were ready to defend themselves. A flesh-creeping silence greeted their arrival. What happened next would haunt Harry for years to come. Suddenly, they were surrounded by an entire tribe of men in full war paint, armed with spears and shields, chanting a blood-curdling war cry.

Leaving the rest of their party well behind, Harry and McKittrick walked slowly towards them, unarmed, sat down on the ground and waited. The natives, disarmed by their behaviour, gradually stopped their noise, and went to inspect them, waving their spears within a centimetre of Harry's nose.

Bateko shouted, "See, we am unarmed, we come for peace, not war," whilst an old N'Gombe man they had brought with them repeatedly jumped backwards and forwards over his spear as a sign of friendship. A bright execution knife made an arc in the sun right next to the old man's head, and Harry was convinced he'd been decapitated, but didn't dare move. In fact, the old man was unharmed, but another tense half hour passed before some of the warriors were prepared to shake hands.

We established ourselves in a little house and lunched as well as might be expected under the circumstances. Towards the close of the meal one of their most prominent men, a powerfully built fellow, with cicatrices the size of a calabar-bean in front of and below each ear, yelled out at the top of his voice, "They love me! Come here. Come here," and by degrees a good many gathered round us and we did a pretty brisk trade in purchasing fowl and eggs.

The old N'gombe man finally convinced the natives they meant no harm, and a big palaver to discuss peace proposals was promised for the following day. The old man would sleep in the chief's tent that night as a sign of goodwill.

As darkness fell Harry began to shiver. He had developed a fever and couldn't stay awake. McKittrick, sensing all was not well, spent a tense night beside the camp fire, jumping at the slightest sound. Suddenly, at five in the morning the old N'gombe man ran towards him waving his arms frantically. The natives were coming to kill them all. They must flee.

They escaped into the forest, the enemy in hot pursuit. McKittrick fired into the air to frighten them, but Harry was so weak he could hardly hold his rifle. On and on they ran, McKittrick dragging Harry, until Bosi Dikolo came into sight at last and they knew they were safe.

Their ordeal might have been over, but for the two villages, it had barely begun. The disastrous expedition heralded a fresh outbreak of violence between the tribes that was finally terminated by the intervention of the state authorities. Officer Peters took a party of his men to Bongwonga and thirty four N'gombe died at the muzzle of a gun.

Harry was too incapacitated by recurrent bouts of fever, too demoralised by the failure of his shambolic attempt at diplomacy, to attempt a second journey. In January 1892 he arrived home, sick and sad, with Dora. Shortly before they left the Congo, his beloved McKittrick had died very suddenly of Blackwater Fever.

He was greeted with the news that his mother had just had a stroke. The rest of the family had rushed to her side, Geraldine from China, Annie from Tasmania, and Lucy from the United States. Harry was too ill to be much help, or to enjoy his new son, Henry Reed Guinness, whom he saw for the first time. But he did send off a detailed report on sleeping sickness to Dr. Patrick Manson.

Manson wrote to Fanny to say her son's research was invaluable, and would almost certainly lead to a breakthrough in treatment. She recovered enough to understand, though whether that was a blessing no one was sure. Despite regaining some of her speech, half of her body was paralysed and useless.

2.

The girls at the night classes bombarded Geraldine with questions. Was Mr. Taylor handsome? Was he kind?

All they could get out of her was, "You would love him."

"You'd be jealous if we did, Miss," Mathilda replied, and the girls shrieked with laughter.

Not a flicker of a smile crossed Geraldine's face. Her relationship with Howard was far too serious a matter.

She spent her two years at home travelling extensively, researching her history of the China Inland Mission, staying long enough to witness the book's immense success. Full of sentimental death-bed scenes, it cloys by contemporary standards, but the Victorians loved it. And the self-sacrifice of the early missionaries was undeniable.

Geraldine was never entirely sure at what precise moment, during their long separation, she knew she had fallen in love with Howard Taylor. She only knew she wanted to marry him the moment she arrived back in China. Leaving Fanny at Cliff in the capable hands of adopted daughter, Leila Dennison, was a terrible wrench, but her staying would have upset her mother even more. At least Fanny had the satisfaction of seeing her children live out her dreams. Harry was fit again, his family continued to expand, as did the work of the Congo and Balolo Mission. Lucy was in demand as a speaker, particularly at the large holiness conventions in Keswick. Whitfield was a doctor at the London Hospital, gaining practical experience before he too left for China.

In April 1894 Geraldine docked at Shanghai. Howard was waiting for her on the quay, as he had waited for her so many times before. But this time, as she walked off the boat towards him, she allowed their eyes to meet. He ached to touch her hand, to take her in his arms, but Chinese custom did not permit improprieties of that kind. He had loved her since she had opened the door to him nearly twenty years earlier, a gawky twelve-year old in pinafore and pigtails. It was seven years since he had first proposed. He had waited almost all his life for this moment, and all he could do was stand and look at her.

They were married in traditional Chinese costume on April 24th by Bishop Cassels in a crowded, flower-filled Shanghai Cathedral. Geraldine wore pale grey, as white was a sign of mourning. Her two bridesmaids were in mauve silk and had real flowers in their hair. As she walked down the red-carpeted aisle the organ played Mendelssohn's glorious setting of "Oh, rest in the Lord, wait patiently for him, and he shall give thee thy heart's desires." Howard had chosen the words from Psalm 37, for they had sustained him on the days he had despaired that this moment would ever come.

The honeymoon was a three-week trip by houseboat up the Imperial Grand Canal. Friends had had the forethought to convert the cabin of a fairly basic junk into an attractive, cosy little nest, draped in red cloth. When they pulled the cloth back they discovered huge cracks in the woodwork separating them from the boatmen's living quarters, large enough for several pairs of prying eyes. But the curtain did provide a certain amount of seclusion, and other wedding presents, a lamp and a miniature tea-set laid out on the table, made Geraldine feel as if she were playing at married life.

The idyll was over all too soon. Back in Shanghai they were catapulted into a major crisis. Fifty Scandinavian missionaries were threatening to resign over Chinese allegations of improper behaviour and Hudson Taylor had set off on a long cross-country journey to try and help them understand the culture. Howard and Geraldine chased after him. He was too old for such a punitive expedition, but when they finally caught up, he refused to change his mind. There was no alternative but to join him.

In eleven days they travelled over 1280 miles, mainly by wheelbarrow. On the twelfth day they arrived at such a steep hill that Geraldine was determined the coolies would not push her. To their utter astonishment she and Howard leapt out of the wheelbarrow and chased each other to the top of the hill, where for a few glorious moments, they threw off the shackles of the culture, and ran around laughing together, revelling in the view and the sweet scent of the wild flowers. The moment of abandon suddenly came to an abrupt end. They rearranged their clothing, patted their hair into place, and with great dignity, walked, a proper distance apart, back to the wheelbarrow. "Oh, China, China," Geraldine lamented later, "We could not stand near together, or sit down side by side to enjoy the beauty and the stillness... Was there ever such a country for a wedding tour?"

The overnight accommodation did not quite meet Geraldine's standards of hygiene, but she thought she was coping pretty well, until one landlord sprinkled sugar all over her rice balls with a pair of the filthiest fingers she had ever seen.

"Oh Howard," she whispered, "I can't eat it now."

"Don't tell him they're dirty," Howard whispered back cheerfully, "No doubt he thinks they're much cleaner than most and quite fit for use as sugar tongs."

Geraldine studied her landlord doubtfully and then caught him licking his fingers with relish. The look on her face reduced Howard to a paroxysm of laughter. No wonder Hudson Taylor had nick-named his son, "The Lifeboat." Howard was unsinkable.

Howard's indomitable spirit kept them going through the weeks of torrential rain, continual drenchings, and impassable flooding. Howard was her inner strength through the bitter disappointment of her first miscarriage. Geraldine would only have one more chance of motherhood, and again, the bumpy roads, continual joltings and miserable conditions of barrow travel brought about the sudden, heart-breaking termination of her pregnancy. For the remainder of her child-bearing years she would have bouts of longing for the two children she never bore.

By the summer, Hudson Taylor had successfully completed his mission and was ready to return home. Howard was anxious to go back to Honan where he was the only doctor in a province the size of England and Wales combined, with a population of thirty five million people. He had decided they would settle in the ancient prefectural town of Cheng-chou, where the local people were so set in their ways that the philosopher Confucius had found them impossible. No missionaries had ever lived there before.

Howard went on ahead and found them "the perfect home," the walls freshly covered in mud, the windows newly papered. Geraldine was in her element—until she saw the dirty little four-roomed shed, with a dilapidated roof that leaked and a dark, prison-like courtyard enclosed on all sides by high walls. Still, she had to agree with the irrepressible Howard that after their recent travels, this was luxury.

She worked hard to make it home and it soon became a refuge for the masses who flocked to Howard day and night for treatment, and for a motley assortment of stray animals. One day a little dog slunk into the courtyard, curled up in a sunny corner and went to sleep. When he saw he was welcome, he came every day, nervous and cowering at first, but gradually his tail came out from between his legs and curled right over his back. She rejoiced in his new confidence, as it symbolised for her the freedoms she wanted for Chinese women, subjugated by the expectations of their culture.

One day, however, he arrived home in a dreadful state, shivering and moaning. Local boys had doused him in scalding water, and he dragged himself to his own sunny corner and died. Geraldine wept bitterly for him.

Though he was a warm, open man, Howard was often puzzled by his wife's emotionalism. Their relationship was never straightforward. They were very different, and in Cheng-chou, where they were thrown on each other for intellectual, emotional and spiritual support, never was that more starkly obvious. Geraldine was excitable and impulsive, Howard more rational and sensible. She was given to great swings of mood. He was steady and even. If her impetuosity bewildered him, his slow methodical reasoning grated on her.

Geraldine had always had her doubts about the advantages of marriage for a woman. Now, she found Howard's concern stifling, and she couldn't escape it- not for a moment. Gradually it dawned on her that she wasn't simply a victim of her destiny. She could chose to struggle against Howard's temperament, or submit positively to the discipline of sharing her life with another. She would never change him, and, after all, would she want to, when he had by far the nicer temperament? So she forced herself, through gritted teeth at first, to harness her wilfulness and give way as generously as she knew how. In time, over many years, she and Howard learned to complement each other, but Geraldine never found it easy.

Though their main base was at Cheng-chou, they also hired rooms at Kai-feng, gravitating between the two, and leaving the smaller station in the hands of two missionary women when they were away. It was at Kai-feng they had their first taste of the horrors to come to that turbulent empire.

There had been a terrible drought. Poverty and destitution were driving the people to despair. Jealous of the missionaries' popularity, a Buddhist nun spread the rumour that they had large sums of relief money to give away. Barrows, carts, and crowds arrived from every part of the district, and the people demanded the money they thought was theirs by right. Howard and Geraldine spent the day explaining the mistake. The disappointed crowds dispersed, but their disgruntlement festered and spread.

One day, while Howard was in the courtyard treating patients, a large mob arrived, howling for revenge. They marched into the house, and began to loot and smash belongings. One of the missionary women managed to slip into a neighbour's property, the other was beaten and her clothes ripped off her back. Geraldine ran to her help, but a woman hacked at her with a hoe and split her head open. As the blood poured down her face and neck, she stood, waiting for the next blow, marvelling at her own sense of calm, when her attackers suddenly froze. An impressive Chinese gentleman Geraldine had never seen before had taken command of the situation.

"My name is Wang," he said to her, as he pushed his way to the front.

Geraldine managed a quick look at her deliverer, which was improper conduct for a woman. But with her clothes hanging off her back, her hair trailing over her shoulders and blood smeared on her face, she was hardly in any position to worry about propriety. She asked him to stay until help came, willing herself not to worry about what had happened to Howard.

Mr. Wang waited until the Mandarin arrived with his men, and most of the mob had fled. Geraldine ran into the courtyard , where she found Howard tied to a post, within seconds of being stoned to death. The Mandarin, a young Manchu and zealous about enforcing law and order, grabbed two of the perpetrators in each hand, shaking them until their teeth rattled. Twenty four were placed under arrest. He was very apologetic about their ordeal.

A month later they were received back in Kai-feng with full civic honours and a triumphal procession worthy of royalty, while the twenty four prisoners knelt in chains by the roadside, awaiting their sentence. Howard begged for their release. The young Mandarin was immensely disappointed. He intended making an example of the culprits and told Howard he would grant him any other request he pleased. Howard insisted he had no other request and finally, the twenty four men were led under armed escort to the mission courtyard and made to kneel in a row. For one awful moment Howard thought they were to be beheaded before his very eyes, but the Mandarin turned to Howard and held out the key to their padlocks. As they cowered in front of him, he walked slowly over, unfastened their chains and to their obvious relief and joy, lifted them to their feet one by one.

Watching carefully was Mr. Wang, Geraldine's mysterious protector. He approached Howard, bowed and told him that if this was Christianity, this dignified behaviour he had witnessed so closely, then it was a noble and worthy calling, one to which he was willing to dedicate his own life.

One Sunday morning, exactly a year later, while Howard was lying ill with a fever, Geraldine went out onto the verandah to watch nineteen men being baptised in the courtyard below, on the very spot where her husband was almost beaten to death. "I returned to my husband's bedside and knelt in silence. As we listened to those songs of praise, I think we scarcely knew whether we were on earth or in heaven."[62]

3.

Harry's photographs of the Congo aroused considerable public interest. No one had seen such strange-looking people before. The camera was more effective than Stanley, vivid as his descriptions were, at shrinking the boundaries of the world. The Grattan Guinnesses turned fairy-tale into reality with their illustrated missionary magazines.

Some, largely within the major denominations, resented their appropriation of the market and accused them of individualism, of setting up their own societies because they were unable to work with anyone else. They, in fact, disliked the imperialistic tendencies of some denominational missionary work. How to deliver the opium eater from his deadly habit without making him a European, how to save the African from the slavers and the worst excesses of tribalism without destroying his identity, the balance between preaching Christianity and respecting other traditions was a fine art. The Guinnesses may not have always got it right, but they made a conscious effort not to import English-style religion or English-style churches.

Harley missionaries were taught to live as simply as possible, identifying with the local people, laying down their lives when the cause required it. They were the "guerilla" priests of their day, defending the indigenous population against imperialist aggression, and never more so than in Harry's fight to free the Congo from Western oppression.

The Congo had been annexed as a Belgian colony in 1884 by King Leopold. Rumour of government atrocities against the local people began to filter back to Harley, but the King's performance as a defender of civil rights was so convincing that Fanny begged Harry to keep an open mind. She told him that the abuses he had seen were probably perpetrated by dissolute local officials and not the direct responsibility of the King.

Harry was convinced the authorities were establishing law and order with far too heavy a hand, but in 1885, however, when sovereignty of the Congo was granted to Belgium, the General Act of Berlin, signed by the world super-powers had guaranteed the natives freedom from slavery.

The discovery of enormous quantities of rubber overturned international rhetoric overnight. Thousands of natives were driven off their land to provide rubber plantations for the agents of the King. The new Belgian plantation owners knew no white man would ever consent to collecting the precious sticky substance in such hot, humid conditions, but soon persuaded the native to give his labour free of charge—down the barrel of a gun.

The first stories of the outrage perpetrated on the African people reached Harry and Lucy at Harley House in 1895, and were confirmed the following year by Mr. Sjoblom, a Swedish missionary and former student. In his written report he said:

> On December 14th, 1895, my friend Mrs. Banks had been crossing the Station Compound at Bolengi when she saw a woman being beaten by a native sentry, and on her enquiring what was the matter, the sentry replied, "She has lost one."
>
> "One what?" enquired Mrs. Banks.
>
> "One of the hands," said the sentry.
>
> And then Mrs. Banks noticed that *the basket on the back of the woman was filled with human hands.*
>
> She immediately called her husband and Mr. Sjoblom, and the hands were counted in their presence. There were eighteen in all, and the angry sentry still asserted that there ought to have been nineteen. Some of these smoked hands were those of children, some of women, and some of men.
>
> "Where are you taking these?" asked one of the missionaries.
>
> "To the white man, the State man, to whom I have to prove that I have been diligent in pushing the rubber business, and who would punish me if I did not compel the people to bring in sufficient quantity."

Harry was so incensed that he set off for Belgium immediately, determined to speak to none other than the King himself.

He was received by King Leopold's private secretary, sent to vet a possible extremist, but he couldn't countermand what appeared to be indisputable evidence of cruelty on the part of the Congo administration, and arranged an audience for the following day.

The King was genial, gracious, patronising.

"You are an excellent young man," he said, patting Harry on the shoulder, "but you mustn't believe all the natives tell you."

Harry found it hard to control his anger.

"It is not a native report, your Majesty," he insisted.

It occurred him that a direct appeal to self-interest might be the only effective way to win his case. He suggested that this kind of behaviour was bound to be counter-productive in the end, if it earned the King international disfavour. And, since the native was the only means available of collecting the rubber, gunning him down or cutting off his hand was actually slaying the goose that was laying Belgium's golden egg.

At last the King began to listen. He was asked what reforms Harry had in mind. Harry had five suggestions to make: an immediate independent enquiry, fair pay for the natives, the removal of the police authorities, a total ban on guns, and an end to murders and amputations.

To his relief, the King conceded. He promised an immediate enquiry and asked for the names of any officials the missionaries thought should be removed. Looking back, Harry realised that gaining concessions that easily should have made him a little more circumspect. But scepticism was not in his nature and he went home well satisfied.

Meanwhile the new Congo and Balolo Mission began to have a more positive impact on the lives of the natives, though the cost was immense. Of the 35 who followed McKittrick out to the Congo, most Harley students and Harry's personal friends, only six survived to see the new century. Their achievement was recorded for posterity by an unexpected admirer, the writer and journalist, Edgar Wallace. Wallace was not a religious man and had little sympathy for the missionary cause until he saw Harry's Congo Mission for himself.

> For me, Bongandanga represents the end of a long and trying journey, a journey that has left me heartsick and bewildered...What the State has done for the Congo and its people, posterity shall judge. What missionaries have done, I am seeing with my own eyes, and seeing, I am prouder of my fellow countrymen and women than I have ever been before.

> Already, the Congo is to me a dreadful nightmare, a bad dream of death and suffering...when every law of man and nature is revolted and the very laws of life are outraged. A bad dream, save only this, that mingled with the bad delirium of lawlessness comes a brighter theme. It is of men and women living their lives and dying their deaths at humanity's need; who are creating a manhood from a degraded race. Hard, bitterly hard is the work... Somebody down river told me it was difficult to get men and women for missionary work in the Congo. I wouldn't be a missionary in the Congo for £5,000 a year. I am grateful to the missionaries for this, that they have made me ashamed of my futile life.

4.

By the end of the nineteenth century Guinness was beginning to encompass the globe—in every sense. The brewing Guinnesses began to expand their enterprise to the West Indies, the banking Guinnesses began to invest overseas, but for breadth of scope, spirit of adventure and sheer audacity, neither branch could match their Grattan cousins.

For a while Lucy had become fascinated by South America and what she saw as a basic denial of human rights there, a theme she explored in her book, *South America, the Neglected Continent*, published in 1894. The country was closed to any religious expression other than Roman Catholicism. A few Harley students had settled in Lima and Cuzco in the only capacity they could, as shopkeepers, but local priests informed the authorities and they were closed down.

With Lucy's encouragement, Harry began to consider expanding his Regions Beyond Mission there, to provide financial backing for those who felt a call to go. He set off for Peru in July 1897, at his own expense as ever, stopping off in the United States, to enlist the support of some of the "giants" there—the famous preacher Campbell Morgan, and Dr. A.B. Simpson, founder of the Christian and Missionary Alliance. His aim was to resettle the missionaries into their same old shop at Cuzco, then link them up with other, independent Harley men working in Brazil and Argentina so that they could support one another. It took all the skills in diplomacy he possessed, but he succeeded, and it turned out to be a first, crucial step towards the passing of a bill which would give Peru its religious freedom in the new century.

Lucy meanwhile sailed with her father for India, yet another of her "neglected" continents, and the land of Kipling. In *Across India At the Dawn of the 20th Century*, published in 1898, she recaptured the towering heights of the Himalayas, the sweltering plains of Madras, the mighty flood of the Ganges, the crowded, dusty streets of Poona, the dark-skinned, turbaned natives thronging the busy bazaars, the overcrowded trains, colourful Hindu Temples, and wretched, heart-rending poverty of the people. One newspaper review referred to her book as, "A most useful and instructive volume, beautifully illustrated...one of the best Christmas gift-books we have ever seen." It ended with its usual challenge—to volunteer for the new Bihar and Orissa Mission, another Harley enterprise founded in 1899.

Fanny followed these comings and goings from her armchair by the fireside at Cliff, looking out on her beloved Derbyshire hills. She could do little for herself, but still insisted on being kept up to date with every new development of the work at Harley, dictating long, loving letters to her children wherever on the globe they happened to be.

In thirty years she had watched the vision that had taken them to Stepney Green grow into an enterprise beyond her wildest dreams. From the very first that vision had cost her all she had, from her two precious little girls buried in the East End, to each of her living children in turn, as they left her to serve God overseas. When Whitfield, her baby, came to say goodbye before leaving for China in 1897, it was the hardest parting of all. She wept uncontrollably as he closed the door behind him, knowing instinctively she would never see any of her children on this earth again. She died on November 3rd, 1898 and was buried in a quiet corner of the churchyard in Baslow.

Only two of her children were present at her funeral, Harry and Lucy. It took months for news to travel across China.

Henry was bereft. In the past six years he had travelled extensively, possibly as an escape from seeing what Fanny had become. But though she had not been a real wife in the fullest sense of the word for some time, she was still his soul-mate, always there to comfort and support him. "As a wife she was exceedingly companionable," he wrote. "Her mind was clear-sighted and capacious, her power of expressing her thoughts unusually great. Her words were always full of good sense and right feeling. Free from exaggeration, from petty selfishness and vulgar egotism, her thoughts and emotions seemed naturally to work on a broad and noble plain. As the months and the years went by, her intellect grew in capacity, and became more and more richly furnished, while her piety took a deeper tone."[63]

Henry had always found travel a diversion and now accepted an invitation to speak at the International Zionist Conference in Jerusalem. Lucy, who had just called off an unfortunate engagement to a much younger man, decided to accompany her father. There had been several proposals over the years, usually from Harley students, too young and immature to be suitable. Lucy was completely unaware of her attractions for the opposite sex. Eugene Stock, Director of the Church Missionary Society later recalled an enchanting young woman who, when she spoke, turned a deadly dull meeting of the Leicester YMCA into a major event. When she played the piano she was captivating. Her very heart and soul seemed to pour out through her fingers. It was small wonder so many men became infatuated with her.

En route to the Middle East she and her father stopped off in Stockholm in response to an invitation from Prince Bernadotte of Sweden. As he showed them around his palace, a large portrait of a lovely young woman caught Henry's eye. The Prince told him she was the daughter of distant relations, but he thought of her as a niece. Her name was Jane af Sandeburg and despite having Stockholm's finest and richest young men at her feet, she had decided to become a missionary in China. Henry made a mental note to write to Whitfield to ask whether he had come across the lady in question.

They stayed in Palestine three months. Lucy rode across the desert and explored, while Henry Grattan spoke at countless meetings. According to Harley student David Baron, the impact of his talk to the Zionist Congress could still be felt in Jerusalem ten years later.

Then they travelled on south through Egypt. Henry had been concerned for some time about the vast unreached areas of the Sudan and wanted to see whether access to this immense, largely unknown territory was possible from North Africa. One evening in May they left Alexandria for an oasis called Fayoom, the "Garden of Egypt" on the edge of the Sahara. According to a letter from Lucy to Geraldine, they had been joined by a "guide, interpreter and general protector," a German by the name of Kumm, who worked with the North Africa Mission. "We are flying down the Delta in a quiet, dreamy light, half grey, half green, half misty blue." Geraldine, who knew her sister's usual meticulous attention to detail, was bemused by the reference to three halves. Did she suspect that they and the "dreamy light" might have something to do with the mysterious new protector?

As they travelled slowly across the desert by camel, exploring the mysteries of the Pyramids together, Lucy had plenty of time to study their guide from behind the heavy veils that hung from her wide brimmed hat. The petite, dark-haired Englishwoman had fallen under the spell of the gentle giant from the Harz mountains.

Born into a Lutheran family in 1874, and nine years younger than Lucy, Hermann Karl Wilhelm Kumm had shown an unusual flair for languages from an early age—a gift which would stand him in good stead when he became an international figure, speaking English, French, Egyptian and African dialects with equal ease. As a post-graduate, he visited England, where he was taken to hear John Glenny, Superintendent of the North Africa Mission. From that moment North Africa was his whole life. He went to Harley College to prepare, though Lucy didn't remember him.

In looks he was not unlike her father, tall, powerfully built with a strong, handsome face and thick mane of hair swept back from a commanding forehead. The jawline was more square and determined, and there was no hint of a twinkle in his clear, blue eyes. This was a man who would never be distracted from his purpose, whatever his attractions for women. Only a few months earlier a young woman had turned up with a ring at the Mission headquarters claiming Kumm had asked her to marry him.

Karl Kumm appears to have been enchanted by Lucy's cultured mind and intelligent conversation. But she also had the added attraction of her pedigree. In missionary work, the name of Henry Grattan Guinness, his old teacher, could open almost any door, and Karl was ambitious.

Lucy had been waiting for a man to sweep her off her feet, someone strong and masterful, with a passion and vision to match her own. By the time Karl escorted them back to Cairo, she was hopelessly, irrevocably in love.

In Cairo all three stayed at the same hotel as Lord Kitchener, fresh from his fight against the Mahdi and about to distinguish himself further in the Boer War. Henry watched him with acute interest from their nearby dinner table, but the main object of Lucy's attention was the intense young man at her side, who was about to take his leave of her to make an exploratory journey up the Nile Valley into the Nubian region. Before they parted they made a tryst. If, in the next months, her feelings for him remained unchanged, he would be waiting for her at Luxor at the turn of the new century.

Lucy returned to England and continued their romance by letter. "Where is my wandering boy tonight? I wish I were in his arms," she wrote.

Karl, however, was more measured. He warned her what her life would be like if she married him. "I must be true to God and my conscience all my life. Are you willing to bear separation if the Lord shall cause it? If I have to work night and day you will not think me selfish? There will be very little "drawing-room" time in my life."

Had she been less in love, Lucy might have realised that this was not a commitment to a relationship. This was a license to stay single within the married state. Karl, whose hero was Livingstone, was wedded to his work, to the freedoms and challenges of the outdoor life, to missionary exploration and pioneering, which he saw uniquely as a man's prerogative. He seems totally unaware of the woman to whom he writes. Lucy Guinness had never indulged in "drawing-room" time herself - in crochet, tapestry or reading, the stereotypical female pursuits. The daughter of Henry Grattan Guinness had never expected to be treated as less than an equal, a co-worker, a fellow pioneer. But she was too involved with Karl to see the potential pitfalls ahead.

In January 1900, having terminated his contract with the North Africa Mission, he made his way back down the Nile to Luxor, wondering how she had responded to his letter, not knowing whether she would be waiting for him or not. But she was there, just as she promised. They were formally betrothed in Aswan in the traditional Sudanese way, joining their hands over the entwined, dark-skinned hands of the two native Bischareens who were teaching Karl their language. In later years Karl would claim that on that very day the Sudan Pioneer Mission was born.

A month later they were married in Cairo, at a civic ceremony at the German Consulate, followed by a service at the American Mission Church taken by Henry Grattan. The wedding breakfast was a tea party for 300 soldiers to whom Karl had been acting chaplain, and the honeymoon a return trip to Aswan in one of Thomas Cooks's discarded Nile steamers. Lucy had never enjoyed domesticity, but she, "learned to cook potatoes splendidly, and to make the most delicious soups (out of tins)." It was the longest time she and Karl would ever spend together throughout their entire married life, and even that was a fact-finding exercise for the new mission.

CHAPTER TWELVE
1900-1902

1

At the end of the twentieth century political tension in China had risen to fever pitch. The young Emperor Kuang Hsu had tried to bring the provincial mandarins to heel, so that he could transform China into a modern constitutional monarchy. But a powerful opposition, led by the diehard dowager Empress Tzu Hsi, overthrew the young emperor and placed him under house arrest. She and her followers, known as "Boxers," despised overseas influence and made foreigners their scapegoats.

Geraldine tried to put the worrying political situation out of her mind. It was exciting to introduce Whitfield, her little brother, to the people she loved in Honan. "I brought him up, you know," she said proudly to everyone they met.

Whitfield Guinness didn't find Chinese traditions easy. The full-length, wrap-round robe with its heavy sleeves cramped his athletic style and made riding a bicycle extremely difficult, shaving the top of his head and tying the rest of his hair into a tight pigtail felt very strange, and the long, thin moustachios at chest level impeded his work.

A year after his arrival one of the local leaders was overheard to say, "Now that Dr. Guinness, it is really wonderful how he has improved! Last year, when he dined with me, he was gauche in the extreme. He hardly knew how to make himself presentable (in Chinese dress); he could not handle chopsticks properly and was unable to reply to a polite remark. But now, in a little more than a year, he is becoming quite a gentleman!"

Whitfield's reputation as a doctor, however, was established almost at once. One day a huge crowd arrived at his door dragging along a tailor who had swallowed his needle. A long piece of thread still attached to the eye was dangling from his mouth, but attempts to pull on the thread had only driven the needle deeper into the poor man's gullet.

By the time Whitfield examined the tailor's throat it was raw, swollen and bleeding. He had never dealt with needle swallowing before, and was flummoxed. Suddenly, inspiration came. He sent one of the crowd for an india-rubber tube, passed a piece of strong silk through it, which he attached to the thread in the man's mouth. Then, he slid the tube gently over the thread and down the swollen throat until it reached the needle. With a little pressure the needle was dislodged and dropped into the stomach where it could dangle freely. To the incredulous gasps of his admiring audience, Whitfield gently pulled on the thread and drew the needle safely out through the rubber tube.[64]

Having another doctor in the province was a relief to Howard. Bouts of fever and dysentery had left him so weak he sometimes had to attend to his patients lying down. Henry Reed had offered him a holiday at Mount Pleasant in Tasmania and now that Whitfield was in Honan, he and Geraldine could leave with an easy mind.

They stopped en route in Australia, where Geraldine, evidently the more gifted preacher of the two, had accepted several speaking engagements. In Adelaide an elderly gentleman offered her his condolences on the loss of her mother.

"Thank you," Geraldine said lightly, "but my dear mother is getting on quite nicely, in spite of the paralysis."

Clearly disconcerted, the elderly man finally managed to stutter, "I'm so sorry. Haven't you heard? Your mother died over a month ago."

Geraldine was devastated and Howard escorted her quickly away.

Whitfield, meanwhile, settled down to life at the station in She-ki-chen, shared with a missionary couple, the Conways, and Miss Watson, a single woman. His bicycle was a source of fascination to the Chinese.

But since it provided no shelter and sometimes had to be carried, they decided it was not nearly as practical as a mule and cart.

Drought and famine were severe everywhere, and in June 1900, the Boxers diverted any public unrest with a decree that all foreigners should be destroyed.

On a sweltering July day word reached the little party in She-ki-chen that the locals were planning to kill them and they must flee for their lives. The waterway to the sea was completely dried up, and overland, a thousand miles of Boxer-infested country separated them from the coast. The Conways had a six-week-old baby. The baby's nurse, a local woman, managed to persuade their neighbour, Li Ch'uen-rong, treated by Whitfield during a near-fatal illness, that he owed his life to the missionaries and must offer them protection.

At five o'clock in the morning the rioters arrived. As they smashed their way through the barricades the missionaries had erected, Whitfield, Miss Watson, and the Conways slipped out of the back door, clambered up a ladder and over a ten-foot wall, ran across their neighbour's courtyard, and climbed another ladder into the relative safety of his attic. As they held their breath they could hear the murderous shouts of the mob, the crash of falling timber, and the crackle of flames as their house burned to the ground.

Then the noise grew louder as Mr. Li's house was overrun by hysterical crowds screaming for blood. They heard the nurse shouting, "You'll have to kill me first!" and realised that she and Mr. Li were all that stood between the mob and the trapdoor.

The protracted argument appeared to lull the crowds into sulky acquiescence, and the little party in the loft heard the sound of retreating footsteps and of shouts gradually dying away in the distance.

Their relief was short-lived. A trembling Mr. Li appeared at the trapdoor. "You can't stay here," he said, "this is my servants' quarters. They will soon be coming up and I can't rely on their secrecy." He couldn't think of an alternative hiding place, until Mrs. Conway pointed to a deserted-looking building in the back courtyard. "The haunted loft?" he asked in disbelief! They were welcome to it.

"The more haunted the better!" Whitfield chortled, as they ran, under cover of darkness, across the courtyard to the disused granary. They managed to build a mountain of wheat held in place with strong cocoa-matting, then, balancing a ladder against it, heaved their way up into a tiny, infested loft.

Tea and bread were suddenly pushed through the trapdoor. After twenty-four hours of heat and high humidity with nothing to eat or drink, it was a feast. A stranger appeared behind the food and urged them to follow him. He had been sent to escort them safely out of the city. They were almost out of the courtyard when Mr. Li came rushing after them. Their guide was the leader of the rioters, a decoy sent to lure them out of hiding.

They ran back to the granary as fast as they could, and as the trapdoor had just closed after them when the dreaded police officer and his men arrived.

The warehouse was ransacked.

"Now search the loft," the officer commanded.

The men refused. The loft was haunted.

"Nonsense!" the officer said.

One of the men fetched a beam and began to ram the trapdoor.

"Rigidly fixed!" he shouted, with relief. "Quite immovable!"

Sitting with his full weight on the trapdoor, Whitfield felt it move beneath him. Mrs. Conway rocked her baby gently. The tiniest cry would have sealed their fate. They waited, holding their breath, sweat dripping from their faces and trickling down their backs.

After a while, all went silent. The officer and his men appeared to have abandoned their search.

The next day the rioters set to work early, smashing everything in their wake. They poured onto the granary roof, peering in the loft window for any sign of life. Whitfield had had the presence of mind to find the one tiny corner of the loft invisible from outside and there they crouched together while the uproar went on around them. And still baby Nora did not cry.

Peeking out of the window, Whitfield saw that the men below had begun to pile wood, grass and bundles of straw around the building. They were about to set it alight when Mr. Li's farm-workers arrived in a fury. Killing foreigners was one thing, destroying their hard work was another. Disgruntled, the mob conceded.

One man went and fetched a ladder instead and the little party in the loft heard the sound of footsteps climbing up towards their window. But the ladder was too short. The man could only reach the window by pulling himself up by his hands for a few seconds. He quickly scanned the room, and though Conway felt his breath on his cheek, he never saw the people hiding in the space right next to him.

They hid in the loft for six more days with almost no food or drink. Every time the trapdoor opened their hearts stood still. On one occasion, to their amazement, two packets of post were pushed through by Postman Lu, grateful for the treatment of a boil on his foot. In the post were newspapers revealing the full extent and horror of the Boxer uprising. They had no choice but to stay in hiding.

Whitfield wrote home on a scrap of paper:

> It is the sixth day of the riot, and we still lie on a dirty floor. The ladies are worn and sick; Conway done. I am well enough thank God, but don't see quite how we are to get away. Clouds lend a hope of rain. If it fell, it would make all the difference. We have no change of clothing; and day by day in a temperature of 90-100 you may imagine our condition—all four in one room with a baby. The Lord grant it may be soon over.

That night they heard the unmistakable pitter-patter of rain on the roof. It grew louder until a torrential downpour drowned every other sound and they were able to leap around for joy. The trapdoor opened and Mr. Li's head appeared. "Truly," he said, "your God is wonderful.

Only this night I have made terms with Mr. Wang, and now under cover of this rain and darkness, I will get you to his house."

Mr. Wang was a leading businessman in the city, probably the only man who could get them to safety. But crossing the city to his house was extremely dangerous. The party was split up, old clothes and blankets wrapped around their heads and the baby taken from them. The paths had turned to mud, and as her guide pulled her along, Mrs. Conway kept slipping and falling.

After a nightmare journey Whitfield and the Conways finally arrived at their destination but there was no sign of Miss Watson or the baby. Mrs. Conway was almost beside herself when one of Mr. Li's farm labourers struggled up the ladder into their new attic with a bundle in his arms. He had blundered into one of Mr. Wang's offices by mistake. "Truly this baby is good," he whispered, "Had it cried when I was in the clerk's office, all would have been spoiled." Miss Watson arrived some hours later. She had lost her shoe in the mud and went back to look for it—in vain. When the Boxers found it, however, it convinced them the foreigners had escaped from the city and they called off their search.

The waterway was still dry, so they were stuck in yet another attic for what seemed eternity. Then suddenly, on the eleventh day, they heard excited shouts below. "Amazing! The dried-up river fills with water!" They could hardly believe their ears. How could the river rise when there had been no recent rain? Two hours later a jubilant Postman Lu climbed into their attic shouting, "The river has actually risen to half its banks. Rain must have fallen way back in the hills."

That night they crept stealthily out of hiding, clambering over soldiers asleep on mats in the courtyard. The baby started to be uneasy, but Mrs. Conway managed to quieten her. Wang had arranged for a cart to take them to the river. That meant passing through the city's iron gates which were heavily guarded. Lying in the cart covered with old blankets and matting, they held their breath while the driver negotiated his way out with a bribe. Finally they heard the gates swing open and soon they were steaming their way to freedom.

The five-day journey took ten. They spent it shut up in the cabin in the heat lest they be seen from the land. Every province had its own Customs Department. Each border encounter was a potential disaster. The women covered their feet and hair and pretended to be asleep.

At last the foreign settlement of Han-k'ou came into view. They kept their heads well down, and the boat glided rapidly downstream past the final customs depot until they were out of Boxer territory at last. Dirty and unshaven, without his Chinese gown, Whitfield went on ahead by rickshaw to the China Inland Mission house to inform them of the arrival of a Honan party, thirty days after the riot.

He was greeted with utter amazement. Gently, they explained that seventy-five of his fellow missionaries and twenty-two children had perished. They had held out no hope for the party.

Weeks later in Shanghai, where he went to rest and recover from his ordeal, he noticed a lovely young woman, tall and slender, with a mass of fair curls caught at the back of her neck. Both were struggling to come to terms with the terrible events of the last months and to understand why they had survived when their colleagues had not. They felt drawn to each other and spent hours talking about their experiences. Her name was Jane af Sandeburg, and she was on her way home to Sweden.

2.

While Whitfield was caught up in the Boxer uprising, his 25-year old cousin, Rupert Lee Guinness was experiencing his own first, great adventure—the Boer War. In Rupert a new brand of Guinness had been born to the brewing side of the family, a Guinness, who in his penchant for travel, innovation, scientific discovery, and ultimately, in his identification with the poor, could well have stemmed from Henry Grattan rather than Edward Cecil's line. Gentle, sensitive, intuitive, there seems little doubt he was a surprise to his father who regarded him as a bit of a misfit.

Years later, convinced he must nonetheless be a product of his genes, particularly in his passion for the sciences, Rupert wrote to another Fellow of the Royal Society, the distinguished scientist Sir Ronald Aylmer Fisher, of Gonville and Caius, Cambridge, who had married Dr. Harry Guinness' daughter, Eileen, to ask him whether there was anyone in the family he might take after. Fisher told him about his own father-in-law's research into tropical diseases, and described his wife's grandfather, Henry Grattan Guinness. "He was a mathematician and an astronomer, but I believe his astronomical interests became centred in the interpretation of biblical prophecies."[65]

Throughout his lifetime some thought Rupert saintly. His headmaster at Eton thought his character "one of the most perfect I have ever met with in a boy here and I can hardly think it possible that he could ever do anything discreditable." Unaware of Rupert's dyslexia, he only wished the boy's academic ability approached his character in excellence.[66]

Although Edward Cecil gave his eldest son £5 million on his 21st birthday, Rupert showed little inclination to join the social jet set. The lavish entertaining of his parents had little attraction for the shy, retiring young man. He was much happier alone with his microscope.

In 1891 Jim Jackson, an Elveden stableman had been bitten by a rabid dog. The only treatment for rabies was the newly-invented course of 40 injections into the stomach, available in Paris at the Louis Pasteur Institute. Research in England by Jenner and Lister had been curtailed for lack of funding. Rupert persuaded his father to go with him and Jackson to Paris so that they could see Pasteur's work for themselves. The stableman survived, and as Rupert guessed, the trip convinced Lord Iveagh he should endow a research institution in England with £255,000. The Lister Institute, as it became, led the world fight for a vaccination against smallpox, dyptheria, and typhoid.

Despite Rupert's scientific ability, Edward Cecil could not believe his eldest son was capable of managing a successful business. Fortunately, his second son, Ernest, still at Eton, showed more promise. Nonetheless, he made Rupert a director of the brewery in 1899, shortly before he set off for South Africa to fight the Afrikaaners. For his service to his country in escorting a field hospital endowed by Edward Cecil, he returned home to receive the Companionship of the Order of St. Michael and St. George.

3

The news of the Boxer massacres reached Hudson Taylor in London where he was recovering from a slight stroke. His devastation was so immense that his wife took him straight to Davos in the Swiss mountains. Here, desperate for news of Whitfield, Howard and Geraldine, joined him.

The telegram announcing her brother's miraculous escape brought Geraldine only temporary relief. The scale of the mission's losses was almost impossible to absorb. Her father in law felt personally responsible and broke down beneath the weight of his grief. He seemed beyond comfort, but Geraldine, who had started her life's work of writing biography, simply worked quietly in his room, while he paced up and down and wept. One day he suddenly walked over to her table and said, "I cannot read. I cannot think...I cannot even pray." She looked up at him with profound sorrow, hunting for words that might help, but after a long pause, he said quietly, "But I can trust."

While Whitfield went to the Chefoo School to support many missionary children who had lost their parents, and to treat the hundreds of refugees who were pouring in daily from the interior, Howard and Geraldine set off for an awareness-raising tour of the United States. Wherever they went Geraldine, with her plummy English voice, refined English-rose appearance, and immense personal charisma was the centre of attention.

This then was the pattern of their lives—Geraldine in the limelight speaking and writing, Howard, shy and self-effacing, in the background looking after her. Every thrilling missionary adventure story she wrote added to her popularity. One of her young admirers wrote, "I met Geraldine in Montreal in my early teens. Even at that age she was my model because of what I knew from her book, *In the Far East*. She so fulfilled my highest ideals, I longed to be like her, so much so that, having seen her, I attempted for some time, by standing before a mirror, to make my mouth to the expression of hers."

Geraldine's heroes were brave, her heroines selfless and flawless. Blemishes had no place in her portraits, partly because she thought it uncharitable to dwell on the weaknesses of another, partly because she happened to be blessed with a generosity of spirit, which saw only their good.

Desmond, one of Harry and Annie's boys, remembered years later that as a child he once told his Auntie Geraldine that a master at his school suffered from asthma. "I hope the boys are kind to him," Geraldine said earnestly. Annie laughed uproariously and said in her matter-of-fact way, "Don't make the boy tell lies, Geraldine dear."

The tendency to lionise Geraldine was so prevalent that she often found it difficult to live up to the ideal of perfect Christian womanhood she projected. Howard alone knew she could be petulant and difficult, that she struggled with the disappointment of not having children, and with the sense of inadequacy which had dogged her from childhood. Without a word of complaint he gave up his career in medicine to care for her. He saw to it that she took daily exercise, went to bed early, ate properly and regularly. Like a child she became completely dependent on him, but sometimes she broke free and played truant. Howard would be hurt. "Darling," he once said to her after a particularly fierce quarrel over something he refused to let her do, "where would you have been by now if I hadn't been taking care of you?"

"In my grave long ago," she admitted ruefully.

While Howard Taylor nurtured and encouraged his wife's vocation at the cost of his own, Karl never allowed Lucy to get in his way. She joined Howard and Geraldine on their returned to Davos, pregnant and desperately sick. In the first few months of their marriage she had worked tirelessly at Karl's side in Aswan. It was imperative to reach the people for Christ, before they were converted to Islam. The race for the souls of the Sudanese was on.

Two workers were quickly found—a young North African, ex Harley student called Samuel Ali Hussein, whom her father had found working behind the post-office counter in Shellal, and Girgis Yacoub, an Egyptian Copt. In the summer of 1900 Karl and Lucy set up the headquarters of the

Sudan Pioneer Mission in Eisenach. Karl needed to travel extensively to establish a network of support. A pregnant wife, who was 35 and suffering from nausea, could only hold him back.

She found the separation harder than she had ever imagined. "I do love you so," she wrote, "and long to creep into your arms...come back soon to both of us." When he failed to appear, her letters took on a more petulant tone. "Naughtie Husbie said he was coming on the 10th and now today is the 11th and never a word to say when he will come or how, at all, and yesterday no letter! Naughty, naughty, naughty, naughty."

Their first son, Henry, was born at Wiesbaden, Karl's home, at the end of February 1901. Karl was there for the birth but set off on a fact-finding mission to Wadi Halfa before the baby was a month old. Rather than stay among strangers, Lucy returned to her father at Cliff, in theory to regain her strength, in practice to raise support for the new pioneer mission in the Sudan.

From Cliff she continued to bombard Karl with desperate demands for expressions of his love.

> Husbie I want you; come to me Husbie—take me in your arms,
> Dear Light, beautiful joy, hide me again in your big heart like the
> old days when you took me there first—in my dream of Paradise.

> Not a dream: It was true once. Tell me it all again, Darling. Write
> to me that I may have it always—write me a little every day—just
> as you remember it all.

In 1901 the old Queen died. The accession to the throne of King Edward VII heralded a new hedonistic era. The Edwardian age, epitomised by the golden lifestyle of Elveden, was gracious and carefree. Interest in missionary work died almost overnight. Not only that but the Boer War robbed the institute of volunteers and severely depleted its funds.

Henry Grattan felt he had no option but to sell Cliff College. All four children were horrified and Lucy begged Karl to let it be the centre for their new mission. Karl knew it was far to big for their purposes, and that they had no money to run it, but in the end he had little choice. Lucy was pregnant again and needed a base while he was in the Sudan. Besides, it had become abundantly clear that his German Mission Board, consisting of respected, but conservative church leaders, did not share Kumm's inexhaustible drive and determination, and could not support his reckless single-mindedness. Saddened, Karl announced his intention of establishing new mission headquarters in England. They would take over Cliff on a temporary basis.

It was there that little Karl was born in 1902. Separated from the husband she adored, Lucy lavished all her affection on her two babies. They were a precious gift she thought would never be hers. The tumult of emotions they aroused in her were poured into poems and prose, "long withheld as too sacred for publication," were eventually published to great acclaim in 1929.

> As long as there are babies in the world the age of miracles will never cease.
>
> All mothers know this.
>
> To look at the dainty, breathing, moving creature lying in its curtained cot with its own energy and volition, its own world and life, its private joys and sorrows, pains and satisfaction—to look at it and think that a few months ago it had no existence and that to you and another its presence on earth is due, is to realise yourself in the presence of a miracle compared with which all but one other pale. For this to which you have given birth is a life which will go on. How far? How long? And whither?

Though steeped in Edwardian sentimentalism, they nonetheless capture the mixture of tenderness and fierceness in the maternal instinct. An almost morbid preoccupation with death appears, the fear that some love is too great to last. Does she love her babies, her Karl too much? A sense of depression, of doom now appears to haunt her.

In 1903, the Wesleyans approached the Kumms and asked if they could have Cliff as a training college for Methodist ministers. It was the perfect proposition. Lucy rented a small cottage in Castleton in the Derbyshire hills near Sheffield, where the Sudan Pioneer Mission held its inaugural English Council meeting in upstairs rooms in the YMCA on November 13th, 1902, with Dr. Grattan Guinness in the chair.

But where was Henry Grattan to live? She wrote about it to Geraldine, who replied, "I know how perplexing the question seems about Father's future home. We cannot fully see how the needs are to be met." But Henry, to his children's surprise, found a most ingenious way of solving the problem.

CHAPTER THIRTEEN
1902-1910

1

On August 14th, 1900 Henry Grattan had scribbled the following words on a piece of paper, which he then kept folded in his wallet.

> After a quiet day of prayer in the woods at Eisenach, had a very vivid dream in the night. I had prayed that God would bring me a wife suitable for me and had endeavoured to trust him to do so. Dreamed she came to me in the night, and sat on my knee and kissed me—with a bright smile, her own act. Not given to dreams! Will wait, and wait on God. Through his grace.

Three years later the following postscript was added in a woman's hand: "...and Grace came and sat on his knee and kissed him! My own act. 11th June 1903."

For a respectable young woman to sit on a strange man's knee was hardly proper behaviour at the turn of the century. That Henry Grattan was 67 and she 25 makes it extraordinary at any time.

Henry's dream became reality in St. Leonards, where he was house-hunting for Lucy. The House of Rest for Christian Workers belonging to his old friend Charles Hurditch, was an ideal place to stay. On the morning of Wednesday, June 11th he called to book a room. Summoned by the bell, Grace Hurditch went to deal with his request. As she walked down the staircase into the hall their eyes met and there was instant, mutual attraction.

Grace was the seventh and youngest child of Charles Russell Hurditch, converted under Grattan Guinness' preaching in Exeter, a leading light in the Plymouth Brethren and professional philanthropist. Although life was rather serious at home, it was a warm and loving family and the Hurditch children invented games that circumvented their parents' religious austerity. By suspending sheets from the bedsteads a four-poster bed was converted into a baptistry, into which a succession of candidates were "plunged" by an "elder" balanced precariously on a bedside table. "I must confess that somewhat unholy mirth accompanied the proceedings when occasionally elder and candidate together suffered total immersion."[67]

Grace's exceptional talent for mimicry was evident from an early age. The victims of her impersonations were usually revivalist preachers or members of their mission hall congregation, whose idiosyncrasies she had plenty of time to observe during the long Sunday services. She was even offered an opening on the stage at a starting salary of fifty pounds—a fortune in those days. "I'd rather see her in her grave," her father was reported to have said.

She grew up to exercise a freedom of choice and independence of mind unusual in a woman of her background and generation. At twenty-six she had evaded all attempts to marry her off and had chosen a career in nursing instead. Shocked by the ignorance of her contemporaries in the basic workings of the human body and equipped with specimens of animal viscera obtained from the local butcher, she delivered a series of lectures in elementary human anatomy:

> I would then proceed to demonstrate the fascinating action of the valves of the heart by pouring water into the auricles and ventricles, and show the workings of the lungs, which I inflated by means of my bicycle pump; when suddenly there would be a thud, thud, thud, as one after another of my audience fainted away at these "ghastly sights."

Grace had to abandon her work when her father opened his "rest home for Christian workers." In all his philanthropic projects Charles Hurditch expected the support of his two unmarried daughters, Grace and Beatrice.

Visitors often took the opportunity to flirt with the vivacious, intelligent Grace. Exceptionally pretty with an oval face, large, mischievous eyes and a mass of light brown curls, held against their will in a bun at the nape of a long and graceful neck, she was never short of admirers. But she wrote to her sister Ruth that she had no time for suitors or people who said stupid things about "ought to be married." Not until Henry Grattan Guinness walked into her life a fortnight later.

In her letter to Ruth, dated Sunday, June 27th, 1903, she describes the transformation:

> My Ruth, my darling sister
>
> At last! The awakening has come, and your little Grace is transformed, and she is really in love. Oh my darling Sister, how I have longed to cable this to you, or at any rate the date of our wedding. July 7th, and yet I date not for fear it would come as too much of a shock to you just now. But the relief to sit down and talk to you about it, knowing that you and Bee will at least understand it all, and so what do I care for all the other criticisms. Fancy, Ruth, that Dr. Grattan Guinness (he is 67 darling!) has been the one to break down the barriers I was building round my little life, barriers I thought insuperable until I met him here just 2 weeks ago.

Henry Grattan Guinness was no stranger to Ruth. It was at Geraldine Guinness' missionary farewell in 1887 that the teenage Ruth decided she was called to be a missionary herself. In time the formidable Ruth was to prove more intrepid than her heroine, becoming the first white woman to climb Mount Kilimanjaro, delivering all five of her babies herself and confronting the legendary Tippu Tib over his slaving activities.

But as Grace knew only too well, admiration for the great preacher was one thing, marriage was another. She would have to persuade her elder sister that what she felt was romantic love, not mere infatuation.

His magnificent presence appealed to me very strongly, his clean-shaven face and white hair brushed back off that great forehead of his. He tells me his first impressions of me were, "What a sweet girl," and from that moment we felt most strongly drawn to each other.

Well after lunch we had tea as usual, and everyone went out but the doctor and me, and strange to say I did not feel in the least afraid of him as the great Dr. Guinness, as everyone else seemed to be. And then he took my hand and asked me a little about myself and what I was doing here, after which he gave me a kiss—such a kiss—and I loved him and felt I never wanted to leave him, but never for a moment thought that he would care for me like that. Such a thought never crossed my mind. I only knew that it was an exquisite day to be with him then and the future never occurred to me.

The next day he followed her around, talking all about his travels, and how he would love to take her with him, and how it would develop her. That very evening he asked her to join him in the office, and told her how for five years he had prayed God to bring him this love she had awakened in him.

Grace, inevitably, was flattered at having a man of his reputation declare his love to her:

Really, darling, I could not have thought it possible to be so happy, yet so humbled, for Ruth I cannot understand why he loves me. Such intellect, and such a soul. I tried to tell him of all my faults, but he only kisses me and says he has never known such love before...Now, my darling, how I shall need your prayers, for I long to be worthy of my high calling, and he wants to teach me so much...He is just now completing a marvellous book on the historical sequence of the Apocalypse (and I don't even know how to spell it!)

Her Henry was even in communication with the Foreign Secretary. "Balfour has written to me," Henry told her, "to say that he is so interested in my books, and has studied them closely." The full significance of these words would not be apparent for another fourteen years. But the growing Zionist interest within government circles was hardly uppermost in Henry's mind at that moment.

The immediacy of their wedding day, less than a month from their first meeting, meant he had to return to straight to Cliff to sort out his affairs and make the necessary arrangements. But he left her a poem he had written to remind her of his love:

> *She has come to my arms, she has come to my heart,*
> *And the dream of my soul is fulfilled,*
> *And the love that unites us shall never depart,*
> *Nor the love that our union has willed.*

> *O thanks to the Giver, O thanks for the gift,*
> *From the gift to the Giver we turn;*
> *From the bliss he bestows to Himself we uplift*
> *The hearts which with gratitude burn.*

> *There is heaven below, there is heaven above,*
> *And they answer like ocean and sky;*
> *For heaven is found in the bosom of love,*
> *In spirit to spirit made nigh.*

In his absence a present arrived almost every day, a compressed cane travelling trunk, a canteen of cutlery, two buckles for waist belts, a long string of pearls and a purse with silver corners. "I have told him I don't care a bit about these sorts of things but he loves me to look pretty fancy," she wrote with undisguised coquetry.

He couldn't bear to be apart from her and wrote from Cliff on June 17th, "I have read and re-read your last letters, which I found on my arrival here last night, with such love and joy, answering to your own—my wife, my life—in anticipation, and in heart, intention, spirit, in reality, how wonderful is the relation—love's secret hidden for a season in the heart, and then, slowly or suddenly bursting into bloom!....I was in the garden this morning and the park, and wanted to gather the best of all the flowers and send them to you. I plucked the leaves of fragrant thyme, or rather lavender and roses and wanted you to have them all. You must come here with me after Switzerland, to see the place where we have lived for so long."

Not everyone rejoiced at their relationship. Grace refers to "not caring for all the criticisms," but at least the two families were genuinely pleased. Geraldine wrote from Switzerland to the future step-mother who was fifteen years her junior that she was glad, for her father's sake that they had decided to marry quickly. "For he loves you Gracie! He has so much to give. The wealth of his great soul and tender heart. And it is yours, all yours. Oh such a heart Gracie! You will explore your treasures as the days go on. And you have much to give dear, your fresh young life and love. But he is worth it all. How did you find our so soon?"

It was decided in the circumstances to keep the engagement as quiet as possible, but when Henry kept a prior appointment to speak at a public meeting at Harley College, the gardens were packed to capacity. Everyone thought Grace would be there and were dying to catch a glimpse of her. But she never appeared, no announcement was made and the disappointed crowds had to be satisfied with excited chatter and speculation.

2

The *Hastings Observer* on July 7th, 1903 referred to the quiet ceremony at the Robertson Street Congregational Church as "A wedding of considerable interest to Nonconformists." After a luncheon at the Queen's Hotel, attended only the immediate relatives of the bride and bridegroom, they left for the continent.

From Brussels Grace wrote to Ruth filling in the details of her wedding day.

In case no one tells you what I wore, here goes. The palest dove grey gossamer voile dress made over silk, with a real lace berthe, a black velvet bonnet, with white net strings, and long pale grey gossamer veil down the back. Everyone said, darling, that I looked rather sweet. My beautiful bouquet was composed of tiger lilies and lilies of the valley. After a bright, happy cheerful time at luncheon we drove off to Westons to be photographed, sweet Geraldine and her husband coming too, in order to pose us (both are very artistic), then we went back to the hotel where Mother and Edith were waiting to get me into a Bolton-tailor-made pale grey coat and skirt. (I am sticking to a bonnet. It becomes me as Mrs. Grattan Guinness!)

Then off we went to the station and had a loving send-off from Geraldine, Howard and Lucy. The two families had stayed at the Queen's the previous evening with their father and did a hundred and one little nice things for me, finishing touches to his toilet. He looked perfectly exquisite in frock coat and white tie and waistcoat and top hat, so absolutely aristocratic with his magnificent face and white hair and upright figure. Really it's not surprising that people stare at us both. We are a little out of the ordinary! And whenever we go into a shop he manages to say something about his "petite femme" so as to see the looks of approval!

The early days of her marriage were more wonderful than Grace had ever dared to hope. In a letter to Ruth dated July 11th, unfettered by the usual prudery of her generation, she wrote about the intimate details of their relationship:

How can I write to you old girl of all my happiness—this wonderful new life—isn't the love, protection, guardianship, sympathy, affection of a good man the greatest blessing that can come with a woman's life? My beloved husband has opened up a new world to me. His love has just touched the spring of that secret chamber which I never knew existed and my happiness is complete.

Ruth, you don't know how humbled I feel when I think of the way God has honoured me, for my darling is so good and clever and wonderful and his marvellous intellect! He reads to me and is educating me all day, but at numerous intervals, whether in the "Grand Parc de Bruxelles," or under the palms on the Hotel verandah, impresses his ideas on me with a kiss, such a kiss, followed by some exquisite expressions of his love...

I remember old girl, the first letter you wrote to me after your marriage you said it was all so natural and no wonderful changes had come. Well, darling, that is just about the truth of it. It is just the most natural thing in the world to be with our kindred spirit, and I'm sure you would have thought that no change had come to me, if you had seen me this afternoon in a marionette tea gown reciting to my dear Grattan, who greatly appreciates all my little funs and frivolities. Don't be afraid of his converting me into some sedate little saint, for he loves me just as I am, at least so he says!

I am keeping a short diary, just writing down the places we visit, because we hope to travel much and it is bound to be an interesting record....While I am writing this there are about a dozen Americans twanging away nineteen to the dozen they are talking such a lot of nonsense and in such loud tones, evidently wealthy people by the way they are talking about their travels. How trivial even travel becomes when done in this way, whereas with my Grattan it becomes an education, creates an interest and leaves a lasting impression.

They travelled much more than she anticipated. With his new young wife at his side filling him with fresh energy and vigour, Henry decided to fulfil a life-long ambition to visit former Harley and Cliff students all over the world. After a short stay in Switzerland with Howard and Geraldine so that Henry could complete, *History Unveiling Prophecy*, they set off for the United States. The honeymoon turned into a world tour. It would be five years before Grace saw her parents again.

For several months Henry maintained an exhausting preaching schedule. He was more popular than ever, and they were feted wherever they went. His books sold in their thousands. *Light for the Last Days* was reprinted over and over again. After a few days recuperation at the Moody Bible Institute in Chicago, they went on to Australia, Japan and China.

In the early hours of a chilly November morning they caught the sight of the outlines of Shanghai. Streams of muddy brown water intermingling with ocean-green indicated their entry to the great Yangtze River. Passengers and baggage were transferred to a river steamer for the remainder of the journey and suddenly Whitfield's familiar face materialised on the quay. With him was his new wife Jane, whom Grace had never met. Whitfield had waited five years for Jane to return to him from Sweden, and when she did, they were married almost at once.

The highlight of their visit was an opportunity for Henry to speak to the Shanghai Zionist Association in the Royal Asiatic Hall. A large number of influential Chinese Jews were present, complete with pigtail, and for over an hour he held them spellbound with one of his most eloquent addresses on "Zionism from a Christian standpoint." The entire text appeared verbatim in a local Jewish newspaper.

At 9.15 pm on the day of their departure, Henry noted sadly in his diary: "Said "Goodnight" to Gershom and Janie." Some years later Grace wrote underneath, "It was their last "Goodnight."

By the time they travelled back to Australia in 1906, Grace was five months pregnant. She stayed on in Sydney while Henry travelled on alone. It was their first time apart and he did not enjoy being without his "pet wife" as he called her.

He was back in Sydney in time for the birth of John Christopher who weighed a magnificent nine pounds. The Australian midwife had never seen such an enormous baby—nor such an easy first delivery. Labour lasted a mere six hours, and as Henry telegraphed the world, Grace, looking radiant, fed their infant son. At 70, Henry was as excited as if he had become a father for the first time. He took endless pleasure in the baby, noting every development with enormous pride and tenderness. "He would delight to carry him out into the warm Australian sunshine, and to pick the flowers from our garden, and see the child's appreciation of beautiful things," Grace noted in her diary. "It was a wonderful gift in light of the heavy blow that was so soon to fall."

3.

1903 was a bumper year for Guinness weddings, each, like Henry and Grace's, attracting its share of newspaper attention. All three of Lord and Lady Iveagh's sons married into the British aristocracy, delighting the public with three grand society occasions. In June the Honourable Walter, 23, the youngest and most dashing of Dodo's boys, married Lady Evelyn Erskine, third daughter of the 14th Earl of Buchan. Walter was elected Member of Parliament for Bury St. Edmonds in 1907.

In July, twelve days after his cousin Henry Grattan created a stir in the non-conformist ranks by marrying a woman 40 years his junior, the reserved, rather conventional Ernest married his opposite, the vivacious socialite, Marie Clotilde Russell, known in the family as Chloe, daughter of Sir George Russell. They set up home at Glenmaroon, next to Farmleigh and Knockmaroon on the Phoenix Park side of Dublin, an area of elegant mansions and sweeping lawns, rapidly becoming a sophisticated Guinness enclave, so that Ernest could be within easy reach of the brewery. Ernest had exceptional flair in engineering and technology, combined with a highly inventive streak, which would lead to the vital modernisation of brewery equipment. Gadgets were one of his greatest loves. At Glenmaroon he installed a mechanical electric organ.

The following October, the Honourable Rupert Edward Cecil Lee married Lady Gwendolen Onslow, eldest daughter of the fourth Earl of Onslow. Gwendolen had been intrigued by the Guinness family for some time before she and Rupert were formally introduced. In 1896, when she met Lord Iveagh for the first time, she was fifteen and despite a sheltered upbringing at Clandon Park in Surrey, was "very full of ideas about social reform and, having consumed much literature on the subject, was impressed by the great gulf between the rich and the poor and the misery and squalor of the slums." Lord Iveagh's reputation for philanthropy had captured her adolescent imagination. He was the living expression of her ideals.

Eventually she received the coveted invitation to Elveden, but she found the house "luxurious beyond any dream," and the Iveaghs disappointingly formidable and distant. Of the sons of the house Rupert caught her attention from the first. He was unlike the other debutantes' dreams, quiet and unassuming, high church and unostentatious.

Shortly after their marriage he was adopted as the Conservative candidate for the Haggerston division of Shoreditch, an area of high economic deprivation, hardly likely to choose a Conservative MP, let alone one with immense wealth and a title. Their parents were horrified when, instead of living in fashionable St. James's Square, in the house Lord Iveagh had bought them as a wedding present, Rupert and Gwenny set up home at 266 Kingsland Road in the heart of the constituency. This was the only way they felt they could contest the seat with integrity. When Dodo had criticised Henry and Fanny all those years ago for raising their children in the East End, little did she guess her own son would one day choose to live there himself. But those seven years in Shoreditch were formative, and in the end, their commitment was rewarded when in 1908 Rupert was voted MP for Haggerston in a by-election.

The couple were in Canada little more than a year later when news reached them that there was to be a General Election. The voters abandoned him, as he knew they would, but by then Rupert felt he had served a reasonable apprenticeship, moved into St. James' Square and accepted the candidature of a safer seat. He became the honourable member for Southend-on-Sea in 1912, a seat he retained for fifteen years, until he inherited his father's peerage and moved into the House of Lords.

Enthusiastic imperialists, Rupert and Gwenny had been deeply impressed by the potential in Canada for enterprising British immigrants who were adequately prepared for conditions out there. In 1912 they bought Woking Park Farm, 550 acres of land near their Pyrford estate and set up the first emigration training establishment. No fees were required, simply token board and lodging costs and a deposit on the fare out. Students were to adhere to a strict code of conduct—no swearing or gambling, no smoking on duty. In the first summer alone, 75 men left for Canada. The similarities with the subsistence farming programme Henry Grattan Guinness had established at Cliff College forty years earlier, are striking. The genetic code was still at work.

4

While Henry and Grace were touring the world and Rupert and Gwendolen were setting up home in Shoreditch, Lucy was living with her babies in Castleton in Derbyshire. Karl came and went and Lucy's letters followed him about, with news of any support she had managed to raise for the mission and expressions of her love and longing for him.

Trying to establish a new missionary society was hard. Lucy made unashamed use of her name and network of contacts, spoke at countless meetings, and visited senior Christian ministers, but every existing British missionary society was already stretched to the limit financially. Well respected ministers like F.B. Meyer told her it was unwise even to consider another non-conformist overseas mission. Undaunted, Lucy organised the first Scottish Council meeting on June 15th, 1904, where the speaker, the great explorer, Dr. Alexander Whyte proposed that the work be called the Sudan United Mission, since it was the only non-conformist missionary society working in that part of Africa.

The first London Council meeting on June 27th 1904 decided to send Karl on a risky fact-finding expedition to the unknown Bauchi Hill Country on the Upper Benue River. There were no funds for the journey, but when Lucy arrived home from Karl's farewell in Liverpool a gift of £1,000 was waiting for her.

Another long separation left Lucy with an inner void which she filled with a frenetic work schedule. As well as attending all mission council meetings in Scotland, Ireland and England, she often wrote the minutes, interviewed prospective candidates, and delivered hundreds of lantern slide presentations on the needs of the Sudan. When she did manage to get home, broken nights with the baby left her in a state of exhaustion. In one letter to Karl she tells him she envies Evan Roberts, the young preacher in the Welsh revival, who is so tired, he has been forced to take a fortnight's rest. "Lucky fellow! I envy him and hope for quiet days in the Blessed Beyond."

But Karl never seems to have appreciated how hard she worked. While he was in Tripoli, a female candidate applied to the mission and was rejected on the grounds that pioneers were needed. Lucy pencilled in the minute book, "It was hoped she might go on later," but it was a very long time before Karl assented intellectually to the equality of women.

The more Lucy demanded to be let into his life, the more he held her at arm's length. He was notoriously bad at keeping in touch. The task was so all-consuming he had not time for minor considerations such as letter writing. It almost broke Lucy's heart.

> Oh my naughty darling, why have I no letter from thee for over five weeks now again? What prevents just one post-card from reaching thy little waiting one? Has my Heart's Dearest been ill? and he doesn't tell me? Maxwell (one of the team) actually says that you said that you couldn't write to me—you were "busy." He says you said you sent me your love. Husdu!

As Christmas approached she wrote to Karl, "In the dim faint hope that possibly you may appear, I am actually beginning to practise a piece of Chopin (his Ballade No.3) which appeals to my mind at present. Always at special seasons of life, there come to me special pieces of music, musical expressions of the thoughts of the time. The present one is very beautiful."

Karl did arrive home to Derbyshire for the happy Christmas of 1905, "the people of the village coming to rejoice with us under the Christmas tree." But around the little family, revelling in rare moments of togetherness beneath the Christmas lights, the shadows were beginning to lengthen.

A few weeks later Karl left for the United States and in April 1906 set up the American SUM headquarters in Germantown, Philadephia. Speaking invitations poured in and when it began to look as if the trip might be prolonged, Henry Mabie, Secretary of the American Baptist Missionary Union, who hadn't seen Lucy since her visit with her father thirteen years before, encouraged Karl to send for her and the boys. She was a gifted preacher and he wanted her to speak to the thousands of young people who converged on the Moody Conference Centre at Northfield for the annual summer convention. Moody's son, Bill, offered the Kumms the use of a delightful chalet, hidden away from the crowds in a secluded spot in woods high above the main auditorium, with magnificent views of the surrounding countryside. Lucy loved it. It was the perfect place to get on with the writing she had promised Harry, alerting the American and English public to the exploitation of the natives in the Congo. It had become apparent that King Leopold had no intention of fulfilling his promises. In March 1904, Harry had helped to establish the Congo Reform Association, determined to expose the cruelty of Belgian state policy.

On July 2nd she got up at 5am to say goodbye to Karl. He was returning to England to speak at the Keswick Convention, then travelling on to the Sudan, and would probably not see her for at least two years. Karl thought she seemed more positive about his departure than usual, committed to her writing project, talking enthusiastically about the possibility of staying on the States for a year or so, as she had received such a warm welcome. She and the boys accompanied him into the woods a little way, then waved him off.

As she was busy writing on July 18th she felt an excruciating stab of pain in her lower abdomen and began to bleed heavily. A doctor was called to see her the following day. He told she had had a miscarriage, and needed immediate curettage to remove the remainder of the foetus. Lucy refused. She had more important things to do.

On July 22nd, she gave an inspired, impassioned appeal for the Sudan in the packed, great auditorium at the Moody Convention. Mabie later wrote to Geraldine, "although I had heard her in previous years, and knew her gifts in that line, this particular address delighted and astonished me beyond measure. It moved on with telling and dramatic power, as she portrayed to us with the aid of a map beside her, the great Soudan, and Christ knocking at the door of his church to find who of his people were willing to go. It was a marvellous address and will never be forgotten by anyone who heard it." She collapsed almost as soon as she finished speaking and had to be carried home.

On July 27th a second doctor strongly advised surgery, but she still refused. She couldn't believe at 41, that she could be pregnant, until the obvious remains of a baby were expelled a week later.

For a while the pain disappeared and she toiled on with her writing day and night, until August 7th, when the pain returned with a vengeance and she scribbled her final sentence. "It is done. Now they can do what they like," she said to Alice Thompson, the children's nurse.

In Castleton on August 8th Karl received a telegram. "Ill. Operation today. Lucy."

"Shall I come?" he cabled back.

Curetting, a relatively new procedure, was performed in the cottage under ether. The operation revealed that an ectopic pregnancy had ruptured the fallopian tube. How Lucy could have coped with the pain the doctors hardly knew. They just hoped the local peritonitis would not spread to the rest of her body.

She regained consciousness three hours later. Bill Moody offered her his own home, but she was too weak to be moved. The slightest noise disturbed her. It was difficult for Alice Thompson to nurse her and care for the children in a holiday chalet. "Helmy and Karl are just as good as can be," Alice wrote to Geraldine. "We have been mercifully favoured with fine weather so they are able to live outside all day long."

Lucy seemed to rally. "Unnecessary," she cabled Karl in response to his question about whether he should come. "But I hope he does come soon," Alice wrote to one of Lucy's friends.

Karl never came. On August 11th he wrote to Geraldine, "Our darling Lu is seriously ill. When I left her she was perfectly well. In her last letter she says she may have to undergo an operation....You may well understand that I am exceedingly anxious. Do join me in prayer. I am so busy with the mission, and now our little one ill."

By then Lucy's condition had deteriorated alarmingly. The peritonitis had become generalised and there was little more the doctors could do. A further operation offered one possible last chance. For the children's sake she consented. At six o' clock in the evening she calmly set about ordering her affairs. Moody's daughter, Emma Moody Fitt acted as her amanuensis. She dictated one last love letter to the husband she had loved so much, reassuring him that she regretted nothing. He had been the light, the joy, the glory of her life. In her will she left her few possessions, her journals, books, a watch, her sonnets on motherhood and a small sum of money, "enough for the journey home," to Karl and the children.

To Geraldine she bequeathed her most precious treasure—her two boys. She explained to her sister that one day Henry was to have her own big Bible, while her father's Bible, with notes in his hand, was to go to little Karl.

I want him to study Daniel, and Revelation and the Lord's closing prophecies of the three Gospels. If he will do that for Mother's sake, when he is fifteen to sixteen, he will understand afterwards why I wanted him to do so. When he is old enough I should like him to know all the time before he was born I had one prayer, one longing, one hunger—that he should continue Father's prophetic studies and research, and in the later days, when he lives he may perhaps see the restored Jewish state, in those unutterable days, he may understand and tell. He is only four now, but I see, I know he is a seer, a thinker. He will look more into the heart of things; will live, I hope, in those days, and he must understand. I wish he could have access to Father's library when he is old enough to hunger for it, to need to know what it contains.

Henry, my angel boy—he does seem that to me, with just an angel's heart, sympathy and devotion—will want to help the suffering, and put wrongs right. He is more called to that I think; perhaps to be a medical man. But that I do not know. Perhaps rather a preacher. Possibly both. I should like that.

I must not write more. I am very restful, very happy in God. How wonderfully good He has been to us—the boys—how can I thank him? My husband, God's gift, blessed and beloved beyond words; and then you, Father, Harry, Annie, Gershom and darling Janie, whom I have never seen. My love, my heart to all of them,

AND TO MY SONS—MY SOUL.

Good night, dear heart,

Without fear, yours, Lucy.

Finally, she dictated one last message for her boys:

I am leaving you, darlings. I am waiting for you with Jesus—waiting till you come. Don't be lonely, darlings. You will come. It is only a little while. I want you to be brave.

I want you to have Auntie Geraldine for your Mamma. She has no little boys or girls, but she is waiting for you. She will be your Mamma—only very, very much better than I have been. Ask Papa to let her be your Mamma—for a little time at least.

And now—you both belong to him. He will safely lead us home.

Good-bye, darlings—heart's darlings. I am waiting for you—There.

Her last words to the doctors were, "I know that my Redeemer lives." As they were operating, a raging thunderstorm suddenly broke over Northfield, shattering the hush which had descended over the conference centre since Lucy's condition had become known, shaking the great auditorium where many had gathered in silent prayer. According to Alice the lightening "was playing around us all the time." Lucy never fully regained consciousness and died five hours later at 1 am on August 12th—"Missionary Day" at the conference, and her father's seventy first birthday.

In the early morning a brief service was held at the cottage by Dr. Torrey and Dr. Campbell Morgan, two of the most respected preachers in America, who were speaking at the conference. Then the coffin was hoisted gently onto the shoulders of Moody's two sons, Charles Kurthalz, American Director of the Sudan United Mission, Harry Mabie, and two ex-Harley students, and carried carefully down the winding path through the woods to the road below, where a hearse was ready to take it to the Moody to await her husband's arrival.

Henry and Karl were taken to Emma Moody Fitt's house. They desperately wanted to go back to the cottage to find their Mama, but Alice did what she could to make their bereavement as bearable as possible.

That evening thousands packed the great auditorium for a memorial service. Dr. Campbell Morgan and Henry Mabie both spoke briefly, explaining what the Guinness family stood for in the world of missions, "and of the part your dear sister had taken in editorial and other practical labours," Mabie wrote to Geraldine, "and of her absolutely fearless and radiant crossing of the river when she reached it."

Karl arrived ten days later and Lucy was finally laid to rest in the Northfield village cemetery. He described the scene to Geraldine and Howard:

> I am sitting by darling Lu's grave. All is silent except for the rustling of the birch leaves and the sighing of the branches in the breeze. I might be in the dead, silent desert. No human habitation is in sight. To the left the quiet fields of Connecticut valley, before me the wooded hills, and to the right the grey-white graves of the cemetery.
>
> Shadows play on Lu's tombstone as the boughs of the trees bend to and fro. I would like to stay here altogether and always. Oh how she loved me.
>
> Six years and six months we were married but less than a year we actually had together. What a difference that year has made in my life, what a depth of fellowship and soul communion.

Lucy would never have lived a long life. While she was in Germantown her hostess was horrified to find her writing at 10 pm one night, with baby Karl lying in the middle of the bed. "She told me her mother had killed herself with work." I said, "My dear Mrs. Kumm, you are doing just the same." "Yes, I know," she replied."

When her precious manuscript was finally placed in Harry and Annie's hands, they made an appalling discovery. It was far too emotive and politically insensitive to publish, and would have done far more harm than good. It ended up on a shelf at Harley House, gathering dust.

But Lucy's efforts were not in vain. The mission she worked so hard to set up is known now as "Crosslinks," and still provides support for the indigenous African church. She would be heartbroken to see the suffering and exploitation of the Sudanese Christians today, for whom she gave her all, yet heartened too by their steadfastness and courage.

5

Geraldine and Howard were waiting at the Liverpool docks when Karl arrived back in England with the children.

> Never shall I forget Karl's face as he came down the long flight of steps by which they had to cross from the vessel to the landing stage, carrying the little one in his arms and leading Henry by the hand. The children were pale and tired with being up so late and looked almost as pale and wan and he did and their whole dress and appearance so pitifully told the lack of a mother's care.

They went together to Castleton to sort out the remainder of Lucy's personal belongings. Geraldine was impressed at the way Karl devoted himself to his children. "They love him and cling to him in a most beautiful way and it is a great comfort to see how thoroughly he understands and how well he can manage them."

It was a rude awakening when she realised that Karl had no intention of leaving the boys with her. It pained her most of all that Lucy's last wishes were not to be fulfilled, but Howard in his usual wise way urged her to keep quiet and wait. An argument at this stage would only hurt the children. After all, Karl was their father. The Taylors bowed to his wishes and left for Switzerland, where Geraldine intended to write an epic biography of her father-in-law.

Worried at leaving his children with his wife's overpowering relatives, Karl asked his sister, Amanda, to come from Germany. Amanda spoke no English, had no control over the children, and was terribly homesick. As soon as she heard that their mother was ill, she insisted on returning to Germany. Karl was due to speak at a huge convention in the United States. He had no alternative but to send an urgent telegram to Switzerland. Howard set off at once to collect the boys.

Howard, kind and considerate, loving and gentle, was the perfect father, but the responsibility of motherhood after all these years made Geraldine nervous. She and Howard were approaching fifty, and the boys were only four and six. "But I loved them just as I had loved Phoebe and Agnes—there was something special about it," she said later.

One day the boys arrived home full of a story they had heard about a mother who had left her baby on a bus. "Do you think a mother could forget a baby like that?" she asked them, intending to teach them about God's love from the verse in the Old Testament which said, "Even a mother may forget, but I will not forget you." But little Henry looked up at her, with such love and trust in his eyes, and said, "I don't know if a mother could, but I'm sure an auntie-mother couldn't," that she somehow she entirely forgot the moral of the story.

She talked to them about Lucy all the time, determined they would never forget her. Small as they were, they remembered her playing the piano. Everyone always did.

6

Henry Grattan received the news of his beloved Lucy's death a month after the birth of his son, John. "I shall never forget his tearless grief as he read the cabled message of sorrow," Grace noted in her journal.

He went for a walk alone along the shore of a quiet bay in New South Wales, and sat for some time on the sands listening to the mournful roar of the ocean. The wave of grief finally burst and he began to weep uncontrollably. Suddenly, he became aware of the gentle pressure of a hand on his shoulder. Raising his head, he found himself looking up into the radiant, wrinkled face of an old Aborigine woman. In a strange, halting accent, she whispered, "Let not your heart be troubled, neither let it be afraid...in my father's house are many mansions." He turned away from her momentarily, allowing the familiar words to sink in, and when he looked up again, she had vanished without trace. For the rest of his life he would wonder who she was and where she had come from, and whether she was not some angelic visitation.

The arrival of little John meant that Henry and Grace's companionship could never be quite as unbroken again. Following an itinerant preacher was no life for a young mother, and Henry frequently had to travel on alone, leaving Grace in lodgings, returning to her as often as he could.

In South Africa, he preached to huge mixed black and white congregations from the seat of an open carriage, but this was little compensation for the separation. Knowing their time together must inevitably be short made it harder. "I seem to miss you most when there is something beautiful to see or hear or tell! I wish I could find words strong and tender enough to tell how much I love you!"

In the end the preaching tour barely paid the bills and they were both more than glad to go home. When they finally reached England in February 1908, Dr. and Mrs. Taylor, Mrs. Harry Guinness and her daughter were waiting for them, along with the press. Grace was now accustomed to the fact that Henry was a source of public interest wherever he went, but couldn't stomach, "the newspaper reporter, with his photographic apparatus, insisting on getting the travellers' impressions of the world in a ten-minute interview." Nor, after five years, could she come quite to terms with "the modern innovations of motor traffic."

Grace was pregnant again, so they settled for a time in St. Leonards, where their second son, Paul Ambrose was born, "a child of energy and purpose, whose vivacious temperament helpfully balances the quiet, more meditative tendencies of his elder brother," Grace noted. At seventy-two Henry Grattan was the proud father of two small boys. His joy was complete. He bought a house in Bath and for the first time settled down with his young family to a life of tranquil domesticity.

While he was abroad, Henry Grattan had acquired four new grandchildren. Whitfield and Janie had a daughter, Isabel, known as Joy, in 1906, and a son, Henry Whitfield in April 1908, a month before Paul was born. Harry and Annie's family had also continued to grow. Since the birth of their third child in Tasmania, there had been seven more, Alexander Fitzgerald in 1893, Margaret, known as Meg, in 1896, who died shortly before her second birthday, Victor Noel in 1898, Ruth Eileen in 1900, Gordon Meyer in 1902, and Howard Wyndham in 1903. By the time Robert Desmond appeared in 1905 his eldest sister Gene was seventeen.

In 1907 Gene accompanied her father to Peru and the book she wrote, illustrated with her father's photographs, was an instant best-seller, making her a popular, if precocious, travel writer.

Since 1904 Harry had worked tirelessly for the Congo Reform Association, speaking all over the country, illustrating his lectures with stomach-churning lantern slides and visual aids such as a chicotte, a whip made of hippopotamus hide, used to beat to death natives who had not collected enough rubber.

He sent documentation to the Foreign Secretary, Lord Lansdowne, went back to see King Leopold twice, and in 1907, on his way to Peru with Gene, went to the USA to demand an interview with the President, Theodore Roosevelt. Harry reminded Roosevelt that since America was the first country to recognise Belgian supremacy in the Congo, the President had a duty to ensure the constitution was upheld.

Finally, in 1909, King Leopold died and his successor, King Albert, unable to resist the strength of public protest any longer, instituted immediate reforms. In 1912 the Congo Reform Association had the satisfaction of dissolving itself, its aims and objectives fully achieved.

Though his doctor warned against it, Harry desperately wanted to see the results of his campaign for himself. Pushing himself beyond his physical limit had turned a strong, athletic young man into a rather worn and ailing reflection of his former self in middle age. He went to the Congo anyway in April 1910, but three months later, was laid low by a mysterious tropical disease and was forced to return home. But three months was enough. "Speaking to an exceedingly intelligent native at Stanley Pool the other day, I asked him his feelings in regard to recent changes at Leopoldville. His reply was unhesitating. "The old, bad times are past, and to-day we are free!"

CHAPTER FOURTEEN
1910-1918

1

Retirement never entered Henry Grattan's head. Preachers did not retire and the demands on him, at 72, were almost as great as they had ever been. Besides, the new century had heralded many exciting new inventions and developments. There was still so much he wanted to do and see, wonderful exhibitions to visit, books he intended to write. His grandchildren found him a stimulating, charming companion. With his thick mane of white hair swept off his high forehead, and the small moustache he had taken to wearing, he cut an impressive figure in his dark frockcoat and high winged collar. His marriage seemed to have endowed him with eternal youth.

From time to time Grace tried to remonstrate with him. She begged him not to overdo things, and encouraged him to paint, but despite his obvious talent, he was incorrigible. One letter began, "You will see from above address that I am at Cliff." Grace had no idea he planned to go up to Derbyshire and had waited up for him until 3 am. After enthusing about the wonderful improvements made to his old home by the new owners, he apologised profusely for causing her such anxiety and promised faithfully to wire her about his movements in future. Henry was still, it would appear, easily distracted from his domestic responsibilities.

Throughout 1909 speaking invitations continued to pour in. He could still pack the St. James Hall in London, as well as an overflow in the Polytechnic, to capacity. Grace had no desire to inhibit Henry in any way, but was very aware of the strain it placed upon him.

He depended on Grace entirely. Separation became an increasing trial. He had always been dreamy, but his absentmindedness was becoming hazardous. On one occasion, taking a train journey with a young couple and a baby, he failed to see the precious bundle his friends had temporarily deposited on the carriage seat. Henry, his thoughts on higher matters, lifted his coat-tails and was about to lower himself onto their little daughter. They caught his arm just in time. In years to come, whenever the mother recounted the story, she would look at her daughter, and say with a sigh, "It would have been a heavenly end for her!" [1]

Following a very popular series of Advent lectures on the Second Coming of Christ, delivered in St. James' Church, Bath, which were reported in detail in the *Bath Herald*, the doctors warned Henry that his heart was severely overstrained. If he continued to tax himself in this way it would prove fatal. Henry had no regrets for himself that his public ministry had cost him his health, but realised that for Grace's sake and the boys he must cancel all engagements for the following year.

One cold, wet night in January 1910 he set out alone to fulfil an obligation to the postman who had begged him to go to his house to say a few words to a gathering of his friends and relatives. Grace was loath to let him go, but he insisted. A promise was a promise, even to the postman. He caught a severe chill which quickly turned to pleurisy and pericarditis.

Though in intense pain, and unable to lie down, he remained as mentally alert as ever. Grace couldn't bear to seem him so weak, but he kept saying to her, "Gracie, can I sink through a rock?"

Howard and Geraldine, Henry and Little Karl Kumm moved to England to be near him, renting a house in Bath. It was to Geraldine that Henry entrusted the care of his beloved wife and two little boys. "What more fitting," he said to Grace, "that my only daughter should be a guardian to you and the children. You cannot find a better friend than you would have in Geraldine. She is like me. I was very like her as a younger man and I am glad she loves my darling boys, I want her to be an influence in their lives."

On the evening of June 20th he had a long discussion with Geraldine about the World Missionary Conference meeting at that very moment in Edinburgh under the leadership of his old friend and student, John R. Mott. It was the first large international, truly ecumenical conference of its kind, and would form the basis of the World Council of Churches. Both father and daughter had dreamed of such an event and were excited about its potential. As she was about to leave the room Geraldine turned back to her father and was struck by his face. As he smiled back at her in the evening light, it almost seemed transfigured.

Later that evening Grace noted in her diary:

We wheeled the invalid couch from the drawing-room, where he was during the seventeen weeks illness and as he spoke to me he was facing that lovely extensive view over the city of Bath which he loved to see from his study window. He smiled at me and said, "I am too weak to talk, but have strength enough to meditate. I think over the history of the world, the history of redemption, the progress of Christ's kingdom, the important issues of this great Missionary Conference at Edinburgh. Then of our own missionary work in the world and all that has grown out of it, work in America, on the Continent, in China and Africa—and I think of what my dear ones have been enabled to do, and of my own life with its shortcomings."

Someone came into the room, and he still smiled that beautiful smile, which so often illuminated his face; and throughout the day we noticed it, the light of his soul shining through. It was the last time we were alone together.

On June 21st, 1910 she wrote: "This beautiful midsummer day my precious Henry passed peacefully and quietly to rest at 10.45 this morning. I was not with him at the end, nor was Geraldine. Strange after we had been with him so constantly. It seemed as if we were not to say goodbye."

Howard alone had been with his father-in-law when he died. He said that Henry had suddenly sat bolt upright in bed and with a rapturous expression on his face, raised his arms to heaven. He kept them raised for some time. Given the fact that he had been too weak to lift them at all the previous day, this was little short of a miracle. Then he let them fall, lay back on the pillow and was gone.

Henry Grattan Guinness died, as he had been born, in the year of Halley's Comet, highly significant for someone who had spent so much of his life studying the signs in the heavens.

Grace wired the Edinburgh Missionary Conference with the news, and Dr. Mott read the telegram to the vast audience assembled in the main auditorium. Almost every delegate there could claim that Dr. Grattan Guinness' ministry had touched their lives in some way or another. The entire congregation rose spontaneously to its feet, and, after a minute's silence, with a volume that almost shook the building, sang, "For all the saints who from their labours rest."

Like Barnardo and many of his nonconformist, evangelical contemporaries, Henry had become an Anglican in old age. After a service in St. James' Church, where he had recently delivered his series of Advent lectures, Henry Grattan Guinness was buried in the Abbey Cemetery overlooking the city of Bath, his grave sheltered by a large, solitary copper beech tree.

Obituaries appeared in *The Times*, *The Daily Express*, *The Daily Telegraph*, *The Westminster Gazette*, *The Yorkshire Post* and *The Sheffield Telegraph* as well as in many other local and religious newspapers. They described his distinguished career as a writer, preacher and founder of missions. Some referred to his brewing connections and to the old story of how his mother's first husband had been killed in a dual at the hands of Daniel O'Connell. Many harked back fifty years to the days when he had preached to thousands from an open carriage in Northern Ireland. All paid tribute to his breadth of vision and achievement. Along with Spurgeon and Moody he was hailed as one of the three greatest preachers of the nineteenth century.

The doctor's commanding figure will no longer be seen about Bath, which he made his residence for the last two years or more, and Bath will be the poorer, for Dr. Guinness was a man of intensely human and wide sympathies, a member of all churches. One who knew him well has described him as a great thinker, a powerful writer and forceful preacher, one who gave up his life to missionary work and found in it the greatest happiness. [68]

Despite the simplicity of his lifestyle Henry Grattan Guinness was, nonetheless, a quintessential Guinness. He had all the drive, industry, energy, initiative, flair and philanthropy of his brewing and banking cousins. But he also had extraordinary personal charisma and presence.

Unlike Sir Benjamin Lee, who was praised when he died in 1968 for the work he had carried out at St. Patrick's Cathedral, "a temple on whose every stone, on whose every shaft and cornice, on whose every embellishment his nature is inscribed," Henry Grattan never built a monument in his own memory—unless St. Sava's in Belgrade can be counted.

In 1895, Francis Harford Mackenzie, missionary, philanthropist and bachelor, converted in his youth by Henry Grattan in Paris, left his old mentor his entire estate, consisting of 12,000 square metres of land in the centre of the city. The land had particular significance for the Serbian Orthodox Church, for it was there on top of Vracar Hill in 1595 that the Turks publicly burned the relics of St. Sava, Serbia's patron saint. In 1895 the Serbians started a fund-raising drive to build a cathedral on the spot, and in 1898, to enable them to do so, Henry Grattan Guinness gave them the land. In the cathedral, which is not yet complete, the name "Henrikh Gratan Gines" is inscribed in cyrillic gold letters on a marble plaque. [69]

No one would have been more surprised at the dedication than Henry Grattan himself, for he gave away his earthly belongings as easily as he had disposed of his Guinness legacy. When Cliff became a financial burden he let it go. His only real treasure there, the eight-inch diameter telescope, was transported back to Harley for the use of the students.

A simple grey stone was erected over his grave. On one side Grace had Fanny's name inscribed. The other side she left blank for herself. In later years, looking back, she saw that it was fitting that there had been no formal farewell between them. For Henry, the after-life was a vivid reality, divided from this world by such a tenuous thread that death involved no real separation for those who truly loved each other.

Grace was 32 when Henry died. She lived a further 57 years, and did not marry again. He left her £4,000, the most money he had personally possessed in his entire life, but not enough to keep her and the two boys. Unlike many middle-class women of her day she went out to work as a school bursar so that she could support herself and the children. With her thick hair swept up into a bun, curls escaping rakishly down a long and elegant neck, she attracted a great deal of masculine admiration—in vain. In seven years Henry had provided her with enough romance and passion to last the rest of her 89 years.[70]

In old age she would sit ramrod straight, a cameo at her throat, reading his poems and letters over and over again. As she did so her face would light up and she would be a young woman once more, deeply in love with the only man who had never really left her. "Even now," he once wrote, "softly falls the whispers of the departed, as they stand in the cloudless light on the other side of death's dark portal, saying, "We wait for you here—we love you still."

2.

With their father gone, Harry and Geraldine feared the next generation of cousins would have little to bring them together and decided to recreate the idyllic summers at Cliff, renting a large house in Newquay for the entire month of August. In the summer of 1912 everyone was there—Harry, now the patriarch, Annie, as efficient as ever, organising the event, their nine children and first grandchild, Karis, daughter of Gene, who was married to Ian Mackenzie, the son of her parents' closest friends; Grace, by far the most liberated of the party, her skirt tucked into her waistband and hair streaming down her back as she paddled with her two boys; Whitfield and Janie on furlough from China with their three children, Joy, Henry and little Mary Geraldine, known by her Chinese name, Pearl; Howard and Geraldine with Henry and Karl; Karl Kumm himself with his new bride, a charming, petite Australian called Gertrude Cato.

The news of Karl's marriage had been a shock. A letter containing the details of his engagement to Gertrude had never arrived. The first Howard and Geraldine knew of it was in a telegram which read simply, "We are to be married at once, and are coming home via the United States." Karl wanted his boys back.

Geraldine was devastated. After six years how could she hand her boys over to a complete stranger? Yet her only real choice was to relinquish them joyfully or reluctantly. The latter, Howard reminded her, would only cause pain all round. She must trust that Karl would choose a good mother for his children and prepare them to love and welcome her.

Geraldine could be prim, she could be straight-laced, but she was never petty or small-minded. The children had been hers—but only for a time. There was no subtle attempt to hold onto them, no malicious or underhand remarks which might divide the children's loyalty. She wanted only the best for them and her total lack of self-interest enabled them to cope with a very unsettling situation.

Karl and Gertrude had in fact booked ticket on the Titanic, but several days before they were due to sail, Karl developed appendicitis and was forced to stay in the USA for urgent surgery. When the day of their arrival finally dawned, Howard and Geraldine took the two boys down the station to meet their new stepmother. Geraldine loved her from the moment she saw her. She was like Lucy, but smaller, daintier, and prettier. But handing over her precious boys was the hardest thing she had ever had to do. "The boys were my very soul," she said later to her niece, Joy.[71] "When I parted from them something died within me. There is a peculiar joy in having children of your own. You live outside yourself, and when it is cut off, you are very solitary. It is different to parting from anyone else." Only Howard fully understood how she felt, for he shared her pain.

The final separation was postponed by the family holiday in Newquay. The children were not aware of any tension amongst the adults despite the almost ceaseless rain. There were still games, walks and endless real-life tales of hair-raising adventures in far away places. Geraldine, wisely, sublimated her feelings by cultivating close relationships with her two little half-brothers and other nephews. Gordon, one of Harry's three youngest sons, adopted her completely and decided that he too would be a missionary one day. Time proved him wrong, though he did become one of the leading evangelical clergymen of his day and a canon of Winchester Cathedral. Desmond, Harry's youngest son, half-terrified by Whitfield's tales of the Boxer uprising decided he would never go anywhere near China. Time proved him wrong too.

Time, however, also proved Lucy right. Henry, and little Karl, coyly cementing their relationship with their new mother would grow up to fulfil her prophetic instincts, Henry as a physician specialising in research into Yaws' Disease, Karl as an Episcopalian minister. Of the sixteen cousins playing together in the house at Newquay, two would become missionaries in China and six would be ordained in the Anglican ministry. With the twentieth century there no sign of any tailing off of the clerical and missionary calling in the Guinness dynasty.

But the world in which the young cousins would fulfil their destiny would be very different to the secure and tranquil world of Newquay in the summer of 1912. Within two years the Great War would bulldoze every remaining nineteenth century value, leaving a less sympathetic environment for Christian ministry in its wake.

The Harley Empire which had started to crumble with the handing over of Cliff, was already on the point of collapse. It was as well Harry had his Congo triumph to sustain him through a time of immense financial uncertainty. Although Harley's annual income had risen, most of it went to the Regions Beyond Missionary Union not to Harley College, to ever-increasing expenditure in the Congo, Peru, Behar and Argentina.

Furthermore the grounds had been leased from London County Council on condition they build a new college by 1908. The condition was met, but at a price. The last few students would always remember his announcement that the new college would have to be sold to cover outstanding debts. "Never get into debt," he warned them sadly. He had tried to listen carefully to what God wanted him to do, but felt he must have misheard.

The new college was temporarily leased to the London Hospital as a nurses' home and Harry and Annie moved their family into a large, rambling house in Sydenham. The last few students moved into the house they vacated, but when war broke out they volunteered and classes finally came to an end. Harley House, home of the Grattan Guinnesses for half a century, was requisitioned as a home for Belgian refugees. Doric Lodge, the deaconesses' residence, and Bromley Hall, the maternity home were also shut down.

Annie was more philosophical than her husband. In the end the war, not their debts, swept the remains of the London Harley empire away. Meanwhile, she and Harry had to face a sickening crisis even nearer to home. It had become obvious that Gene's six year marriage to the son of their closest friends was over. Divorce was anathema, and this was the first in the family—and it was on the missionary, not the brewing or banking side. An agreement was reached that their little granddaughter would stay with her father, while the new baby would stay with Gene, and a veil drawn over the whole affair.

Harry had never been well since his return from the Congo five years earlier. Some unknown tropical disease was slowly destroyed his internal organs. When told that he was terminally ill, he accepted the news quietly. "Still young—life has been short," he said, "I might have had another thirty years."

He died in the early morning of May 26th 1915. After the funeral Annie disappeared for three days, then emerged from her room, just as suddenly, in long black widow's weeds, her mourning done, ready to raise the rest of her family alone.

3.

The Grattans were only one of the three branches of the Guinness family to lose a patriarch in the year 1915. Lord Ardilaun had died on January 20th, aged 74, not as deeply lamented in the land of his birth as he might have been, had his resistance to Home Rule not been quite so obsessive.

Lord Ardilaun's will, drawn up in 1902, left most of his land to Lord Iveagh, "fearing that the care of my estates would impose too much upon my wife." Nonetheless, upon his death, Lady Olive inherited their London house in Carlton Terrace, the Dublin house in St. Stephen's Green, and St. Anne's, Clontarf. She sold the Carlton Terrace house at once to Lady Iveagh's cousin, Benjamin Seymour Guinness of Guinness Mahon, and retired to eke out her days in her beloved Ireland.

At her salon in St. Stephen's Green in Dublin she entertained the cream of artistic society during the particularly tense era between the Easter Uprising of 1916 and the civil war of 1918. Officers from the castle rubbed shoulders with leading members of Sinn Fein, and W.B. Yeats read his poetry, leaving the entire company wildly enthusiastic, but completely bewildered.

When Dodo became the chief benefactress of the Adelaide Hospital, Lady Ardilaun took on the Mercer Charity Hospital, visiting the patients regularly, sitting at the end of a bed, regaling them with tales of her glorious past. It was a time when Sinn Fein was in the habit of stealing cars. Looking out of the window of an upstairs ward, Olive Ardilaun observed that she couldn't see hers. "What should we do if it has been taken?" she asked.

"But, my lady, the tram passes your gate," piped up an old man from one of the beds.

"I've never been in a tram," she replied, causing a sensation on the ward.

"How would you be going then?" the patients asked her, and she explained that she had always had a coach, a head coachman, horses, and a reserved carriage on the train if she had to travel as far as London.

For most of the patients it seemed unreal, a fairy tale, and they begged her to tell them more, which she did, on each successive visit, with increasing Irish verve.

"Tell us, my lady, did you ever see the King?"

She said she had, at various garden parties and dinner parties. She had attended the jubilee, and two coronations.

The patients were always loathe to let her go. "Did you ever see Queen Victoria?"

"Yes, of course, often in London; but the old Queen didn't treat Ireland too well. When she was young she and the Prince Consort came and stayed with my mother's people at Muckross, and about fifty years later she came a gain and paid me an afternoon visit."

"Did you give her a cup of tea?"

Olive laughed. "Yes, and a bunch of flowers."

"She'd like a cup of tea as well as any old woman, wouldn't she?"[72]

Unlike future generations of Guinnesses, Lady Ardilaun was a true blue aristocrat, never self conscious about status or wealth, though it did cramp her style at times. "I should have enjoyed doing some actual work," she once said, "But it wasn't possible." Her strength was her ability to accept the limitations of her position, while using its possibilities to their full potential, as imaginatively as she knew how. Wealth brought responsibility and she took that seriously to the end of her life. She lived another ten years after the death of her husband, and with her passing the Ardilaun peerage became extinct.

4.

The war which spelt the end of the Harley College empire did not spare the gracious world of Elveden. For almost three decades to 1914, despite two changes in monarchy, the routine there continued much as it had always done. The new King George V regarded Lord Iveagh as his unofficial advisor in all matters relating to Ireland, his escort when he went to Dublin with Queen Mary in 1911, and saw the Guinness Trust housing project and Lady Iveagh's new nursery and play centre.

Elveden had become the glamorous, glittering focal point of an extended family network, a coveted venue for a new young generation of Guinness cousins intent on being seen by the rich and important, on making their way in society. "It was a well-ordered, formal life, leisurely but disciplined, regulated by the shooting season and untroubled by any suspicion of its essential impermanence. Looking back on it now, it seems like one long summer—the last summer but endlessly drawn out." [73]

It could not last indefinitely. Events outside Lord Iveagh's control began to encroach upon the ordered world he had created. Lady Iveagh became increasingly incapacitated. At times she seemed well and in her right mind, but those times became less frequent as her early dementia increased. The depth of Edward Cecil's pain and embarrassment can be gauged from the fact that it was the family's best kept secret. No one was ever allowed to speak of it. Dodo was left to her twilight world in a private wing, largely content, playing games of hide and seek with the maids and valets.

In the end political rather than personal circumstances brought Elveden to a standstill. In 1914 many of the estate workers volunteered and went to the front. The shooting parties ceased and were never revived. Nor was the lavish entertaining. When Lady Iveagh died in 1916 the great era was almost over. The few staff left rattled around like ghosts of former days. Eventually, most of the rooms were closed, and the furniture covered in dust sheets. Elveden, the epitome of all that was serene and self-confident about Edwardian England, had fallen asleep.

5.

London, June, 1917. General Sir Beauvoir de Lisle, KCB, KCMG, DSO, on leave for ten days from his command in the trenches, is reading *the Times* over breakfast when an announcement catches his eye. His old friend, Field Marshall Sir Edmund Allenby has been appointed Commander-in-Chief of His Majesty's forces in the Middle East.

The British intention was to establish supremacy in all territory around the Suez Canal, and Allenby's brief was to deliver the Holy Land from a hundred years of domination by the now crumbling Ottoman Empire. Those who thought it a relatively simple task after the conquest of the Sinai Peninsula had been forced to change their minds. With German support the Turks held on with the iron grip of a drowning man. The Allies had fought a long and bitter campaign under Sir Archibald Murray, suffering a humiliating defeat at Gaza.

Few would envy Allenby his appointment, or rush to congratulate him, but Beauvoir de Lisle has a rather different perspective and decides to see the new Commander. He dresses quickly and takes a cab to the Grosvenor Hotel where Allenby is staying. This is how he later described their conversation.[74]

No cause for congratulation," Allenby said in his gruff way. "Had to give up a jolly fine army to take over a rotten show. Archie Murray is a good man and if he could not succeed, I don't see how I can."

"My dear Allenby," I replied, "you are on velvet. You may make all the mistakes in tactics or strategy, but nothing can prevent you from being in Jerusalem by the 31st December."

"How do you make that out?" he asked.

I told him of the book *Light For the Last Days* by Dr. Grattan Guinness in 1886, in which he had stated that the interpretation of the three prophecies in Daniel, Ezekiel and Revelation all pointed to the same year, 1917, as the end of the Gentile times, a period of 1260 years—Time, times and a half a time. "At the same time," I added, "don't forget your big guns."

Beauvoir de Lisle had said his farewells and was at the door, when a sudden thought occurred to him and he turned back. "When you get to Jerusalem, Allenby, I hope you will not ride in state, for that is reserved in the future for One higher than you."

The significance of the year 1917 had not passed unnoticed in the national press. In January, at the advent of the year, a correspondent in the *Daily Mail* reminded readers that Henry Grattan Guinness had written, "There can be no doubt that those who live to see this year will have reached one of the most important, perhaps momentous, of these terminal years of crisis."

Light for the Last Days was reissued for the sixteenth time in July and had to be reprinted in August. Guinness' words provided a glimmer of hope in the fourth year of a disheartening world war.

In his lifetime Henry Grattan knew that the politician, Arthur Balfour, had read his books. Balfour, Foreign Secretary in 1917, had also been a regular guest at Elveden once Rupert was helping to put the guest list together. On November 2nd he signed a historic Declaration:

> His Majesty's Government views with favour the establishment in
> Palestine of a National Home for the Jewish people, and will use
> their best endeavours to facilitate the achievement of this object,
> it being clearly understood that nothing shall be done which may
> prejudice the civil and religious rights of the existing non-Jewish
> communities in Palestine.

On December 11th Sir Edmund Allenby rode at the head of his victorious troops right up to the gates of Jerusalem. Then he stopped, got down from his horse, and holding her by the bridle, walked into the Holy City.

Geraldine Guinness Taylor opened her Bible and read to her 14-year old nephew, Gordon, words he never forgot: Therefore say to the house of Israel, "Thus says the Lord God, it is not for your sake, O house of Israel, that I am about to act, but for the sake of my holy name. For I will take you from the nations, and gather you from all the countries, and bring you into your own land."

With her dying words Lucy Guinness Kumm had said her boys would live to see, "those unutterable days," and she was right. But Henry Grattan Guinness had alluded to an even later date. The last, scribbled in pencil beneath the final paragraph of the book of Ezekiel in his large black Bible, was 1948.

CHAPTER FIFTEEN
1918-2000

1

On May 14th 1948, sitting in her armchair in a room in the retirement home where she had lived since her stroke, three years earlier, Geraldine Taylor heard on the wireless that the independent Jewish State of Israel had been born. She was eighty five and it seemed she had waited all her life for this. She picked up her pen and wrote to her niece, Joy, "From a full heart words will hardly come this morning; yet I long to write to you. It is like trying to express the inexpressible."

This was her Nunc Dimittis. She was ready now to meet her maker.

Howard's death in 1947 had been a terrible blow. He had been devoted to her for over seventy years. Few women could lay claim to such a love. She missed him terribly, but couldn't wish him back, for the man who had always been her lifeboat had suffered with intense depression at the end. "Now, he seems nearer, really, you know, than before," she admitted to Joy, "It's more like the old relationship. All the weakness and weariness is gone, and there is the same bright, cheery, loving spirit one had come to depend on so much. There is the consciousness that he is there, waiting, nearer, dearer than in far years."

Their last thirty years had been far from uneventful. In fact, for a rather sedate couple in late middle age, Howard and Geraldine's escapades were positively hair-raising. One particular adventure, which necessitated major diplomatic negotiations, captured the newspaper headlines for weeks.

In 1919, after the publication of Geraldine's hugely successful biography of Hudson Taylor, the China Inland Mission arranged for her to go on a lengthy tour encouraging missionaries in the furthest outposts of China. In three years she and Howard covered thousands of miles in carts and sedan chairs. Often, they rose before dawn, and journeyed long after dusk, stopping off in dozens of uncomfortable, vermin-infested inns. It was a punishing existence, their difficulties compounded by the fact that Howard was now so deaf he heard little without the use of an ear trumpet.

Their first Christmas was spent with Whitfield and Janie in Kaifeng. In her journal she wrote, "No notes. I was absorbed in dear little Mary's life story." Whitfield's youngest daughter, her namesake, Mary Geraldine, had died the previous year at the age of nine. The beautiful little girl with the mass of golden curls, whose Chinese name was Pearl, had shown a simple, but total trust in God throughout her ordeal, and her aunt decided to record her story for posterity. She had never written a children's book before, but the response to "Pearl's Secret" was overwhelming. It was translated into more languages than any of her other books, and thousands of young readers from all over the world wrote to tell her how much the book had meant to them.

The Christmas of 1920 was harrowing for both of them. They were staying in Lanchow, very close to a huge earthquake that cost 200,000 people their lives. Thousands more were left homeless in bitter winter weather, their possessions swept away by the floods which followed the dereliction. For five months Geraldine and Howard tirelessly helped with relief and salvage work, but that was merely a prologue to what was to come. They finally set off south through brigand-infested mountains to the next missionary outpost, but before they got very far, were ambushed and taken hostage. The brigands only wanted Howard, but Geraldine insisted they take her too, as Howard was too deaf to understand what was going on.

For two days they were held at the brigands' headquarters to await the arrival of the leader, P'u Kiang-kuin. There was little food and they were forced to sleep on the ground at night without any covering to keep out the penetrating cold, but otherwise, they were not harshly treated.

When P'u arrived on their second day in captivity, he made it clear that he would kill them if government troops attacked his men, but release them if his terms were met. The next day Geraldine was sent on alone to Yunnanfu to negotiate. Parting from Howard was one of the hardest things she had ever had to do. Blinded by tears, she kissed him goodbye, for the last time for all she knew.

For five weeks Geraldine worked tirelessly for his release, begging local officials to take action, but they remained unmoved. Money, it appeared, was the only way to melt their hearts, but Geraldine had nothing to bribe them with. Her sympathy for the bandits grew by the minute. The British Consulate tried to help, but its powers did not extend to a dispute between a Chinese provincial government and its outlaws. The British newspapers covered the story in full and demanded action—to no avail.

Eventually, to her relief, a letter from Howard got through. She could hardly believe her eyes. He urged her not to exaggerate his difficulties. Opium fumes, vermin, the suspense and monotony, and not being able to hear his possible fate were all very trying, but on the other hand, open air life and a compulsory diet had much improved his figure and he had never enjoyed such rugged health in his life. The lifeboat, it appears, was as unsinkable as ever.

Then suddenly, China's highly volatile political situation changed overnight, turning Howard into redundant captive—but not before he had helped P'u become a follower of Christ. Back home, Geraldine wove their experience into a little booklet called, *With P'u and the Brigands*, a sympathetic portrait of a group of pathetic young rebels who were simply looking for something better.

Geraldine sensed that she had said a last farewell to her beloved China. She poured out her sorrow for the people in a longer, more detailed account of those three years, *The Call of China's Great North West*. Reading it made her nephew, Desmond Guinness, decide to follow in her footsteps.

2

Life for Harry's family changed dramatically after the First World War. Domestic help was hard to come by and Annie, who was nearly fifty, took up cooking for the first time—with varying degrees of success. The three youngest boys, Gordon, Howard and Desmond, greeted her scones with demands for a hatchet, and fed her semolina to the chickens. Keeping livestock, providing shelter for several missionary children, and unsuccessful attempts to cultivate a plot of spare land at the back of the house to feed them all, were Annie's lot in life. She was also the first woman in Upper Norwood to attach a 1□ horsepower motor to the back of her bicycle so that she could deliver home-made soup to a larger number of housebound elderly neighbours.

The boys had been introduced to the Church of England when they first moved away from Harley House, simply because Christchurch, Upper Norwood had a reputation for the best preaching in the area, and preaching was everything. Annie told the boys their grandfather had been used to convert thousands, their father hundreds. The achievement of their forefathers was an unspoken expectation hanging over their heads throughout their adult lives.

Unlike their older brothers and sisters who had lived through the Great War and struggled to find any faith until late in life, all three boys were profoundly influenced by Crusader Boys Clubs, and along with friends who became Christians at the same time—Max Warren, Brian Green and Stafford Wright—became leading evangelical clergymen in the 1940s and 50s.

But the world in which they exercised their ministry was far less sympathetic than their father's or grandfather's. The last flickers of religious revival were finally doused by a blanket of post-war scepticism. Robust evangelicalism with its absolute certainties was no longer fashionable. Liberal theology was in the ascendancy—particularly in the Church of England, and Gordon, Howard and Desmond often found themselves with their backs against the wall, rather than enjoying the kind of acclaim their grandfather had known.

Nonetheless each made their own mark. Gordon established a reputation for taking on dwindling congregations and building them into the most vibrant in the city. Howard, who was also an outstanding preacher, was sent by his fellow London University students to Canada in 1928 to form a Christian student movement like the British Inter-Varsity Fellowship. He went on to pioneer evangelical student movements in Australia and New Zealand and had a powerful influence on students throughout the world.

That Desmond, her youngest son, had taken up the call to China was a source of immense satisfaction to Annie. Now that one of her children was a missionary abroad, she said, she would not be ashamed to meet her maker. She died in 1933, shortly after his departure.

The political situation in China had been volatile since the turn of the century. Whitfield had been responsible for building a hospital in Kaifeng, the first in the Honan region. In the 1920s, when law and order broke down yet again, and the wards were filled with the wounded and dying, he and Janie were often driven to the limit of their resources. "Janie wondered at a patient's lack of interest in her new-born baby," he wrote to his sister in America. It was a bandit baby.

In 1926, he southern army descended on the northern troops, leaving Honan in the middle, like a walnut in a nutcracker. Despite the increasing tension in the province, Whitfield remained his old self, calm and unruffled, playing his violin for his medical students to help them relax, enjoying an occasional game of golf or chess. But though he missed them terribly, he was very relieved that both the children, Henry and Joy, were at school and safely out of the country.

Early in 1927 gunfire could be heard in the distance, and the wounded began to arrive in droves. When there was no more room at the hospital, he nursed patients in his own home. At the same time, he worked hard to keep up the spirits of the staff. On February 6th, in his daily letter to his children, he wrote:

> This afternoon I took the old jumping pole and taught the students to do the high jump, or rather pole jump. They greatly enjoyed the fun. I drew the line for myself at a little over six feet, as I am too old now, 58 in April! But I remember doing eight feet six at Cliff years ago.[75]

One night a man arrived at his door obviously suffering from typhoid fever. It was a freezing night and he couldn't turn anyone away, but nor could he risk an epidemic. A fellow missionary offered to prepare a hut nearby, and Whitfield stipulated that he alone would take care of the patient.

By the time the order to evacuate reached Kaifeng, Whitfield was seriously ill with typhoid. With Janie at his side, he travelled by train on a camp bed for two days through the war torn state, becoming increasingly feverish and confused. When they finally reached the Union Medical College in Peking on April 8th, the first day of Holy Week, Whitfield had slipped into a coma. Janie wrote in her diary:

> My heart is breaking with sorrow, but full of peace. I stand by his side and praise God for all the love of these twenty two years. Such perfect happiness. There is peace in this little room and Whitfield is too ill to feel any pain...He put his hand between mine this forenoon.

He died on April 12th at the age of 58, and was buried on Easter Day in the English cemetery in Peking.

Geraldine was now the only surviving child of Henry Grattan and Fanny Guinness. The other three had all died before the age of sixty of conditions directly related to their missionary service.

3

Edward Cecil Guinness, the first Lord Iveagh, also died in 1927. His last gesture, two days before his death, was to make his eldest son, Rupert, chairman of the company. Rupert had never taken any real interest in the business. Ernest, his middle son, on the other hand, had been a vice-chairman for years. But despite being the only real brewer of the three, Ernest was first and foremost an engineer, and Edward Cecil doubted his leadership ability. Walter, the youngest, was already pursuing a successful political career and was Minister for Agriculture. The line of command must pass through the eldest son, though the controlling financial interest was to be divided between all three. Their father, in true patriarchal Guinness fashion had dictated the firm's future from beyond the grave.

Rupert inherited his father's peerage, as well as his mantle, and moved into the House of Lords. In the resulting by-election in Southend Gwenny was elected in his place. One of only seven women MPs in the country, she had a distinguished political career of her own, increasing her majority substantially at each succeeding General Election, until she retired from the Commons in 1935, handing over her seat to her son-in-law, Henry "Chips" Channon. Effectively the seat belonged to the Guinness family for 85 years.

The eldest son also inherited his father's favourite property—Elveden, which was rapidly becoming more trouble than it was worth. Its upkeep drained Rupert's resources, but there was no question of selling it when 1000 employees depended on it for their livelihood. Besides, at his first meeting with Rupert after Lord Iveagh's death, as the King offered his condolences, and said, "I hope you're going to keep up the shooting at Elveden. I shall hope to come next year and I think the Queen would like to come too."[76] A wish from a monarch is as good as a command, though it made his heart sink. In 1928 Rupert and Gwenny opened the house for one last shooting party, an Indian summer before setting in motion a wildly ambitious agricultural experiment.

Convinced of its importance in combatting TB, they had been producing tuberculin-tested milk from their herds at their estate, Pyrford, for some years. Now they planned to extend the scheme, reclaiming 8,000 acres of barren Elveden shrub land in an attempt to prove that what appeared to be wasteland could be effectively used in the production of food.

The project's success was largely due to Rupert's absolute determination to improve British agricultural methods. His pioneering work earned him an array of honorary degrees, and during the Second World War Elveden became an invaluable example of agricultural reclamation, not to mention, a precursor of organic farming.

Meanwhile, the Guinness brewing business was in the doldrums. When Edward Cecil died, he was the second wealthiest man in the British Isles, but there was now stiff competition, and Guinness had never been able to capture the vital, highly lucrative market across the Atlantic. This left his three sons with only one option—to resort to advertising.

Advertising had always been a bone of contention in the family. The first Lord Iveagh believed it was unnecessary since Guinness should sell on its own merits. Ernest agreed with his father, but Rupert went ahead anyway, and the most successful advertising history of all time began. In the end it was probably the single major contributing factor to the company's success in the 1930s, ensuring its survival through the war.

The first advert which appeared in the national newspapers on 7th February, 1929, gave no hint that Guinness might taste good, or even make you feel good, especially after a pint or two above the recommended dose. It simply did you good. The first two Arthur Guinnesses would have approved. It was entirely in keeping with their non-conformist philosophy.

Years later, when one indignant peer complained in the House of Lords that everywhere he went he was unable to enjoy the beauties of the British countryside for billboards proclaiming "Guinness is good for You," the Earl of Iveagh rose to his feet, and made his one and only "speech." "Guinness *is* good for you," he shouted back.

The second most important decision made in those vital pre-war years under Rupert's leadership was the establishment of a brewery at Park Royal, just outside London. The building programme was shrouded in secrecy so as not to upset the Irish, or the punters, who might not like the idea that their pint was no longer brewed beside the magical

Liffey waters, but in a London suburb just off the A40. They needn't have worried. The Guinness mystique survived.

4.

News of Israel's independence may have been the culmination of Geraldine's hopes and expectations, but for the brewing side of the family, it was bitter sweet. On November 6th, 1944, Walter Guinness, first Baron Moyne, was assassinated in Egypt by Jewish terrorists intent on freeing Palestine from British domination.

Walter Guinness had picked the name Moyne for his title from a map of Loch Corrib, near his uncle Arthur's Ashford estate. In 1940, when Churchill became the leader of a nation at war, Lord Moyne became Secretary of State for the Colonies, and in 1941-2, Leader of the House of Lords. In 1942 he joined the Cabinet as Minister of State in Egypt, and in 1944 became Minister resident in the Middle East, responsible for an area stretching from Tripoli to eastern Persia.

Though a prestigious appointment, it was an unenviable one. Palestine presented an almost unsurmountable problem. The British government was both protective of the indigenous Arab population, with whom relations were cordial, yet appalled by early stories of Jewish persecution emerging from Europe.

On November 4th 1944, Chaim Weizman the future first President of Israel, then a lecturer at Manchester University, was invited to lunch with Churchill at Chequers. The Prime Minister wanted to discuss the possibility of partitioning Palestine into two independent states, Jewish and Arab, with Jerusalem as a free city. Moyne had apparently been involved in delicate negotiations with Arab and Jewish representatives to this effect. Weizman appears to have welcomed the idea, delighted that his dream of a Jewish homeland might become a reality.

Churchill suggested Weizman go and see Lord Moyne and enlist his support, but two days later, before Weizman had left England, Lord Moyne was dead. He was returning home from the British Embassy in Cairo to his residence on Gezira Island, separated from the city by the Kasr-el-Nil bridge across the Nile, when two young men suddenly appeared with revolvers in their hands. One thrust his gun through the driver's window and fired at almost point blank range, hitting Lord Moyne in the neck and the stomach.

Parliament was informed at once, but eleven days passed before Churchill could trust himself enough to speak of it in public. Churchill was at heart a colonialist, and it was difficult enough for him to hand over control of Palestine, let alone to a people responsible for the death of one of his closest friends.

In 1985, looking back at those events, his son, Bryan Guinness wrote, "It can be no more than speculation to suppose that if my father had not been murdered by Stern Gang terrorists, and if he could have achieved agreement before the end of the war on a partitioned Palestine...the many cruel wars that have since beset Israel and her neighbours might have been avoided." [77] But as his forefathers had foreseen only too well in Ireland, a partitioned country is no guarantee of peace.

5.

Geraldine Taylor's joy over the establishment of state of Israel was dampened a little in succeeding months by news of the Communist takeover of her beloved China.

Whitfield's son, Henry and his wife, Mary, were there, and in grave danger. At eighteen Henry had decided to bypass university and go straight to the Bible Training Institute in Glasgow so that he could prepare to leave for China as quickly as possible. Such was Henry's daredevilry that he had narrowly escaped expulsion from his school, St. Lawrence College in Ramsgate. In China, it would enable him to survive.

He sailed from Tilbury with seventy other new recruits, including his cousin, Desmond Guinness, in 1931, starting his missionary career in the same rural prefecture as his parents—Honan. Walking or cycling between villages, he would stop on street corners, wearing local costume as his father had always done, and play his silver cornet, the family heirloom he taught himself to play in Glasgow. Then he would preach in fluent Mandarin to the assembled crowd.

Politically, the country was no calmer. By the time the Japanese invaded Shanghai in 1933, civil war between Chiang Kai Shek's Nationalists and the Communists had weakened the Chinese army's ability to defend itself against foreign onslaught. Taking advantage of a new outbreak of anti-foreign feeling, communist soldiers began to vent their anger on Christian missionaries. Some, like John and Betty Stam, were executed. Others were forced to trudge thousands of miles on Mao's infamous long march.

One night, after holding a meeting at an inn, Henry overheard a plot to throw him down a well. With an instinctive nose for danger, he had taken stock of the place before preaching and noticed a small niche in the courtyard wall—one solitary, possible foothold. Walking nonchalantly across the courtyard in the direction of the toilet, he suddenly scaled the ten foot wall, jumped down the other side and outran his captors and their dogs to the next town, four miles away.

In Kaifeng, his childhood home, he couldn't cope with the many opportunities to share the faith and prayed God would send him a co-worker. One night he was awoken by a noise, and crept downstairs in his pyjamas to discover a burglar about to make off with a sackful of his possessions. He barred the exit and invited the burglar to sit down, so that he could read him John's Gospel and explain what he had to do to become a Christian.

Next morning, the would-be burglar was left in charge of the house with instructions to prepare the lunch. When Henry arrived home the house was immaculate, the meal waiting on the table, and Henry had his new co-worker.

He married Mary Taylor, the daughter of CIM missionaries, in 1938. A qualified doctor, she was working at the hospital her father-in-law had founded in Kaifeng. A gentle, practical woman, she was as brave and resourceful as her husband, which was just as well, given the demands of their calling. After the bombing of Pearl Harbour and the threat of a

Japanese invasion, life was unbearably hard. Drought, famine and flood were followed by a plague of locusts of almost biblical proportions. Raging inflation meant that money only bought a little rice. Starving local people discarded their youngest children and the Guinnesses took them in, sharing out their own meagre supplies with an ever-expanding family.

Between 1940 and 1943 they had three boys of their own, Gerald, Oswald and Reginald, following an established Chinese family custom by giving them a common ending to their names But the difficult conditions took their toll and Gerald died of dysentery when he was only two. Reginald, born shortly after the death of his brother, died at seven months and was buried alongside him. There was no time to grieve. The Japanese were closing in and they had to flee the day after Reginald died, carrying Os, their remaining toddler, in a basket on a pole the 1,000 miles to Bombay and the boat home.

In 1947 Chinese friends in Honan begged them to go back. Communist thought was gaining ground, but many students and intellectuals wanted to hear about the Christian faith. Leaving Os with Gordon Guinness and his growing family, Henry and Mary went out to Nanjing where they started a Bible study group which grew as fast as the political vice tightened. Communist indoctrination meetings were followed by mass shootings outside the city gate—300 people at a time, every day. The presence of foreigners became increasingly untenable. Chou En Lai said ominously, "While China is putting its house in order, it is undesirable for guests to be present."

They were forced to flee south in 1949, and spent the next three years under house arrest on meagre rations—tea on Sundays, water the rest of the week. It was here that they heard the news on June 6th 1949 that Aunt Geraldine had died. When Mao came to power all foreigners were finally expelled. Henry and Mary had held out as long as they could and were among the last foreigners to leave in 1952.

6

Two weeks before Geraldine died, my husband, Peter, the youngest grandchild of Henry Grattan Guinness, was born. He was the son of Henry and Gracie's younger son, Paul, whom Geraldine took under her wing in the 1930s, when he was studying at Dallas Theological Seminary. Like many impecunious theological students in the USA, he needed preaching opportunities to fund his studies, so Aunt Geraldine introduced him to bemused congregations in her refined English accent as, "may brother." She looked more like his grandmother.

He soon became engaged to Jean Elliott of Montreal, whom he had met when he was speaking at the Canadian Keswick Convention. Jean, the daughter of strict Baptists and a real rebel, had an aversion to these powerful preachy Guinnesses. As a teenager she had been left alone in a room with Howard Guinness, the well-known student evangelist. This could mean only one of two things: he had been encouraged by her parents either to convert her or propose to her. Fortunately it was the former, but whichever, she had already determined to send him away with a flea in his ear.

But Paul was tall and mouth-wateringly handsome, with the same gift of oratory, the same presence, the same penetrating eyes of his father, the legendary Henry Grattan Guinness, though Paul had been only two years old when his father had died.

After their engagement he took his fiancee to meet Howard and Geraldine. Howard, she said, was "a perfect pet," so deaf she would have to repeat her social chit chat multo voce into his ear trumpet. Geraldine, however, the family matriarch, aware of the demands involved in marrying into the clan, interrogated her in depth. "Jean, dear, can you cook? Jean, dear, can you sew? Jean, dear, can you type?"

"What a cheek!" my mother-in-law said indignantly years later. "She had never done any of those things for herself in her life."

Even in retirement, Mathilda, who never forgot Geraldine's kindness to her, cared for them.

From the moment of his own conversion to Christianity, as a young farmer in New Zealand, Paul had felt a strong calling to continue his father, Henry Grattan's work in Jewish Christian relations, but his half Aunt Lucy had given that commission to her youngest son, Karl, on her deathbed, and that was a puzzle to him.

In the early days of the Second World War, the two cousins, Paul and Karl, one British, one American, both army chaplains, met for the first and only time on a troop ship in the mid-Atlantic, apparently by chance.

"I have always wanted to meet you," Paul said to Karl, "to ask you whether you have any sense that it is your ministry is to fulfil your mother's last words and carry on my father's work?"

Karl said he didn't, and Paul heaved a sigh of relief.

"I'm glad," he said, "because I do." [78]

I do not believe it is purely co-incidence that I am Jewish, and nor did Paul. When I went home to tell my parents, practising Jews, that I planned to "marry out," I intended to soften the blow by showing my father the Guinness family tree, and the place he would now have in it as, "father of..." After all, not many girls can take home their intended's pedigree. My father took one look at it and said, with a twinkle in his eye, "And you had to pick one of the poor relations!"

In recent years Peter, who became a clergyman in the time-honoured tradition, [79] has not been quite so proud of his family name, as endless scandals and tragedies have beset the brewing side, culminating in the arrest of the Chief Executive, Ernest Saunders, in 1986 for insider dealing. Saunders had tried to save the company from being taken over by a multinational. He succeeded only in postponing the inevitable, for now Guinness, once the quintessential family business, is merely part of Diageo, and has no family involvement.

The media insists on thinking that the only real Guinnesses are directly descended from one of the peerages and must, by definition be mind-numbingly rich. "There is no such thing as a poor Guinness," said biographer Hugo Vickers in an article by Anne de Courcy in the

Daily Telegraph.[80] "If any of them do happen to be poor it's because they've squandered their inheritance." Peter never had an inheritance to squander. It was given away by his grandfather when he became a teetotal itinerant preacher in the last century. Some family members might think we are poor, dependent as we are on a Church of England stipend, but we think we're probably the richest—but then, it's all relative.

THE END

(FOOTNOTES)

1   *In Memoriam,* Henry Grattan Guinness, by his son, Harry Guinness; Regions Beyond, Vol. 32, 1911.

2   *In Memoriam*, op cit., RBMU, 1911, p. 3

3   This account of the duel is based on several newspaper cuttings, including "Grattan Guinness; An Echo of a Great Duel," *TP's Weekly*, July 8th, 1910. The details of their stories vary according to their Protestant or Catholic sympathies. One of the most accurate accounts appeared in *The Irish Times*, Monday, February 1st, 1965. It was written by Fergus Pyle, a descendant of John Norcott D'Esterre's daughter, Amelia, who married Captain John Grattan Guinness' second son, Arthur Grattan Guinness.

4   An inaccuracy repeated as late as 1910 by T.P. O'Connor in *TP's Weekly*

5   The pedigree of the Guinness family was subject to detailed scrutiny by Henry Seymour Guinness in his book *Richard Guinness of Celbridge.* Only a few copies exist in private circulation within the family. Jonathan Guinness, the third Lord Moyne, in his book *Requiem for a Family Business* (Macmillan, 1997) prefers the more common explanation that Richard Guinness was descended from a humble part of the Magennis clan, far removed from the earldom, which dropped the "Mac" (meaning "son of") at some point in history, possibly around 1690 to avoid penal laws against Catholics.

6   Letter quoted in *The Guinness Brewery in the Irish Economy, 1759-1876,* P. Lynch and J. Vaizey, CUP, 1960, p. 72

7   Lynch and Vaizey, op cit, p. 58

8   Lynch and Vaizey, op cit, p. 104

9   Lynch and Vaizey, op cit, p. 104

10 1st August, 1813, Lynch and Vaizey, op. cit., p. 110

11 According to local records, a John Guinness and Susan Hatton had a son, Benjamin, in Dumfries. Benjamin did not survive babyhood.

12 Undated letter to Mrs. Jane Guinness, Farmleigh Manuscript.

13 Records of the Battle of Waterloo refer to an English officer's drinking a glass of Guinness.

14 Plunkett Papers, February 9th, 1816

15 Plunkett Papers, March 12th, 1849

16 Lynch and Vaizey, op. cit. p. 106

17 Lynch and Vaizey, op. cit. p. 167

18 M. S. Alexander to Arthur Guinness, 1842, Park Royal Manuscript

19 Farmleigh Manuscript, November 2nd, 1851

20 Lynch and Vaizey, op. cit. p. 108

21 W.E. Adams, quoted by S Blake and R Beacham in *The Book of Cheltenham*, Buckingham, 1982.

22 *In Memoriam*, op. cit.

23 *In Memoriam*

24 *Henry Grattan Guinness, In Memoriam*, op cit, 1911

25 *In Memoriam*, op. cit. p9

26 Letter in the author's possession

27 A Sketch of the Life and Ministry of the Rev H G Guinness, from *Thirteen Sermons*, John Farquar Shaw, 1859

28 A Sketch, op. cit.

29 Lynch and Vaizey, op. cit. p178

30 From an Elveden manuscript

31 F.S.L. Lyons, *Irish Historical Studies*, 1962-3, p374

32 J Edwin Orr, *The Second Evangelical Awakening in Britain,* Marshall, Morgan and Scott, 1949

33 *Enter Thou, Pages from the life of Fanny E Guinness*, RBMU and Paternoster, 1899

34 Mrs. S Barnado and James Marchant, *Barnado*, Hodder and Stoughton, 1907, p17

35 Farmleigh Manuscript, June 1st, 1862

36 Ibid, January 1st, 1863

37 Lynch and Vaizey, op. cit. p181

38 *Lucy Guinness Kumm, Her Life Story*, by her father, H Grattan Guinness, Morgan and Scott, 1907

39 February 16th, 1866, from the Hudson Taylor Archives of the Overseas Missionary Fellowship, sent to the author by Taylor's cousin and archivist, the late Jim Broomhall.

40 A.J. Broomhall, *Hudson Taylor and China's Open Century*, Book 4, Survivor's Pact, Hodder and Stoughton, 1984, p122

41 Tom Barnado had decided to stay in England, feeling he needed more time to consider his calling.

42 *She Spake of Him*, Being Recollections of the Loving Labours and Early Death of the Late Mrs. Geraldine Dening, an essay by Fanny E Guinness, 1872

43 An obituary of Mrs. Geraldine Dening in *The Christian*, Thursday August 2nd, 1872

44 From an obituary booklet published on the death of Pastor Claude Degremont in 1912. Degremont became pastor of the French Protestant Church of London in Soho Square in 1894. Some of Guinness' preaching in France was shared with the well-known French evangelist, Theodore Monod.

45 Kate Drew, *The Escape Upward*, Drummonds' Tract Depot, Stirling, undated

46 *Barnado,* op cit. p104

47 *The East London Institute, Our First Year,* 1872. Fanny liked to keep their supporters informed. She wrote to them on a regular basis, and her letters were compiled into a series of annual reports.

48 Joy Guinness, *Mrs. Howard Taylor, Her Web of Time*, China Inland Mission, 1949

49 These and subsequent quotes are from The East London Institute Reports, 1874-9

50 Introduction to *The Approaching End of the Age*, viewed in the light of history, prophecy and science, Hodder and Stoughton, first published in 1878, with twelve editions by 1896.

51 Over the years a variety of cranks, sects and amateur biblical sleuths have claimed that Henry Grattan Guinness foretold "the end of the world." In an article as recent as 1988 in *The Asbury Theological Journal*, entitled, *The World Will End in 1919*, Professor Stanley Walters of Knox College, Toronto University claimed that Henry Grattan Guinness died in 1910 "without knowing he was wrong." But Grattan Guinness intentionally never used the phrase "the end of the world." In *Light For the Last Days* he expressly asks his readers not to use his book in that way. No mention of the year 1919, or the end of the world, was ever made within the family.

52 Piers Brendon, *Head of Guinness*, privately published in 1979 for family circulation only

53 G Martelli, *A Man of His Time—A life of the First Earl of Iveagh KP GCVO*, private publication, 1957, p111

54 Martelli, op. cit. p92

55 G Martelli, *Rupert Guinness: a Life of the Second Earl of Iveagh, KG, CB, CMG, FRS*, private publication, p5

56 Mary Reed's reminiscences of Lucy Guinness are taken from *Pools In the Glowing Sands* by Irene V Cleverdon, The Specialty Press, Melbourne, 1936,

57 The Regions Beyond Magazine, 1885, p110

58 See *The Story of Faith Missions*, Klaus Fiedler, Regnum Books International, 1994.

59 A private account given to Piers Brendon and described in his book *Head of Guinness*, p149

60 J. Martelli, *The Elveden Enterprise*, Faber and Faber, 1932, p50

61 Frederick Mullally, *The Silver Salver*, Granada, 1981 p43.

62 Joy Guinness, *Mrs. Howard Taylor*, China Inland Mission, 1949, p160

63 *Enter Thou, Pages from the Life Story of Fanny E Guinness*, RBMU, op cit

64 The technique is still performed in accident and emergency departments to this day

65 12 June, 1925, in *Head of Guinness* by Piers Brendon.

66 Martelli, *Man of His Time*, op cit, p13

67 *Peculiar People* by "Septima," Heath Cranton, 1935. Septima was a pseudonym for Grace Hurditch.

68 *The Bath Herald*

69 I am indebted for this information to Dr. Michael R Palairet of the Department of Economic and Social History at the University of Edinburgh, who has written a short biography of Francis Harford Mackenzie.

70 My husband, Peter, was 18 when his grandmother, Grace Guinness died in 1967. He received a first-hand account of a life shared for seven years with his remarkable grandfather.

71 Joy Guinness, *Mrs. Howard Taylor, Her Web of Time*, CIM, 1949

72 Katherine Everett, *Bricks and Flowers*, Reprint Society, 1951, p162

73 Martelli, *The Elveden Empire*, op cit p102

74 *Reminiscences of Sport and War*, Eyre and Spottiswood, London, 1939, p229-30

75 Mrs. H Taylor, *Guinness of Honan*, China Inland Mission, 1930, p307

76 J. Martelli, *The Elveden Enterprise, op cit*, p 87

77 Bryan Guinness, *Personal Patchwork*, Cygnet, 1986, p219

78 Paul Guinness, Vicar of Christ Church, Ashton-under-Lyne and later Ecumenical Officer for Greater Manchester, spent a lifetime involved in Jewish-Christian dialogue, culminating in his writing a book called *Hear O Israel*, which showed the crucial role his father and other Victorian leaders had played in the creation of a Jewish state.

79 Robin, Garry and Christopher, Canon Gordon Guinness' three sons, are all ordained as well.

80 Saturday 20th November, 1997.